SUPPLY CHAIN STRATEGY

SUPPLY CHAIN STRATEGY

UNLEASH THE POWER OF BUSINESS INTEGRATION TO MAXIMIZE FINANCIAL, SERVICE, AND OPERATIONS PERFORMANCE

SECOND EDITION

EDWARD H. FRAZELLE, PhD

New York Chicago San Francisco Athens London Madrid
Mexico City Milan New Delhi Singapore Sydney Toronto

1 2 3 4 5 6 7 8 9   LCR   22 21 20 19 18 17

ISBN   978-0-07-184280-8
MHID   0-07-184280-2

e-ISBN   978-0-07-184281-5
e-MHID   0-07-184281-0

Library of Congress Cataloging-in-Publication Data

Names: Frazelle, Edward, author.
Title: Supply chain strategy / Edward H. Frazelle.
Description: Second edition. | New York : McGraw-Hill Education, 2017. | Revised edition of the author's Supply chain strategy, 2002.
Identifiers: LCCN 2017022777 (print) | LCCN 2017037953 (ebook) | ISBN 9780071842815 | ISBN 0071842810 | ISBN 9780071842808 (hardback : alk. paper) | ISBN 0071842802 (alk. paper)
Subjects: LCSH: Business logistics. | Industrial procurement. | BISAC: BUSINESS & ECONOMICS / Leadership.
Classification: LCC HD38.5 (ebook) | LCC HD38.5 .F735 2017 (print) | DDC 658.7—dc23
LC record available at https://lccn.loc.gov/2017022777

RightChain™, RightScores™, RightServe™, RightStock™, RightBuys™, RightTrips™, RightHouse™, RightSource™, RightTech™, RightTeam™, RightPlan™ and related terms are trademarks of RightChain™ Incorporated.

This book is dedicated to my Lord and
Savior Jesus Christ; my intimate ally
and beautiful wife Pat; and our children,
Kelly, Andrew, Travis, and Gabriela.

CONTENTS

CHAPTER 9

CHAPTER 10

CHAPTER 11

PREFACE

It's been nearly 20 years since I wrote the first edition of *Supply Chain Strategy*. In those two decades, this book has been read in seven languages and adopted in many corporations and universities as the standard for supply chain decision making. In many supply chain circles it is simply referred to as "the red book."

Ten years ago we packaged our "red book" principles, methodology, and analytics into a proprietary offering known as RightChain. RightChain Analytics is home to supply chain pattern recognition, scoreboards, and optimizations. RightChain Consulting is home to our methodology and strategic consulting services. RightChain Research is home to our investigation of new supply chain algorithms, benchmarks, trends, and vendor performance. RightChain Institute is home to our supply chain education curriculum. RightChain Portal is home to our subscription-based analytics, assessments, and academics. RightChain Alliance is home to our joint ventures in Asia, Europe, and South America.

RightChain principles, methodology, and analytics have been implemented in nearly every major industry in nearly every part of the world. The supply chains for merchandise, food, beverage, costumes, textiles, and service parts in Disney theme parks in Orlando, Los Angeles, Paris, Hong Kong, and Tokyo have all been guided by our principles, methodology, and analytics. Honda service parts, the world's most profitable, efficient, and accurate automotive supply chain, is guided by our principles, methodology, and analytics. Our principles, methodology, and analytics are also guiding the global supply chain for airplane engine assembly at Pratt and Whitney; toothpaste at Colgate-Palmolive; hair care products at P&G; mining products at Rio Tinto in Australia; textiles at BP; beverages at Coca-Cola; coffee in Starbucks's Japanese outlets; greeting cards at Hallmark; milk and dairy products at H.P. Hood; medical devices at Abbott Laboratories; office products in 3M's Latin American operations; e-commerce foods at Nutrisystem; telecommunications hardware at Hills Australia; light bulbs at GE; beauty aids and cosmetics at NuSkin; cable products at AT&T; mined commodities at England's Anglo-American; pens and pencils at BIC; plastics at Korea's SKC; frozen food at Schwan's; retail and e-commerce at Alshaya in the middle east; camping goods in L.L. Bean's omni-chain; consumer electronics at Edion Japan; mail-order goods at Scroll; bedding at Serta-Simmons bedding supply chain; air conditioners at Carrier; convenience and grocery products in 15,000 Oxxo stores in Mexico; shoes at Payless; and books at LifeWay.

In addition, RightChain has been taught and in some cases adopted as a full supply chain curriculum at Georgia Tech in Atlanta, the University of Costa Rica in San Jose, Northwestern in Chicago, Cornell in Ithaca, the National University of Singapore in Singapore, Meiji University in Tokyo, Swinburne University in Melbourne, and the University of the Pacific in Lima. Through those universities, seminar settings, and online education, more than 50,000 professionals have been taught RightChain principles. Through this book and the other books in this series, more than 10,000 professionals have read about RightChain.

Since the first edition of *Supply Chain Strategy*, the logistics landscape has changed dramatically. What was considered science fiction a mere 20 years ago has now come upon us. Autonomous vehicles were a Jetsons cartoon fantasy as opposed to a real disruptive potential cure for truck driver shortages. Uber had not yet even made it into the most innovative Silicon Valley imaginations. Drones were reserved for black dagger military missions. Omni-channel would have been mistaken for a new cable TV network. E-commerce and its Amazon icon were infants. Next-hour delivery was reserved for pizzas and Chinese food. Supply chain outsourcing was considered risqué. Robotics were tucked away in university laboratories and along a few automotive assembly lines. Electric cars and solar-powered plants were left-wing conspiracies. Subscriptions were for magazines. Terrorism was only in the movies. Social networking required literally meeting someone. Streams were small flowing bodies of water. A cloud was a puffy white thing in the sky. A chat was a brief face-to-face conversation. Donald Trump was a real estate developer.

Though the decision-making landscape has changed radically, the decision-making principles, methodology, and analytics have remained basically the same as those I authored in 2000. Those same principles are presented here and shared through a mix of methodology, principles, analytics, anecdotes, and client case examples most appropriate for the context at hand.

What's Solomon Got to Do with It?

Authors quote many different sources. Some quote historical figures such as Ben Franklin or George Washington. Some quote military figures such as Patton or Napoleon. Some quote philosophers such as Aristotle or Socrates. Some quote political figures such as Reagan or Churchill. Some quote contemporary business or tech gurus like Steve Jobs, Bill Gates, or Jeff Bezos.

My favorite author to quote is bit older—Solomon. Solomon was the wisest man who ever lived and was humble and wise enough to ask for wisdom to lead people when he could have asked for and received any attribute or riches known to man. From that wisdom, Solomon became the world's wealthiest and most influential man. Solomon wrote the book of Proverbs in the Bible; one of my favorite resources and oddly applicable to *Supply Chain Strategy*. I use those Proverbs as a truth filter for RightChain principles and recommendations (Table I.1). That's what Solomon's got to do with it.

Table I.1   Solomon's Proverbs and RightChain Principles

	Solomon Says	RightChain Principle
RightServe *Supply Chain Service Optimization*	"The king's favor is toward a wise servant."	A quantified supply chain service policy segmented by channel, ABC customer, and ABC SKU addressing fill rate, response time, returns policy, value-added services, change orders, and minimum order quantities is in place, updated, and used to monitor customer satisfaction.
RightStock *Inventory Optimization*	"In the house of the wise are stores of choice food and oil, but a foolish man devours all he has."	Inventory financial and service performance is maximized by optimizing SKU turn and fill rates and by optimizing forecasting, lead times, purchase order and setup costs, lot sizes, and inventory carrying rates.
RightBuys *Supply Optimization*	"She considers a field and buys it; from her profits she plants a vineyard."	Source(s) are selected that minimize total cost of ownership, maximize return on invested capital, and integrate with our supply chain systems.
RightTrips *Transportation Optimization*	"Whoever travels life in integrity and straight lines travels securely, but whoever travels crooked paths will be found out."	The transportation network, routes, delivery frequencies, schedules, modes, and carriers are selected and managed to minimize total supply chain cost and meet the requirements of the supply chain service policy.
RightHouse *Warehouse Optimization*	"Develop your business first before building your house. A house is built by wisdom, and by understanding it is entirely put in good order."	Warehouses that meet supply chain service policy requirements and minimize total supply chain cost by optimizing storage density, labor productivity, inventory accuracy, shipping accuracy, and throughput rates are in place.

	Solomon Says	RightChain Principle
RightScores *Metrics* *Optimization*	"God desires honest weights and measures."	Spanning, balanced, minimal, benchmarkable metrics and ambitious, achievable, and incremental targets are used in a fair performance measurement program to impact decision making and assess individual performance.
RightSource *Outsourcing* *Optimization*	"Blessings on all who play fair and square."	Each of the supply chain logistics activities are currently right-sourced and continually under review for right-sourcing, and the best possible provider has been selected for outsourced activities.
RightTools *Technology* *Optimization*	"Buy truth, and do not sell it; buy wisdom, instruction, and understanding."	Data mining, decision support, planning, and execution systems meeting required functionality are in place utilizing the right breed (ERP vs. BOB), host (in-house vs. ASP), and form (package vs. SAAS) for supply chain service, inventory management, supply, transportation, and warehousing.
RightTeam *Organization* *Optimization*	"Do you see a man skilled in his work? He will serve before kings; he will not serve before obscure men."	A chief supply chain officer is supported by directors of supply chain service, inventory management, supply, transportation, warehousing, planning, and security/compliance whose staffs include professionals trained in that area of expertise.
RightPlan *Planning* *Optimization*	"The plans of the diligent lead surely to plenty, but those of everyone who is hasty, surely to poverty."	A short, middle, and long-term internal and external collaborative planning process is in place to maximize financial, service, and operations performance.

CHAPTER 1

RightChain
Supply Chain Strategy

"Strategy is the key to warfare."
—SOLOMON

I begin all our seminars with a discussion on the motivation to attend. In the case of our RightChain strategy seminar, the foundation for this book, it's easy. Based on formal and informal research with our clients and seminar attendees, less than 30 percent of all supply chain projects are successful. In harsher terms, *approximately 70 percent of supply chain projects fail!* If the project involves software, the failure rate climbs to 85 percent. It's hard to imagine embarking on any project if the probability of success is only 15 percent. With all the research that has been conducted, all the software tools that have been developed, all the education programs that have been offered, all the books that have been written, and all the conferences that have been conducted, the probability of success for supply chain projects is unacceptably low and has not improved. The reasons and excuses are many and various.

- The complexity and scope of supply chain decision making is increasing much faster than decision support resources—models, metrics, education, methodology, management, and software tools—are developing.

- Though improved, the coordination and communication between marketing, sales, manufacturing, procurement, and distribution is still lacking and sometimes dysfunctional.
- Supply chain performance metrics are often at odds with one another and frequently exacerbate the very problems they are designed to solve.
- Supply chain benchmark targets are often unreliable and unreasonable.
- The few key resources who are candidates for supply chain projects are stretched so thin on dizzying arrays of projects that they have limited to no capacity to handle the true requirements of supply chain strategy initiatives.
- Consultants retained as supply chain guides are often young and inexperienced; follow regimented problem-solving approaches; and are more interested in and financially motivated by selling or integrating large, expensive software projects.
- Third-party logistics firms that are looked to for supply chain strategic advice are really only qualified to provide advice pertaining to their supply chain niche, and even that may be biased toward their own products and services.
- The decision support tools used to help supply chain professionals often do not properly reflect financial objectives and service constraints, are often only operable by the software developers themselves, and are currently operated by harried professionals with little or no training.
- Less than 10 percent of supply chain professionals have any formal education or training in supply chain management, and that education is often outdated and/or impractical.

- Competing, short-term executives grasp for supply chain silver bullets, shortcuts, and get-rich-quick schemes, fostering a culture of mistrust and hostility.
- In the name of "cost avoidance," procurement is still looking for the cheapest first price and are costing double that in hidden inventory carrying, lost sales, transportation, and poor quality costs.

These are observations synthesized over three decades of working closely with supply chain organizations in nearly every industry in nearly every part of the world. There has to be a better way. We developed and have been quietly working with that better way for many years. We call that way RightChain.

Based on more than two decades of supply chain strategy consulting, executive education, and research, the RightChain program includes the definitions, methodology, tools, curriculum, principles, metrics, processes, and delivery mechanism required to address the major decisions in supply chain strategy development. RightChain is successfully guiding the supply chains of large, medium, and small companies in nearly every major industry around the world and is responsible for more than $5 billion in bottom-line impact through optimized combinations of higher sales, lower expenses, and improved capital utilization. RightChain typically *puts between 1 percent and 5 percent of sales on the bottom line.*

1.1 RightChain Definitions

Nearly 20 years ago we were helping a large food company develop a supply chain strategy. One of the our recommendations was that they create a supply chain steering committee. The company accepted our recommendation and asked me if I would facilitate the first meeting.

The meeting began at 8:00 a.m. on a Tuesday morning. The meeting went very well for the first six or seven minutes. It then started to sound like our minivan used to sound about five hours into a long trip with our kids. There was something about that five hour mark. Maybe it was that two DVDs had finished playing. Whatever it was, it was bad, whiny, and loud.

That's what it sounded like in the conference room with eight six-figure executives and a bewildered facilitator. I remember thinking, "I need to refund the consulting fees because I'm doing such a poor job facilitating this meeting." To be candid, I would have been delighted to return the fees and exit stage left. By the grace of God there was a scheduled break at 9:00 a.m. During the break I remember thinking, "Lord, why am I having such a hard time facilitating this meeting?" Then it dawned on me what the problem was.

The executives in the meeting that day included the heads of manufacturing, transportation, warehousing, materials management, finance, marketing, and IT, and the nephew of the chairman of the board. Of those, none had worked for any other company and none had worked outside the areas they were currently in. So, if an "expert facilitator" starts talking about supply chains, and you've only worked in transportation (fill in the blank with any other area), guess what you think he's talking about? One of two things. Either you think he's talking about transportation or some other strange world that you can only conceive of through the perspective of transportation. Once I had that revelation (aha or duh!), I realized they (and most other companies) really had no idea what supply chain logistics was. I changed my meeting strategy.

When we reconvened, I told the group that we were not going to meet any longer. They were taken aback and asked if they had done anything to offend me. I assured them they had not, and that I might have done something to offend them. I apologized for doing such a poor job facilitating, and I asked them if they would give me another chance. They were gracious to do so. We then restarted with a half-day seminar on supply chain strategy. Once that groundwork and common language had been established, the meeting and the project went smoothly. From that day forward we have commenced every RightChain supply chain strategy project with a seminar workshop introducing the client's executive and management team to the RightChain definitions, models, principles, and trade-offs of supply chain logistics. Our ConsulCation (consulting blended with education) approach has been so successful that we now integrate the RightChain curriculum with all our consulting engagements.

The Supply Chain Tower of Babel

The real issue in the aforementioned story is more memorably gleaned from a much older story. Remember Adam and Eve? Despite their transgressions, they and their offspring had a lot going for them. One thing going for them was that they spoke the same language. Their children, children's children, and several subsequent generations spoke that same language. What happens to the creative, economic, and industrial development of a society or organization when everyone communicates with the same language? Real, rapid, sustainable progress happens!

We think we are highly sophisticated with our modern entertainment, technology, and medical advancements. Adam and Eve's early descendants weren't too shabby themselves. They developed music, art, metallurgy, urban planning, and architecture. Eventually they became so successful in their own minds that they decided to build a monument to themselves. That's when the trouble started.

One day I was reading the story in the book of Genesis, and two things jumped off the page at me. The first thing that jumped out was a quote. God is looking down observing what is happening and says, "If they can speak the same language, there's not anything they can't accomplish." My first thought was, "That comes from a highly reliable source." My second thought was, "That will work! That will work in a business organization, a sports team, or a family." I was so inspired that I wrote what may be the most boring book ever written, *The Language of Logistics*, to help establish a common language for supply chain professionals. I also got started on a plan to develop a series of seminars on supply chain logistics to teach a common language of logistics. That series of seminars, the RightChain Management Series, has run for nearly 20 years. More than 10,000 professionals from more than 1,000 companies from more than 20 countries have been in our seminars on-campus, on-site, or online.

Another thing that jumped off the page at me was the sad end of the biblical story. Unfortunately, the society forgot who had given them the ability to accomplish so many great things. The Lord knew that rapid and massive progress with evil and prideful intent would culminate in rapid and massive destruction. God compassionately intervened by scrambling their language. They got halfway up with the tower, the project stopped, and the people scattered. That is not unlike what happens with many supply chain projects that can't overcome thresholds of political infighting, prideful turf wars, and/or the inertia and apathy of human nature.

The inability to communicate naturally breeds frustration, blocks trust, and creates barriers to progress and creativity. The point of the contemporary and ancient stories is that we need a common, unifying language to communicate and to make lasting, collaborative progress. It starts with a common definition of the field—supply chain logistics.

What Is Supply Chain Logistics?

To develop the definition of supply chain logistics, we're going to break it into its component parts. We'll start with logistics as the foundation.

There are many definitions of *logistics* floating around out there. We developed a simple one nearly 20 years ago. "Logistics is the flow of material, information and money between consumers and suppliers."

Some very important supply chain lessons can be learned from the three phrases in that simple sentence. First, logistics is "flow." Flow is a good thing! What happens to water when it stops flowing? Stagnation, scum, insects, and possibly death. What happens to blood when it stops flowing? The nerds in the group always say, "coagulation." The non-nerds usually just say, "somebody dies." The point is, when things stop flowing, something or someone dies (or loses their job, customers, and/or shareholders). In logistics three things need to flow: material, information, and money. Ideally those three flow simultaneously, in real time and without paper.

We can also learn a lot about logistics from the origins of the word itself. The root word for *logistics* is "logic." According to Webster, logic means "reason or sound judgment." RightChain leans heavily on reason and sound judgment in walking through the decisions that compose a supply chain strategy. The root word for *logic* is *logos*, a Greek word meaning "Word of God, divine reasoning, wisdom, balance." RightChain also leans heavily on Godly wisdom for working through complex supply chain trade-offs. (Our Japanese team, a joint venture of RightChain and Mitsubishi, is called the LogOS Team in honor of this approach.)

If that's *logistics*, what is a *supply chain*? There seems to be just as much confusion about the definition of *supply chain* as there is about the definition of *logistics*. Everyone seems to have their own. Here's ours: "The supply chain is the infrastructure of factories, warehouses, ports, information systems, highways, railways, terminals, and modes of transportation connecting consumers and suppliers."

Putting the two together, "Supply chain logistics is the flow of material, information and money in the infrastructure of factories, warehouses, ports, information systems, highways, railways, terminals, and modes of transportation connecting consumers and suppliers." To use a sports analogy, "Logistics is the game, and the supply chain is the stadium."

What Is a Supply Chain Strategy?

Just like there are a plethora of definitions of *logistics* and *supply chain*, there are also a plethora of definitions of *strategy*. "Vision" in one world is "strategy" in another world. "Strategy" in one world is "tactics" in another world. In the RightChain world, a supply chain strategy (Figure 1.1) is the answer to the following 10 questions (Table 1.1).

Table 1.1   RightChain Methodology

MISSION	1. What **metrics and targets** should we use to define supply chain success? 2. What should our **supply chain service** strategy be?
SUPPLY	3. How much **inventory** should we carry and where? 4. Who should we **buy and source** from and in what quantities?
LOGISTICS	5. What **transportation** flows, nodes, modes, and loads optimize our supply chain? 6. What **warehouse** designs and levels of automation optimize our supply chain?
SUPPORT	7. What supply chain activities should we **outsource** and to whom? 8. What supply chain **information systems** functionality and technology are required to support our supply chain?
MANAGEMENT	9. How should our supply chain **organization** be aligned and developed? 10. What supply chain **planning** program optimizes and integrates our supply chain?

Figure 1.1   RightChain Strategy Model

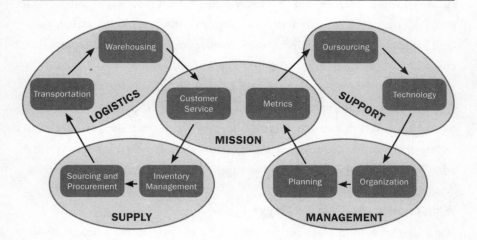

1.2 RightChain Models and Frameworks

According to Webster, a *model* is "a simplified representation of a system," and a *framework* is a synonym for a model meaning "an integrated structure of concepts or words used to explain the operations of complex systems". Models and frameworks represent physical and ideological systems. They are helpful aids in explaining complex phenomena. To help explain the complex phenomenon of supply chain logistics decision making, I developed a variety of RightChain models and frameworks. (I stopped at four because any more would have required a model to explain the models and a framework to explain the frameworks.) Those high level models and frameworks include (1) the RightChain Star Model of Supply Chain Logistics (the RightChain Star), (2) Frazelle's Framework of Supply Chain Logistics, (3) the Wrong Chain Model of Supply Chain Suboptimization, Dysfunction, and Conflict, and (4) the RightChain Supply Chain Integration Model.

The RightChain Star Model of Supply Chain Logistics

Our Star Model of Supply Chain Logistics (Figure 1.2) is an answer to a desperate prayer for a means to explain to a mean-spirited, cynical CEO of a very large chemical company why he did not need the $15 million warehouse and hundreds of jobs he had just gone on TV promising to a downtrodden local economy. I had to have something to explain that a physical warehouse was not the best answer to the absence of a customer service policy, excess inventory, unintegrated sources of supply, and uncoordinated transportation operations. The answer was to eliminate or minimize the need for physical warehousing by (1) developing a supply chain service policy, (2) determining the amount of inventory required to support that service policy, (3) optimizing and coordinating manufacturing schedules, and (4) optimizing the transportation operations. Whatever role remained for physical inventory defined the requirements for the (5) warehouse. Once that supply chain strategy was developed, the excess

**Figure 1.2   The RightChain Star Model of Supply Chain Logistics—
descriptive and prescriptive**

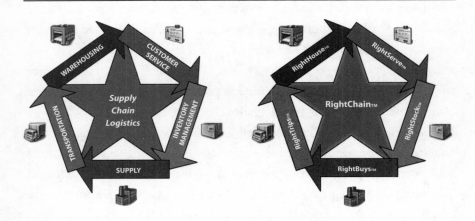

inventory and need for an additional warehouse were eliminated, customer service was improved, and profits increased.

Our RightChain Star represents two important features of supply chain logistics. First, there is a formal scope to supply chain logistics. We include customer service, inventory management, supply, transportation, and warehousing. In the absence of a scope, scope creep, a potential cancer for all projects (and what we call people who want to pile onto projects), can overwhelm a supply chain project. Second, there is an optimal sequence to consider the supply chain decisions when developing a supply chain strategy. Facing myriad decision interdependencies, in the absence of the optimal sequence, supply chain decision making becomes like a cat chasing its tail.

The RightChain Star Model begins with customer service for many reasons. First, a humble attitude of service and serving customers is the foundation for supply chain success. Second, the constraints developed as a part of customer service policy are the foundation for supply chain optimization.

It is fascinating to observe the faces and body language of the managers and executives in the RightChain project kickoff meetings. When the CEO, COO, or CSCO makes his or her remarks to kick off the project, you can immediately identify the marketing and sales group. They are the ones slumped down in their seats with downtrodden body language and a skeptical countenance. They assume that the project will be all about "cutting heads" and heavy expense reductions through declining service offerings. That's not what RightChain is about. *It's about determining the most profitable way to service customers and to take the burden of worry about supply chain logistics off the sales and marketing team so they can focus on sales and marketing.* In the end, the strongest proponents for our RightChain programs are often the sales and marketing teams, the dealer support groups in automotive service parts, the chefs in our restaurant programs, the doctors in our healthcare programs, etc. *RightChain begins with service!*

The second consideration in RightChain strategy development is inventory planning and management. Many assume that the goal is to minimize the amount of inventory in the supply chain. That's not the goal. *The goal is to determine the mix, amount, and deployment of inventory that satisfies the requirements of the customer service policy and maximizes the financial performance of the inventory.*

The third set of RightChain decisions are in the area of supply. The RightChain needs suppliers and sourcing decisions with those suppliers whose performance meets the requirements of the supply chain service policy and yields the maximum supply chain financial performance. Since the supply chain has to make up the gap between supplier service and customer service with excess inventory and/or excess transportation costs, the supply chain needs high-performance, service-oriented suppliers.

The fourth set of RightChain decisions are in the area of transportation. (Notice that we are describing the world of supply chain logistics and are just now getting to transportation, which many consider to be supply chain logistics.) The goal of transportation is to connect the sources of supply with customers within the guidelines of the supply chain service policy at the lowest possible total supply chain cost. In that way, transportation is a critical component of a supply chain strategy. It is not just a non-value-added, inconsequential expense line item whose manager's sole focus is to reduce expenses to the bare bones via hard-core carrier negotiations.

The fifth and last set of RightChain strategy decisions have to do with warehousing. It's my personal favorite, but I have to admit for many reasons it's the last activity that should be considered when developing a supply chain strategy. First, a clever trip through the first four RightChain initiatives may eliminate, should minimize, and will correctly determine the need for warehousing. Unfortunately warehouses often play a role as the physical manifestation of the lack of coordination, integration, and planning in the supply chain. Second, the warehouse is like a goalie in a soccer game. Like it or not, the warehouse is often the last line of defense for the supply chain against poor quality suppliers. Third, we need the service, inventory, and distribution mission requirements from the supply chain strategy to properly plan and operate the warehouse. Lastly, we may learn that a third party should be operating the warehouse.

We call these five RightChain elements the RightChain initiatives. In order they are to optimize supply chain service (RightServe), optimize inventory (RightStock), optimize supply (RightBuys), optimize transportation (RightTrips), and optimize warehousing (RightHouse). The RightChain enablers of those initiatives are to optimize the supply chain metrics and targets (RightScores), optimize supply chain outsourcing (RightSource), optimize supply chain technology (RightTech), optimize the supply chain organization (RightTeam), and optimize supply chain planning (RightPlan). These 10 elements of supply chain strategy comprise the outline for this book.

The Wrong Chain Model of Supply Chain Dysfunction and Conflict

At the request of a recent client, we developed the Wrong Chain Model of Supply Chain Suboptimization, Dysfunction, and Conflict (Figure 1.3) to help them understand the suboptimization and internal conflict they had created in their supply chain. It also happens to be the reason why there is

Figure 1.3   The Wrong Chain Model of Supply Chain Suboptimization, Dysfunction, and Conflict

suboptimization, dysfunction, frustration, and internal conflict in nearly every supply chain.

Think about a typical supply chain including sales, manufacturing, sourcing, transportation, and warehousing.

First stop: sales. Let's assume that the sales force creates the forecast and works on commission. What's the worst thing that could happen to a commission salesperson? Running out of product. So, guess what kind of forecast they will most likely turn in? You guessed it—an inflated forecast that will not run out of product. The result: more safety stock inventory than you know what to do with.

Second stop: manufacturing. How are most plant managers measured? The large majority of plant managers are evaluated based on the unit cost, plant yield, and/or machine utilization within the four walls of the plant. How do you go about achieving those objectives? Long production runs creating lots of inventory are the norm.

Third stop: sourcing. How are most buyers measured? The large majority of buyers are measured based on how low a price they can pay a vendor for the product. How do you get a low price? Large purchase quantities creating lots of inventory are the norm. (Is it any wonder it's called a *lot size*?)

Next stop: transportation. How are most transportation managers measured? Most transportation managers are evaluated based on transportation cost as a percent of sales, cost per mile, and/or vehicle utilization.

How do you minimize transportation cost and maximize vehicle utilization? By making sure the outbound containers and vehicles are as full as possible—in other words, by maximizing the in-transit inventory.

Last stop: warehousing. How are most warehouse managers measured? Most warehouse managers are measured on space utilization and labor cost per unit. How do you maximize space utilization? By filling up the warehouse. How do you minimize the labor cost per unit? By holding orders and releasing large batches of work to the warehouse floor. Those two objectives work together to increase four-wall inventory.

Is it any wonder there is excess inventory in nearly every supply chain?

One day I received a call from the chief operating officer of a large food company. He said they were struggling with the inventory levels in their supply chain. I asked him if he minded if I guessed what their problem was. I took him through the illogic of what I just took you through. There was an awkward silence on the line, and then he burst out laughing. I asked him why he was laughing. He said it was because they had been struggling with their excess inventory levels for years, had paid millions in unfruitful software licenses and consulting fees, and in less than a minute I had diagnosed their inventory ills without ever stepping foot in one of their offices or operations. He said, "You must be some kind of supply chain Sherlock Holmes."

I'm not Sherlock Holmes. What I shared with him and just shared with you is the root cause of most inventory ills in every supply chain. The illness is the misalignment of the metrics and decision making in the elements of the supply chain.

Supply Chain Integration

There are many and various mistakes in the wrong chain model described above. Sometimes it's helpful to learn from mistakes in creating the correct model.

One critical mistake in the previous supply chain model is the silos of decision making. We correct that mistake in the RightChain Integration Model (Figure 1.4) by having all the activities of the supply chain under one

Figure 1.4   RightChain Supply Chain Integration Model

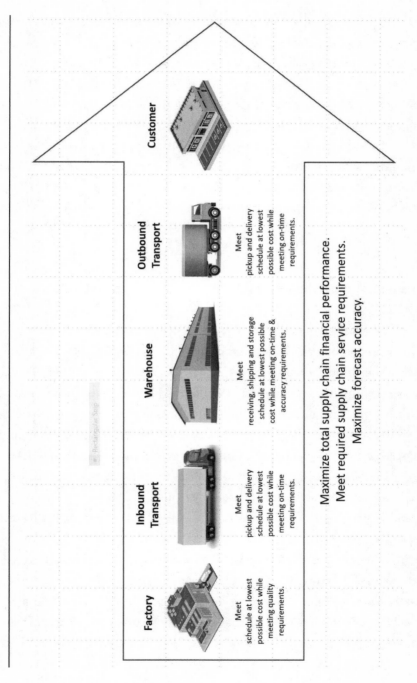

decision-making roof. Another major mistake in the wrong chain model is the focus on unit cost reduction achieved primarily by the utilization of resources in the supply chain. RightChain corrects that by developing and implementing an overarching objective function to minimize total supply chain cost while simultaneously meeting the requirements of the supply chain service policy. Our RightChain definition of total supply chain cost includes the expense and capital costs of inventory carrying, lost sales, inbound and outbound transportation, and warehousing. The RightChain Integration Model uses optimization to reflect the mission of the supply chain and to determine the proper role and schedule for each supply chain activity.

1.3 Supply Chain Simplification

We have a large semiconductor client in Silicon Valley. Our first project with them was an overall assessment of their supply chain. Their RightChain score was 71 percent, a C-minus. When I shared that with their COO, he was none too happy. He said that he didn't like his grade. I told him that I didn't like his grade either, but that was his grade. He complained that I didn't understand the complexity of his business. I agreed to redo the assessment. I flew back to Atlanta, reran the numbers, and computed the assessment grades. The overall grade was the same, C-minus. I flew back to San Jose, California, and shared the result. The COO was just as upset, complaining again that I did not understand how complex his business was. I shared with him that I had worked with lots of clients, empathized with his complexity, but stood my ground with the assessment. He asked us and paid us to redo the assessment one more time. I flew back to Atlanta, redid the assessment, and the grade came out the same, a C-minus. The next thing I knew I was flying back to San Jose worrying and praying about how to explain the result to the COO. In what could either be described as an aha or duh moment, it dawned on me:

Some supply chains are inherently more complex than others. However, some organizations have heaped self-inflicted, non-value-added complexity on top of their inherent complexity. Those are the under-performers. To help explain this phenomenon to the COO, I created the RightChain Complexity Index, a quantification of supply chain complexity. The index uses 10 factors that contribute to the complexity of a supply chain and grades a supply chain from 1 to 5 in each area, 5 being the highest level of complexity. The factors and their mitigating optimizations are named in Table 1.2.

Table 1.2   Supply Chain Complexity Factors and RightChain Simplification Initiatives

Supply Chain Complexity Factors	RightChain Simplification Initiatives
Number of SKUs and Commodities	RightSKUs: SKU Optimization
Number of DCs	RightNodes: Supply Chain Network Optimization
Number of Carriers	RightLines: Carrier Optimization
Number of Suppliers	RightCore: Supplier Optimization
Number of Handling Transactions	RightFlow: Flow Path Optimization
Demand Variability	RightCast: Forecast Optimization
Threats of Disruption	RightRisk: Risk Optimization
Regulatory Requirements	RightDocs: Documentation Optimization
Response Time Requirements	RightTimes: Leadtimes Optimization
Number of Software Applications	RightTech: Technology Optimization

I used the index to compute the supply chain complexity of a wide variety of our clients. The highest scores on our ranking so far are NASA (49 out of 50) and the U.S. Defense Logistics Agency (48 out of 50).

With these complexity concepts on the table, our client's COO began to understand what I was getting at. Then I showed him his RightChain score relative to logistically similar companies with comparable supply chain complexities. Relative to his inherent complexity, he had created much more. He was beginning to see the light.

Figure 1.5   Supply chain complexity vs. supply chain performance

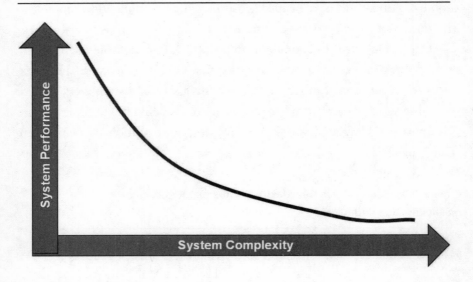

This degradation of system performance with increasing system complexity (Figure 1.5) holds regardless of the type of system (including personal life). The phenomenon is related to the thermodynamic principle of entropy, which states that *any system running without intervention will eventually run into chaos.* All systems need intervention. To help explain the phenomenon, I often ask our seminar students to imagine what would happen in their houses if they never did spring cleaning. One lady got it and stood up and said, "It would look like my house."

Complexity is the plaque in supply chain arteries. It has to be removed, and it takes an ongoing battle to prevent it and remove it once it builds up. In the case of this particular client, they had never intervened in the complexity. In fact, their culture took pride in and rewarded over-coming self-inflicted complexity instead of reducing it. Once I got that point across, the work with our client became one of our most successful engagements.

Pruning for Profit

We have a joint venture with Mitsubishi in Japan. I travel there once or twice a year to teach a series of seminars, consult with clients, and check up on the business. During one of my trips, my Japanese partner promised to take me to one of the best places to eat in Tokyo—the basement of a department store near our Tokyo office. I did not understand until I got to the produce section. He showed me some of the most beautiful fruits and vegetables I have ever seen. One cantaloupe was $100. They were also the most expensive fruits and vegetables I have ever seen (Figure 1.6). A small bunch of grapes was $14. A single strawberry was $5. Three peaches were $9. I asked my partner why the fruit was so expensive. He explained that when the fruit is just budding on a plant, the farmers identify the most promising 10 percent and prune the remaining 90 percent. The full resources of the plant are then focused on the best 10 percent of the fruit.

The fruit was so expensive that I declined to buy any. I could only imagine what it tasted like until a client invited us into his home for dessert. My wife and children were with me. We sat on the floor in his dining room, and he proceeded to serve what I guess was $5,000 worth of fresh fruit. It was the best fruit I have ever eaten, so good that it was almost like I had never eaten fruit before.

What does all of this have to do with supply chain strategy? We call it "pruning for profit." According to Webster, "pruning" means "to reduce especially by eliminating superfluous matter, to remove as superfluous, to cut off or cut back parts of for better shape or more fruitful growth, to cut away what is unwanted or superfluous" (Figure 1.7). The purpose of pruning is to focus the resources available to the plant in the healthiest limbs and branches in order to maximize the quality of the fruit produced by the plant.

Pruning is not easy. It is painful. You probably know from your personal life when you have had to cut out certain activities or cut off certain relationships that are not profitable or are even harmful. It comes up in supply chain strategy when someone in marketing and/or product

Figure 1.6   Hundred-dollar cantaloupe

development faces the fact that certain customers, SKUs, and orders are no longer profitable.

Simplification is never easy. It goes against the grain of human nature and the pride in the complexity or difficulty of what we do. During one of our seminars in Tokyo an attendee asked me what she would do if her company took all the complexity out of the work. I said, "You won't have to work nights and weekends. Your husband and your family need you." My translator started crying. Then the attendee started crying. Then I started crying.

I recently wrote an article titled, "Complexity Is the Plaque in Supply Chain Arteries." I have learned the hard way that complexity is the plaque in many arteries of life.

Figure 1.7   Pruning is a critical supply chain discipline.

When we begin a RightChain project, we typically find that about one-third of the customers, SKUs, and orders are profitable, about one-third are breaking even, and about one-third are losing money. Perhaps the most fruitful first step to take in developing a supply chain strategy is to remove the unprofitable customers, SKUs, and orders. With those customers, SKUs, and orders removed, the same amount of inventory investment is much more profitably allocated to the value-added customers, SKUs, and orders. Supply chain expenses decline dramatically as the cost of non-value-added complexity decreases. Forecasting becomes more accurate because the same forecasting resources are focused on fewer more forecastable customers, SKUS, and orders. Fill rate and market share increase as a result.

1.4 Supply Chain Optimization

A few years ago, I received a phone call from the head of supply chain for one of the world's largest laptop computer companies. After a few pleasantries, I asked about the nature of the call. The individual explained that as part of a new service initiative there was a requirement to radically reduce door-to-door times and they wanted my advice on how to go about it. I suggested the typical options of parallel processing, automation, and next-day shipping. The individual shared that each of those had been proposed, but as a part of a new Lean austerity initiative the company was unwilling to invest the time or money in any of those options. I suggested the obvious, that without the investment in time or money to re-engineer processes, automate, and/ or increase transportation costs, they had put themselves between a rock and a hard place. The individual became despondent and started crying. I gently asked a question I already knew the answer to. "What's wrong?" The individual shared that this kind of pressure had been ongoing for the past year, and that the last person in the position had only lasted six months. I suggested that no one was meant to stand up under that pressure and that they were unfortunately at the intersection of two mutually exclusive philosophies—higher service at any cost and lower cost at any price. For that particular company the "cost" and "price" in their philosophy were the emotional and physical well-being of their employees. It's easy for managers to fall back on mantras like "Just make it lean." or "The customer is king." instead of doing the hard decision making work of considering the short and long-term impact of any new initiative on employees, customers, and shareholders. That's why we say, "Don't philosophize, optimize."

Since supply chain logistics is replete with complex trade-offs, optimization—RightChain's claim to fame—is one of the most critical, yet elusive concepts for supply chain professionals. Let me take a stab at simplifying the concept.

If I asked you to tell me the best way to travel from Atlanta, Georgia, to Los Angeles, California, what would you say? When I ask that question in our seminars, most say by plane. When they say that so quickly they are making assumptions about the trip, that there is sufficient money available to buy a plane ticket, that time is of the essence, and that air travel is preferred. (That says a lot about our culture.) The real answer is, "It depends."

Suppose I add something to the question and ask you to tell me the best way to go if you only have $100. What would you say? Now the range of options may be limited to hitchhiking or stowaway. Suppose I add that money is no object and you must arrive within 12 hours. What would you say? Now the only option is to go by plane, and since money is no object, why not charter a jet? Suppose I say that you must arrive in 12 hours and spend the least amount of money possible. What would you say? Now the range is even narrower and probably means getting the cheapest possible coach plane ticket. In that example, the "12 hours" is a constraint and the "least amount of money possible" is the objective function. In optimization format it would look like this:

- Objective Function = Minimize Expenses
- Constraint = Arrive Within 12 Hours

In any decision-making environment, without an objective function *and* constraint(s), any answer is right and any answer is wrong. Since most business and supply chain decisions are not framed this way, how are business or supply chain decisions made? It often comes down to who can write the most caustic e-mail, who has the boss's ear, who has the most political clout, who is the most upset customer, what the stock analysts said, and so on.

Every optimization has two components—an objective function and constraints. In supply chains, the objective function is usually to minimize total supply chain cost or to maximize some aspect of supply chain financial performance. The constraints should be the requirements of the supply chain service strategy for fill rate, response time, delivery frequency, and delivery quality. In less formal terms, optimizing a supply chain means maximizing the supply chain's financial contribution to the business while satisfying the terms of the supply chain service policy. Supply chain optimization is not possible if the supply chain financial performance and costs are not defined and computed (they rarely are) or if the supply chain service policy is not defined and computed (it rarely is).

SUPPLY CHAIN CONSTRAINTS

Optimization would be easy if all we had was an objective function. Admittedly facetious, but unfortunately common, what follows is a story line that is played out in many companies. Let's consider each component of the total supply chain cost in isolation. First, transportation. Transportation has become so expensive and complex that we may just decide to stop trying. Fuel costs. Regulatory hassles. Poorly performing carriers. The list goes on. Second, warehousing. All the JIT, Lean, and Six Sigma books suggest that warehousing is non-valued-added, and just plain bad for business. Let's close the warehouses. Third, inventory carrying. Even though inventory is still an asset in accounting, we all know it's a liability (borderline forbidden in some companies) and politically incorrect in the current JIT, Lean, Six Sigma environment. We need to stop carrying inventory. Then, since there is no inventory, there will be no customers. Since there are no customers, lost sales cost is eliminated. These all work together to completely eliminate supply chain cost. We win, right? Wrong!

What should stop a company from going down that path? A supply chain service policy that provides the constraints for supply chain optimization.

The RightServe strategy is segmented by channel, ABC customer strata within a channel, commodity, and SKU strata within a commodity. It establishes optimal targets that must be met or exceeded for supply chain fill rate, response time, delivery frequency, delivery quality, packaging, and any other element of the supply chain service policy. Those requirements serve as the constraints in supply chain optimization. An example supply chain optimization statement follows. An illustration of the optimization is in Figure 1.8.

Figure 1.8   Supply chain optimization surfaces

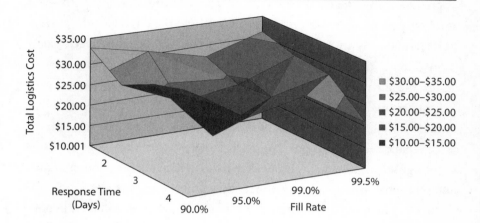

Example RightChain Objective Function

- Minimize Total Supply Chain Cost
- Total Supply Chain Cost = Total Logistics Costs + Inventory Policy Costs
- Total Logistics Costs = Inbound Transportation Costs + Total Warehousing Costs + Outbound Transportation Costs
- Inventory Policy Costs = Inventory Carrying Costs + Lost Sales Cost

Example RightChain Constraints

- Fill Rate > 99.2 percent
- Response Time < 48 Hours
- Delivery Frequency = 3x per Week

SUPPLY CHAIN OPTIMIZATION IN CONTEXT

Optimization is a facet of our RightChain program (Table 1.3) that most clearly differentiates it from other quality, operational, and/or philosophical approaches to supply chain logistics including Lean, Six Sigma, Pull,

Just-in-Time, Kanban, and the Toyota Production System (TPS). Those approaches all have their roots in the Toyota Production System—and implicitly assume that all inventory is bad (or illegal), that 100 percent perfect quality is always the goal, and that moving things between places more often is always better than batching and carrying inventory.

In the late 1980s I had the unique privilege to lead a major study for the U.S. government comparing U.S. and Japanese logistics systems. As a part of that study I interviewed business and supply chain executives in many large Japanese organizations. Not surprisingly, one of those was Toyota. I spent significant time with the developers of the Toyota Production System and their professor. One of the stories they shared explains more about the Toyota Production System than all the books I have ever read on the topic.

The Toyoda (the company name was created from the family name) family was a rice farming family. They became wealthy when they invented mechanical harvesting equipment for rice. At some point they decided that if they could make rice harvesting equipment so well, they could also make cars. Unfortunately the production concepts did not translate very well and the auto-making venture almost bankrupted the family. The head of the family decided to hire a new engineer from outside the family and to give him one year to develop a new way to make cars. To make a long story short, that young man came up with a way to profitably make cars in an island nation (self-contained), with few natural resources (no waste), limited inhabitable land (no space), and locust-like industrial congestion (perfectly orderly). The Toyota Production System was born out of those unique geographic, business, and cultural conditions. Those are not the same conditions that exist in the United States, western Europe, eastern Europe, China, Brazil, and so on. There are many good ideas and concepts in the Toyota Production System and its paradigm children, but they are not all applicable and they are not all best practices. They are for Toyota, but not for everyone. *Don't philosophize, optimize!*

Table 1.3   RightChain Table of Optimizations

	Optimizations	Description	Typical Benefits
RightServe **Service Optimization**	RightSales	Customer Portfolio Optimization (CPO)	Identifies and dispositions non-value-added customers.	*1% to 5% of Sales*
	RightPrice	Sales Order Optimization (SOO)	Identifies and dispositions non-value-added orders.	5% to 15% lower total cost to serve
	RightFill	Fill Rate Optimization (FRO)	Computes the financial and service optimal fill rate for each customer.	1 to 4 points higher customer satisfaction
	RightStops	Delivery Frequency Optimization (DFO)	Computes the financial and service optimal delivery frequency for each customer.	
	RightTerms	Service Terms Optimization (STO)	Optimizes channels, segments, dimensions, and levels of service.	
RightStock **Inventory Optimization**	RightSKUs	SKU Portfolio Optimization (SPO)	Identifies and dispositions non-value-added SKUs.	
	RightCast	Demand Forecast Optimization (DFO)	Optimizes forecast accuracy.	
	RightLots	Lot Size Optimization (LSO)	Optimizes production run and procurement lot sizes.	10% to 30% lower inventory levels
	RightFill	Fill Rate Optimization (FRO)	Computes the financial and service optimal fill rate for each SKU.	1 to 6 points higher fill rates
	RightTurns	Turn Rate Optimization (TRO)	Computes the financial and service optimal turn rate for each SKU.	
	RightPloy	Inventory Deployment Optimization (IDO)	Computes the financial and service optimal deployment for each SKU.	

(continued on next page)

Table 1.3   RightChain Table of Optimizations, *continued*

	Optimizations	Description	Typical Benefits
RightBuys Sourcing Optimization	RightSource — Source Selection Optimization (SSO)	Computes the financial and service optimal source(s) for each SKU.	*1% to 5% of Sales*
			5% to 15% lower total cost of ownership
	RightTimes — Leadtime Optimization (LTO)	Computes the financial and service optimal leadtime for each SKU.	
			1 to 3 points higher customer satisfaction
	RightBuys — Buy Quantity Optimization (BQO)	Computes the financial and service optimal buy quantity for each SKU.	
	RightRisk — Supplier Risk Optimization (SRO)	Computes and optimizes supplier risk portfolios.	10% to 40% less supply risk
	RightTerms — Purchase Terms Optimization (PTO)	Computes the financial, service and compliance optimal INCOTERMS and purchase terms.	
RightTrips Transportation Optimization	RightLanes — Lane Optimization (LPO)	Determines financial and service optimal flow lanes for each SKU.	
	RightNodes — Logistics Network Optimization (LNO)	Determines financial and service optimal logistics network for each flow path.	5% to 15% lower total transportation cost
	RightModes — Transportation Mode Optimization (TMO)	Computes the financial and service optimal transportation mode for each shipment.	
	RightShip — Shipment Plan Optimization (SPO)	Computes the financial and service optimal shipping frequency for each lane.	1 to 2 points higher customer satisfaction
	RightFleet — Transportation Fleet Optimization (TFO)	Computes the financial and service optimal transportation fleet size and configuration.	

(continued on next page)

	Optimizations	Description	Typical Benefits	
RightHouse Warehouse Optimization	RightStore	Storage Mode Optimization (SMO)	Computes the cost and space optimal pallet, case, and broken case storage mode for each SKU.	10% to 25% lower total warehousing cost	1% to 5% of Sales
	RightFace	Pick Face Optimization (PFO)	Computes the cost, labor, and space optimal pick face size for each SKU.	1 to 7 points higher inventory accuracy	
	RightSlot	Slot Location Optimization (SLO)	Computes the cost, labor, and space optimal slot location for each SKU.		
	RightZone	Pick Zone Optimization (PZO)	Computes the cost, labor, and space optimal order picking zone configuration.	1 to 8 points higher shipping accuracy	
	RightFlows	Flow Path Optimization (FPO)	Computes the cost, labor, and space optimal warehouse layout and material flow paths.		
RightPlan		Supply Chain Plan Optimization (SCPO)	Computes the financial and service optimal monthly supply chain plan.		

Optimization quantifies and translates unique marketplace objectives and constraints and determines a supply chain decision solution for each element of supply chain strategy. We developed our RightChain Optimizations to assist our clients in the ongoing optimization of their supply chains. RightChain Optimizations include optimization tools that address the major decisions in supply chain strategy in customer service, inventory, supply, transportation, warehousing, and the supply chain as a whole. Our RightChain Optimizations have their roots in our decision support tools developed as early as the mid-1980s, and they have been successfully used in nearly every major industry in nearly every part of the world.

Through optimization, RightChain takes into consideration the unique financial goals, service requirements, competitive environment, and logistics conditions for each business to help determine the most effective supply chain strategy. Though it may sound heretical, the optimal solution may involve carrying more inventory. That was the case in three of our largest and most successful supply chain strategy engagements last year. In each case, the strategic increase in inventory led to higher profits, higher market share, and higher levels of customer satisfaction. Though it may sound heretical, the optimal solution may not mean perfect quality, but optimal quality. We use a computation of the cost (expense, capital, and lost revenue) of poor quality to help our clients determine the optimal level of quality and the reasonable investment in quality improvements. The optimal supply chain strategy may involve fewer, less frequent movements using less expensive transportation modes. It is the cost of fuel and freight relative to the cost of carrying inventory and the customer service requirement that should determine the frequency, length, and modes for supply chain moves—not the philosophical or operational paradigms of supply chain mantras.

In summary, via optimization RightChain quantifies and monetizes marketplace objectives, dynamics, and constraints and yields a supply chain decision solution for each element of supply chain strategy.

CHAPTER 2

RightScores
Supply Chain Performance Strategy

"God desires honest weights and measures."
—SOLOMON

We have a variety of contests in our seminar programs. One that I particularly like is the *Question of the Day* contest. The seminar students vote on the best question asked during the day. During our recent RightScores seminar, the vice president of supply chain for a large telecommunications company won the contest. His question was, "What is the quickest, cheapest, and most effective way to get a supply chain up to world-class performance?" The first thing I thought was, "Only in America would someone even ask such a question." The second thing I thought was, "I'd better come up with something." The answer I gave him is what I passionately believe to be true. *Develop, implement, and maintain a world-class set of performance metrics and targets.*

People for the most part behave based on the way they are measured. If you give people the right definition of success embedded in a healthy set of performance measures and targets, the right behaviors will normally follow. Unfortunately, most metrics exacerbate the very problems they are meant to solve, often introduce new problems, and go hand in hand with targets so aggressive as to be discouraging or so lame as to be irrelevant. The systems of metrics and targets in most businesses are so dysfunctional that the average life span of a performance metric in American business is six weeks. Professionals rarely think and ponder; they tend to measure and target, and crisis begets crisis.

So before we delve into the metrics and targets themselves, let's consider a few of the most important characteristics of healthy metrics and targets in general and then apply those characteristics to supply chains in particular.

2.1 Metrics and Targets

In our RightScores seminars I ask the seminar attendees to name the characteristics of healthy metrics and targets. I'm writing a synopsis here of the most important characteristics.

Metrics and targets are frequently confused. Metrics are the dimension of measurement. Targets are the numerical goals. You can have a great metric and a terrible target and vice versa.

Effective Metrics

Though there are many characteristics of effective measures, the most important that I have experienced in our consulting and research answer the following.

- Are the metrics **meaningful**?
- Are the metrics **controllable**?
- Are the metrics readily **comprehensible**?
- Are the metrics **aligned** vertically, horizontally, and externally?
- Are the metrics **consistent**?
- Do the metrics **span** the activities being measured?

Meaningful

Meaningful metrics are both memorable and relevant.

During a recent visit to an automotive client I asked the vice president of supply chain how many metrics they used to monitor their supply chain performance. I don't know why the number stuck with me, but it did. He proudly stated that they had 349 supply chain performance metrics and pointed to the six-inch-thick notebook on the shelf behind him that had details on each of those metrics going back for the prior five years. I wasn't quite sure how to respond, and so I said what I often say when I don't know what to say and I don't want to be derogatory. I simply said, "That's amazing." That is amazing.

There is no way anyone could keep track of 349 metrics. (I suspect that they, like many, use metrics as a substitute and/or pretense for management.) At some point, having too many metrics dilutes the meaning of any single metric. The right number of metrics is the fewest needed to do the job. I typically recommend that no more than seven metrics be used for any activity. People can only remember up to seven things about anything. As long as they are the right things, fewer is better than more!

Being meaningful also means being relevant. According to Webster, *relevant* means "having significant and demonstrable bearing on the matter at hand." If a metric is irrelevant, either because it is buried under so many other metrics that no one can find it, or because no one is accountable to it, or because when the performance of the metric changes no behaviors or decisions change—then it should not be incorporated in a supply chain performance measurement program.

Controllable

Several years ago I was invited to address the supply chain management team of one of the world's largest grocery companies. I was first up, and before I got up to speak the CEO asked to talk with me. After a little chit chat, he shared with me that he was going to speak to the group about their new supply chain performance indicator. I asked him about it. He shared that after some extensive research they had developed the metric of all metrics to define their supply chain performance. They had researched all of their SKUs and found the one that was the average weight, cube, and cost of all the other SKUs. It was a can of Starkist tuna. He said that they were just going to monitor the supply chain cost as a percent of sales for that one SKU and, based on that, reward or discipline their supply chain management team.

My internals were going haywire trying to come up with a way to react that would not be offensive. I just said, "That's amazing." I then shared with him a make-believe story that popped into my head to help get the point across in a semi-humorous way.

I knew the CEO was a movie buff, so I asked him how many Rocky movies there had been. He said correctly that there had been six (that was correct at the time). I asked him to imagine *Rocky VII*, where Rocky and Apollo Creed are roused from their assisted living facilities to duke it out one more time. I asked him to imagine the scene at the end of the fourteenth round, and it's not looking too good for Rocky. He can hardly walk back to his corner stool to rest for the fifteenth round. When he plops down on his stool, his manager, Mick, exhorts to him to "man up" for the final round. Rocky, exhausted and wavering, has a boyhood flashback of his favorite cartoon hero—Popeye the Sailor Man. In the flashback he remembers that in dire situations, Popeye could pop open and swallow a can of spinach and miraculously transform into a strong fighter. Rocky asks his manager, "Hey Mick, got a can of spinach?" Mick says, "No, but I have a can of Starkist tuna." Rocky pops open and downs the can of Starkist tuna, pops up off his stool as the bell rings for the final round, walks into the center of the ring, and knocks Apollo Creed out cold. Rocky wins the world senior heavyweight championship, 10 million dollars, and a new Mercedes. The movie is wildly popular and audiences begin associating success with Starkist tuna. The sales of Starkist tuna skyrocket. The supply chain cost as a percentage of sales for Starkist tuna plummets. The supply chain managers at this grocery chain all receive promotions and bonuses. And what in the world does any of this have to do with supply chain performance? *Nothing!*

What's the point of this roundabout story. What if Rocky had downed the can of Starkist tuna and collapsed? What if people had begun to associate Starkist tuna with failure? What if the supply chain cost as a percent of sales for Starkist tuna had skyrocketed and the grocery company's supply chain management team was disciplined or even let go? What does any of that have to do with supply chain performance? *Nothing!*

The point and principle is that metrics must be influenceable by the people held accountable to them. There are very few phenomena that will discourage a workforce more than holding them accountable to metrics they can't control or influence.

Comprehensible

During a recent project I was standing at the end of a client's bottling line. I asked the plant manager how they measured the performance of the line. He looked at me with an expression that suggested that I should know the answer, and he proudly stated that they used the QUAX index. I remember thinking, "I'm supposed to be an expert in this field, and I have never heard of the QUAX index." I thought that maybe I had missed the day the QUAX index was covered in class or that I had skipped that chapter in my operations or statistics textbook. The only thing I could think of pertaining to the QUAX index was a day when my son was three years old. He came running up the stairs to meet me and was upset, saying that he had a QUAX. I said, "Son, what's a QUAX?" He said, "It's a hairball that gets stuck in your mouth." It made think that perhaps they had hairballs in their production process. I was embarrassed to ask about that, so I finally just asked, "Do you mind explaining the QUAX index to me?" He looked at me like I didn't know anything and condescendingly explained that QUAX stood for four things: Q for quality, U for utilization, A for accuracy, and X for the "x factor." "Q" was determined by multiplying 16 aspects of quality times one another. "U" was determined by adding 16 elements of utilization together. "A" was determined by averaging 16 elements of accuracy together. "X" was determined by taking the geometric mean of 16 miscellaneous factors. The results of Q, U, A, and X were added together to make the QUAX index. I asked him how many of their plants used the index. He explained that the index was used in all of their plants around the world. All I could say was, "That's amazing."

One of the main reasons metrics programs are abandoned is a lack of trust in the metrics, the process, and/or the people. Trust is best established in metrics that are simple, understandable, and easy to explain.

Alignment

Several years ago the vice president of supply chain for one of the world's largest auto companies called me. The conversation went something like this: "Dr. Frazelle, our CFO is upset about inventory levels. He believes they are too high. What should we do?" I recommended what I almost always do in that situation. I recommended they determine their optimal turn and fill rates and establish the metrics, processes, and systems required to hit both targets. He said, "That sounds like good advice." Three months later he called again. This time the conversation went something like this: "Dr. Frazelle, our dealer network is upset. They believe our fill rates are too low. What should we do?" I recommended that same approach—determine the optimal turn and fill rates and establish the metrics, processes, and systems required to hit both targets. He said, "That sounds like good advice." Three months later he called again. The conversation went something like this: "Dr. Frazelle, our CFO is upset about our inventory levels. He believes they should be lower. What should we do?" I said, "I think you should stop calling me because you are either not listening to or not implementing what I am recommending. You are on the inventory seesaw; lowering inventory levels to satisfy finance until sales complains about service levels, and then raising inventory until finance complains." He said, "You're right. Will you come talk to our CFO?" That was the start of a significant supply chain journey for this company—a journey to the land of balance and optimization.

Since "a house divided against itself cannot stand," alignment is one of the most important characteristics of a healthy system of metrics. The metrics need to align the objectives of the supply chain with the business, to align the objectives of the supply chain activities with one another, and to align externally with metrics that allow benchmarking with peers.

Spanning

Imagine a bridge that reached 70 percent of the way from one side of a river to another. What use is the bridge?

That seems like a ridiculous question, but many systems of metrics only span a portion of the activities or concerns they are meant to cover. For example, supply chains have three main groups of constituents—employees, customers, and shareholders. If a system of supply chain metrics excludes the concerns of one of those groups, it is incomplete and potentially dangerous. Supply chains have five main activities—customer service, inventory management, sourcing, transportation, and warehousing. If a system of supply chain metrics excludes one of those activities, then the system of metrics is incomplete and potentially misleading. I could continue, but I think you get the message. Incomplete systems of metrics always lead to sub-optimization and a lack of integration.

Effective Targets

Though effective targets have many characteristics, the most important that I have experienced in our consulting and research answer the following.

- Are the targets reasonably **achievable**?
- Are the targets **motivational**?

Achievable

If someone invited me to play golf and told me my target score was 72, I would assume the person was talking about nine holes. If the target was for 18 holes, I would be so discouraged I wouldn't play. Many corporate cultures are demotivating performance and discouraging people by demanding ridiculous and unreasonable performance accompanied with no timeline, plan, or resources. Challenging performance targets can be effective as long as they come with reasonable time, plans and resources.

Is it ever effective to have stretch goals? Absolutely—if the goals are accompanied with sufficient resources and a wise project plan, and especially if they are given incrementally. If someone told me that I need to lose 24 pounds (and I do), I would be discouraged. If someone told me that I need to lose 2 pounds per month for 12 months, I would be encouraged. Incremental goals reflecting reasonable, sustainable progress work best!

Motivational

When I was a sophomore in college, I was in the scholarship program of one of the large automotive companies. In addition to paying my tuition and fees, they also provided a summer job. My first assignment was to reset a time standard on a lathe operation with an operator who had been working on that lathe before I was born. Needless to say, he had his way with me.

During that time I noticed that when I went out on the plant floor to conduct the work samplings between 3:00 p.m. and 5:00 p.m., no one was there. When I went to find the workforce, I soon figured out that they were hanging out at the exit doors and in the cafeteria. I was curious about how this worked and wondered if this was normal. It was my first factory job, so I asked my boss about it. He said that they had developed standards that defined "eight hours' worth of work." As soon as someone had made the "eight hours' worth" of product, he or she could stop. Employees were not allowed to go home, but they could stop working and "hang out." That's not motivational or helpful. I have never seen a workforce work so hard to not work. A critical aspect of effective leadership is providing helpful performance goals.

2.2 Supply Chain Scoreboard

So how do you develop and implement a set of metrics and targets that meet all those criteria? Our best attempt is the RightChain Scoreboard depicted in Figure 2.1. Let's go through it.

1. Note that the scoreboard is organized according to a servant leadership culture, thereby aligning the metrics with our client's corporate culture. The metrics are organized into three major blocks—employee-facing metrics to reflect the desire to serve employees with a great place to work; customer-facing metrics to reflect the desire to serve customers with excellent customer service; and shareholder-facing metrics to reflect the desire to serve shareholders with a high return relative to their risk.

2. The scoreboard spans each of the supply chain activities and culminates in summary metrics that tie the workings and motivations of the supply chain together.

3. Like sports teams, organizations perform based on the way they practice. If a team has poor practices, their performance will reflect them. If a team has excellent practices, their performance will reflect them. The practice score for each supply chain activity is incorporated.

4. Organizations also perform based upon the intrinsic or self-imposed complexity they face. RightChain performance targets are adjusted accordingly.

5. Reasonable performance targets have been selected based upon the client's current practices and from benchmarks available from RightChain Research. The client's score relative to target and past performance is incorporated for each metric.

6. We recently completed a supply chain scoreboard for an element of the United States Army. They were pleased with all the aspects of the assessment except one—RYG. To be honest I didn't even know what

Figure 2.1 RightChain Scoreboard

Year	2010
Month	July
Channel	Grocery
Category	Waters
State	TN

Category	Sub-Cat	Selling	Planning	Manufacturing	Sourcing	Transportation	Warehousing	Delivery	Merchandising	SUPPLY CHAIN
Service (Customers)	Quality	94.0% PSO	56.0% Fcast Accuracy	99.0% PMQP	81.0% PPQP	92.0% PDP	72.0% PWHQP	98.0% PDP	93.0% PMCO	72.0% PDP
	Cycle Time	1.9 SCT	4.7 IPCT	7 MCT	14.3 POCT	8.2 TCT	2.4 VTS, WOCT	5.4 DCT	12.8 MCT	17.3 SCCT
	On Time	93% % on-time	92% % adherance	92% % adherance	92% % OT Pos	92% % loads on-time	92% % order on-time	92% % loads on-time	92% % merch on-time	92% adherance
GPTW (Employees)	Safety	4,250.0 MH/I	7,653.0 MH/I	3,822.0 MH/I	8,788.0 MH/I	9,145.0 MH/I	9,997.0 MH/I	9,650.0 MH/I	8,998.0 MH/I	9,001.0 MH/I
	Satisfaction	81.0% % yes	91.0% % yes	93.0% % yes	94.0% % yes	91.0% % yes	81.0% % yes	79.0% % yes	98.0% % yes	85.0% % yes
	Development	9.2 out of 10	8.1 out of 10	9.3 out of 10	8.5 out of 10	8.7 out of 10	7.3 out of 10	9.2 out of 10	8.8 out of 10	8.7 out of 10
Finance (Shareholders)	Cost	1.23 $s/case	1.22 $s/case	2.99 $s/case	0.99 $s/case	1.88 $s/case	2.11 $s/case	1.82 $s/case	4.21 $s/case	12.24 $s/case
	Capital	12,000,000 $s	48,000,000 $s	207,000,000 $s	2,000,000 $s	50,000,000 $s	60,000,000 $s	70,000,000 $s	80,000,000 $s	529,000,000 $s
Productivity	ROIC	6.00% SROA	12.00% GMROI	33.00% GMROA	21.00% GMROI	9.05% GMROA	45.00% GMROA	33.00% DROA	8.00% MROA	19.00% SCROIC
	Labor	67 orders/MH	43 $s/FTE	78 cpmh	34 cpmh	124 cpmh	112 cpmh	100 cpmh	21 cpmh	18.99 cases/FTE
	Space	0.998 GM/cube	0.876 GM/cube	0.776 GM/SF	0.601 GM/cube	0.398 GM/cube	21.3 cases/SF	0.511 GM/cube	0.991 GM/cube	18.99 cases/SF
Utilization	Labor	90.0% % labor util	92.0% % labor util	91.0% % labor util	65.0% % labor util	73.0% % labor util	82.0% % labor util	82.0% % labor util	93.0% % labor util	81.0% % labor util
	Capital	28.0% % buy util	34.0% % labor util	81.0% % prod util	99.0% % buy util	34.0% % fleet util	44.0% % cap util	39.0% % fleet util	89.0% % buy util	82.0% % cap util
	Space	91.0% % space util	80.0% % space util	78.0% % space util	79.0% % space util	77.0% % space util	80.0% % space util	69.0% % space util	89.0% % space util	80.0% % space util
TOTAL		18.91 TSLC/PSO	13.45 TIC/PHO	11.10 TMC/PMO	9.97 TSC/PSO	8.88 TIC/PTO	9.12 TWC/PWHO	11.10 TDC/PDO	12.55 TMCC/PMO	26.93 TSCC/PNetOrder
	Practices	2.1 out of 5	2.8 out of 5	2.8 out of 5	2.8 out of 5	2.8 out of 5	2.8 out of 5	2.8 out of 5	2.2 out of 5	2.4 out of 5
	Complexity	2,000 orders	500 SKUs	3,000 SKU-lines	2,000 SKU-suppliers	3,000 SKU-stops	5,000 locations	1,000 SKU-stops	10,000 accounts	26,500 complexity
	Risk	4.1 Out of 5	2.8 Out of 5	3.1 Out of 5	2.1 Out of 5	4.6 Out of 5	3.5 Out of 5	3.2 Out of 5	2.5 Out of 5	3.1 Out of 5

they meant by the acronym, so I asked. They simply explained the RYG stands for "red-yellow-green," a hyper-critical aspect of the presentation of their indicators. When I pressed further they explained that in battle they may be making scenario assessments with little to no sleep, little to no food, and bullets flying around. In trying to make quick, logical decisions under those circumstances it is helpful to know if things are OK (green), in trouble (red), or somewhere in between (yellow).

2.3 The Golden Metric

Another question I get in our seminars goes like this: "Dr. Frazelle, is there just one metric we can use instead of that whole table?" The short answer is yes, but you have to compute all the others to get there. The next question is, "Well, what is it?" We have studied this for some time and have developed what I believe is a reflective single indicator of supply chain performance—the total supply chain cost per perfect order. In that single indicator we capture the major elements of financial (total supply chain cost) and service (perfect order) performance.

Total Supply Chain Cost

Our definition of total supply chain cost (TSCC) is much broader than that used in many organizations. It incorporates the revenue, expense, and capital aspects of financial performance as follows.

Total supply chain cost (TSCC) is the sum of total logistics cost (TLC) and inventory policy cost (IPC).

Total logistics cost (TLC) is the sum of total transportation cost (TTC) and total warehousing cost (TWC).

Total transportation cost (TTC) is the sum of inbound transportation costs (IBTC) and outbound transportation costs (OBTC) including all fuel, labor, space, capital, freight, and third-party charges.

Total warehousing cost (TWC) is the sum of all labor, space, capital, and third-party costs expended in warehousing.

Inventory policy cost is a term we coined a few years ago. Inventory policy cost (IPC) is the sum of inventory carrying cost (ICC) and lost sales cost.

Inventory carrying cost (ICC) is the product of average inventory value and inventory carrying rate (ICR).

Lost sales cost (LSC) is the product of true demand, unit selling price, unfill rate, and shortage factor. Unfill rate is computed as one less the unit fill rate percentage. The shortage factor is the percentage of the selling price lost when demand is unfillable.

Retailer Total Supply Chain Cost

The total supply chain cost computations for one of the world's largest retailers is illustrated in Figure 2.2. The rows correspond to the locations of their major distribution centers.

Healthcare Total Supply Chain Cost

The total supply chain cost computations for a large healthcare company are illustrated in Figure 2.3. The rows correspond to their major and minor business regions and supporting supply chain activities.

Perfect Order Percentage

According to the *American Heritage Dictionary, accurate* means "deviating only slightly or within acceptable limits from a standard." Supply chain logistics encompasses customer service, inventory planning, manufacturing and procurement, transportation, and warehousing. Defining the right measurement focus, defining the right standard, and defining the acceptable limits of deviation from the standard for an integrated set of activities as broad as supply chain logistics is complex work.

Figure 2.2   Retailer total supply chain cost computations

DC	Inbound Transportation Cost	Outbound Transportation Cost	Total Transportation Cost	Total Warehousing Cost	Total Logistics Cost	Inventory Carrying Cost	Lost Sales Cost	Inventory Policy Cost	Total Supply Chain Cost	% of Sales	SCC per Order	SCC per Order Line	SCC per Piece
Paris	$ 64,655,663	$ 102,736,030	$ 167,391,692	$ 124,476,570	$ 291,868,262	$ 195,540,967	$40,825,433	$ 236,366,400	$ 528,234,662	17.16%	$ 2,384	$ 17.48	$ 2.75
London	$ 68,301,252	$ 109,451,752	$ 177,753,004	$ 124,757,368	$ 302,510,372	$ 187,706,564	$41,761,337	$ 229,467,901	$ 531,978,273	16.36%	$ 1,362	$ 14.43	$ 2.46
Madrid	$ 31,014,013	$ 62,363,105	$ 93,377,118	$ 61,693,955	$ 155,071,073	$ 90,917,371	$21,089,529	$ 112,006,900	$ 267,077,973	18.08%	$ 1,651	$ 14.65	$ 2.17
Barcelona	$ 51,725,440	$ 70,785,106	$ 122,510,547	$ 81,057,699	$ 203,568,246	$ 129,699,998	$27,266,696	$ 156,966,694	$ 360,534,940	14.64%	$ 2,176	$ 14.06	$ 2.46
Munich	$ 41,039,375	$ 79,860,655	$ 120,900,031	$ 83,465,426	$ 204,365,456	$ 139,070,956	$39,104,662	$ 178,175,618	$ 382,541,074	19.57%	$ 2,427	$ 23.27	$ 2.05
Rome	$ 58,422,654	$ 136,833,989	$ 195,256,644	$ 106,665,124	$ 301,921,768	$ 173,263,595	$34,886,671	$ 208,150,266	$ 510,072,034	18.33%	$ 3,862	$ 17.22	$ 2.62
Prague	$ 68,227,281	$ 125,940,008	$ 194,167,289	$ 106,016,521	$ 300,183,809	$ 198,509,961	$40,741,433	$ 239,251,394	$ 539,435,203	16.60%	$ 2,609	$ 15.49	$ 2.47
Amsterdam	$ 54,293,989	$ 100,007,913	$ 154,301,902	$ 73,130,322	$ 227,432,224	$ 154,621,243	$32,266,142	$ 186,887,385	$ 414,319,609	16.03%	$ 2,499	$ 14.94	$ 2.46
Basel	$ 32,105,696	$ 71,285,359	$ 103,391,056	$ 63,752,296	$ 167,143,352	$ 93,971,704	$27,656,764	$ 121,628,468	$ 288,771,820	18.89%	$ 2,803	$ 15.46	$ 2.59
Manchester	$ 39,574,071	$ 46,560,001	$ 86,134,072	$ 82,122,952	$ 168,257,024	$ 131,021,149	$64,901,477	$ 195,922,626	$ 364,179,650	19.33%	$ 2,341	$ 13.94	$ 2.90
Berlin	$ 33,011,956	$ 49,455,444	$ 82,467,400	$ 76,084,574	$ 158,551,973	$ 101,573,235	$12,497,383	$ 114,070,618	$ 272,622,591	17.34%	$ 6,563	$ 17.79	$ 2.66
Athens	$ 29,919,420	$ 40,706,798	$ 70,626,219	$ 64,076,009	$ 134,702,228	$ 92,028,818	$33,467,009	$ 125,495,827	$ 260,198,055	18.26%	$ 3,454	$ 15.53	$ 2.61
Milan	$ 32,975,709	$ 85,508,638	$ 118,484,347	$ 71,955,283	$ 190,439,630	$ 103,276,358	$18,984,587	$ 122,260,945	$ 312,700,575	19.91%	$ 3,895	$ 17.22	$ 2.63
Brussels	$ 57,802,597	$ 98,613,756	$ 156,416,352	$ 100,977,820	$ 257,394,172	$ 162,149,577	$33,938,382	$ 196,087,959	$ 453,482,131	16.48%	$ 1,938	$ 14.50	$ 2.23
Warsaw	$ 33,799,447	$ 61,432,249	$ 95,231,696	$ 84,769,140	$ 180,000,836	$ 114,044,150	$36,310,263	$ 150,354,413	$ 330,355,249	20.53%	$ 2,686	$ 14.92	$ 3.08
Moscow	$ 44,131,695	$ 93,158,543	$ 137,290,238	$ 106,867,581	$ 244,157,818	$ 158,470,762	$46,779,597	$ 205,250,359	$ 449,408,177	21.39%	$ 3,277	$ 19.37	$ 2.91
TOTAL	$741,000,259	$1,334,699,245	$2,075,699,604	$1,411,868,639	$3,487,568,244	$ 2,225,866,408	$552,477,365	$2,778,343,773	$6,265,912,017	17.76%	$ 2,455	$ 16.02	$ 2.54
% of Sales	2.10%	3.78%	5.88%	4.00%	9.88%	6.31%	1.57%	7.87%	17.76%				

Figure 2.3 Global healthcare total supply chain costs

RightChain™ Scoreboard | Healthcare

File Edit View Insert Format Data Tools Add-ons Help All changes saved in Drive

fx Region

	A	B	C	D	E	F	G	H	I	J	K	L	M
1	Region	DC	Inbound Transportation	Outbound Transportation	Total Transportation	Warehousing	Total Logistics Cost	Inventory Carrying Cost	Lost Sales Cost	Inventory Policy Cost	TOTAL SUPPLY CHAIN COST	Sales	Supply Chain Cost to Sales Ratio
2													
3	EMEA	Netherlands	$4,876,000	$5,041,000	$9,917,000	$6,544,000	$16,461,000	$13,605,400	$1,792,170	$15,397,570	$31,858,570	$179,217,000	17.78%
4		Finland	$93,500	$199,827	$293,327	$428,500	$721,827		$0	$0	$721,827		
5		UK	$506,027	$1,092,000	$1,598,027	$1,739,000	$3,337,027	$704,000	$187,050	$891,050	$4,228,077	$18,705,000	22.60%
6		Poland RDC	$672,480	$625,190	$1,297,670	$558,963	$1,856,633	$2,995,600	$752,250	$3,747,850	$5,604,483	$75,225,000	7.45%
7		Spain	$294,800	$1,004,000	$1,298,800	$819,937	$2,118,737	$1,504,200	$506,290	$2,010,490	$4,129,227	$50,629,000	8.16%
8		Italy	$300,300	$951,741	$1,252,041	$781,810	$2,033,851	$2,097,600	$822,770	$2,920,370	$4,954,221	$82,277,000	6.02%
9		Distributor CCC	$0	$986,858	$986,858	$0	$986,858	$0	$0	$0	$986,858	$0	
10		Distributor MEA	$0	$1,185,000	$1,185,000	$0	$1,185,000	$0	$0	$0	$1,185,000	$0	
11		**REGION TOTAL**	**$6,743,107**	**$8,913,758**	**$15,656,865**	**$10,872,210**	**$26,529,075**	**$20,906,800**	**$4,060,530**	**$24,967,330**	**$51,496,405**	**$406,053,000**	**12.68%**
12		% of Sales	1.66%	2.20%	3.86%	2.68%	6.53%	5.15%	1.00%	6.15%	12.68%		
13		% of Total	13.09%	17.31%	30.40%	21.11%	51.52%	40.60%	7.89%	48.48%			
14													
15	Asia-Pacific	Japan	$537,222	$573,999	$1,111,221	$884,561	$1,995,782	$2,287,400	$210,495	$2,497,895	$4,493,677	$42,099,000	10.67%
16		Australia-Sydney	$1,554,000	$988,156	$2,542,156	$1,529,000	$4,071,156	$1,643,800	$148,505	$1,792,305	$5,863,461	$29,701,000	19.74%
17		New Zealand	$791,672		$791,672		$791,672	$150,400	$28,615	$179,015	$970,687	$5,723,000	16.96%
18		Australia-Perth			$0	$108,300	$108,300		$0	$0	$108,300		
19		Singapore	$492,187	$4,256	$496,443	$710,169	$1,206,612	$2,321,600	$138,445	$2,460,045	$3,666,657	$27,689,000	13.24%
20		China	$39,601		$39,601		$39,601	$387,000	$44,540	$431,540	$471,141	$8,908,000	5.29%
21		India	$24,676		$24,676		$24,676	$217,800	$5,750	$223,550	$248,226	$1,150,000	21.58%
22		Korea	$54,575	$0	$54,575	$0	$54,575	$25,852	$47,570	$73,422	$127,997	$9,514,000	1.35%
23		Distributors	$204,411	$0	$204,411	$0	$204,411	$0	$0	$0	$204,411	$0	
24		**REGION TOTAL**	**$3,439,358**	**$1,566,411**	**$5,005,769**	**$3,232,030**	**$8,237,799**	**$7,008,000**	**$576,350**	**$7,584,350**	**$15,822,149**	**$115,270,000**	**13.73%**
25		% of Sales	2.98%	1.36%	4.34%	2.80%	7.15%	6.08%	0.50%	6.58%	13.73%		
26		% of Total	21.74%	9.90%	31.64%	20.43%	52.06%	44.29%	3.64%	47.94%			

Americas EMEA APAC Global

Let's consider each aspect in turn. First, the right measurement focus. The link and common deliverable of customer service, inventory planning, manufacturing and procurement, transportation, and warehousing is an order. Supply chains exist to fill orders. Second, the standard. The standard has to be perfection, otherwise the pursuit of the standard will not yield the order of magnitude improvements needed in all areas of the supply chain. The focus: an order; the standard: perfection. Alas, the perfect order. The perfect order is logistically perfect, meaning it is:

- Perfectly **entered** (the entry is exactly what the customer wants) by the means the customer desired (web, tablet, telephone, direct entry) in a single entry
- Perfectly **fillable** with the exact quantity of each item available for delivery within the customer-specified delivery window
- Perfectly **picked** with the correct quantities of the correct items
- Perfectly **packaged** with the customer-designated packaging and labeling
- Perfectly **shipped** without damage
- Perfectly **delivered** in the customer-designated time window and to the customer-designated location
- Perfectly **communicated** with order status reports available 24 hours a day
- Perfectly **billed** with on-time payment
- Perfectly **documented** with customer-specified documentation including paper, fax, EDI, and/or Internet

Suppose each of these nine supply chain activities were performed correctly 90 percent of the time (assuming performance independence for each activity). Then more than 60 percent of the orders would be imperfect. If each of these activities were performed correctly 95 percent of the time, 40 percent of the orders would be imperfect. If each of the activities were performed correctly 99 percent of the time, 90 percent of the orders would be perfect. If each of these activities were performed correctly 99.95 percent of the time, then 99.5 percent of the orders would be perfect.

To get an idea of your own perfect order percentage, take the product of your performance in each area you define as making up perfect order performance. Formally, with P_n the performance in one of n elements of perfect order performance, the perfect order percentage is computed as

$$POP = \prod(n = 1 \text{ to } N)\, P_n$$

An example perfect order percentage computation is provided in Figure 2.4. There are many lessons in this little exercise. First, you may not even track performance in the nine activities described above. It is difficult to improve something that you don't measure. Second, you may not recognize the interdependence of these logistics activities. They all contribute to the ultimate supply chain objective of filling a customer order perfectly. In fact, the perfect order percentage can only be as high as the lowest performance of its composite elements. Truly, a supply chain is only as strong as its weakest link! Third, you may not believe how low the number is. Most of our clients have a perfect order percentage lower than 50 percent. If you want to know why your customers always seem dissatisfied, that's the reason. Imagine walking into your boss's office and telling him or her that you got less than half the orders right last month. What kind of conversation would that be? (Possibly very short and/or the last one?)

Unfortunately, very little benchmarking data exists on perfect order performance. Admittedly it is difficult since there are so many parties involved in perfect order performance, including suppliers, manufacturers, wholesalers, inventory planners, carriers, third-party logistics companies, and so on. But that is the point. To deliver a perfect order requires integrated and coordinated performance by and across all these parties. World-class supply chains require this same degree of integration and coordination.

Figure 2.4   Perfect order computations

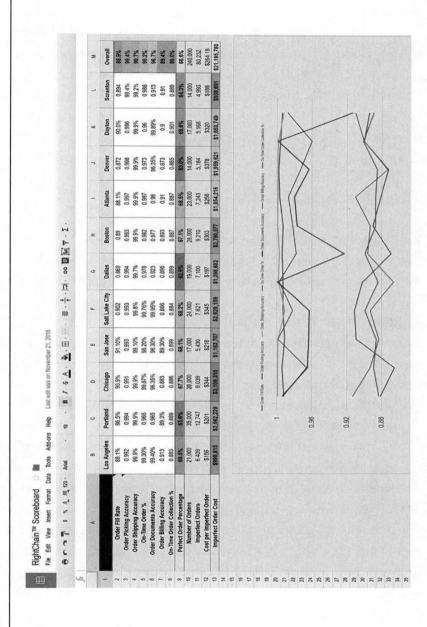

Total Supply Chain Cost per Perfect Order

The total supply chain cost per perfect order brings together the two indicators that together best reflect the financial and service performance of a supply chain. It is simply computed as the ratio of the total supply chain costs expended to the total perfect orders delivered. An example computation from a recent client engagement is provided in Figure 2.5. We have recently been including this metric in the performance bonus computations for chief supply chain officers and for supply chain service providers.

2.4 Justification and Valuation

With those metrics in hand, we use the RightChain Practices Assessment, RightChain Performance Assessment, and RightChain Financial Assessment to estimate a justifiable investment in a client's supply chain.

RightChain Practices Assessment

There is a saying in sports that a team performs based on the way they practice. It is the same in business. A business or activity within a business performs based on the way they practice. *Supply chains perform based on their practices.* Practices predict performance! That's why RightChain puts so much emphasis on practices.

Based on more than two decades of supply chain consulting and research in every major industry in many parts of the world, we have developed a database of more than 1,000 RightChain practices in customer service, inventory, supply, transportation, warehousing, metrics, outsourcing, technology, organization, and planning. We use those practices as a part of our RightChain Practices Assessment Program. Individual practices assessments for each of the 10 RightChain areas are conducted using our RightChain Practices Assessment System (Figure 2.6).

Figure 2.5 Total supply chain cost per perfect order

ACTIVITY	Los Angeles	Portland	Chicago	San Jose	Salt Lake City	Dallas	Boston	Atlanta	Denver	Dayton	Scranton	Totals	% of Total	% of Sales
Supply Chain Service	$ 575,400	$ 378,560	$ 434,760	$ 492,400	$ 499,560	$ 459,360	$ 383,120	$ 434,880	$ 311,080	$ 376,920	$ 376,920	$ 4,661,080	1%	0.12%
Inventory Management	$ 21,268,265	$ 23,164,844	$ 14,865,337	$ 11,486,489	$ 17,618,078	$ 30,302,191	$ 21,927,389	$ 21,062,741	$ 27,323,878	$ 25,446,023	$ 29,202,978	$ 242,658,213	52%	6.49%
Sourcing	$ 1,018,600	$ 1,089,600	$ 1,066,600	$ 1,013,600	$ 1,008,600	$ 1,055,600	$ 910,600	$ 1,066,600	$ 1,022,600	$ 1,047,600	$ 1,047,600	$ 11,861,600	3%	0.32%
Transportation	$ 12,059,096	$ 4,212,761	$ 12,049,003	$ 7,346,000	$ 5,950,723	$ 6,968,601	$ 5,821,003	$ 11,913,079	$ 11,732,805	$ 29,586,152	$ 4,366,903	$ 112,026,227	24%	3.00%
Warehousing	$ 9,458,684	$ 6,660,760	$ 10,618,375	$ 8,320,076	$ 6,605,880	$ 8,191,770	$ 6,821,916	$ 8,324,589	$ 6,924,601	$ 10,618,320	$ 10,618,320	$ 91,042,651	20%	2.44%
Total Supply Chain Cost	$ 44,370,046	$ 35,706,525	$ 39,034,175	$ 28,658,565	$ 31,682,841	$ 46,977,523	$ 35,864,028	$ 42,821,889	$ 47,315,164	$ 67,075,015	$ 44,632,721	$ 462,249,771	100%	12.36%
% of Total	10%	8%	8%	6%	7%	10%	8%	9%	10%	15%	10%	100%		
Cost/Sales	13.67%	7.16%	14.48%	11.58%	9.92%	8.93%	9.07%	13.14%	16.21%	23.94%	17.22%	12.36%		
Cost/Order	$ 2,112.36	$ 1,020.19	$ 1,394.08	$ 1,686.80	$ 1,320.12	$ 2,472.50	$ 1,280.86	$ 1,861.82	$ 3,379.65	$ 3,945.59	$ 3,188.05	$ 1,926.04		
Cost/Perfect Order	$ 3,040.93	$ 1,604.60	$ 2,056.62	$ 2,476.94	$ 1,394.33	$ 3,947.66	$ 1,908.65	$ 2,717.65	$ 5,367.06	$ 5,668.93	$ 4,955.36	$ 2,893.25		
Cost/Line	$ 211.29	$ 102.02	$ 139.41	$ 168.58	$ 132.01	$ 247.25	$ 128.09	$ 186.18	$ 337.97	$ 394.56	$ 318.81	$ 192.60		
Cost/SKU	$ 1,479.00	$ 1,190.22	$ 1,301.14	$ 955.29	$ 1,056.09	$ 1,565.92	$ 1,195.47	$ 1,427.40	$ 1,577.17	$ 2,226.83	$ 1,467.76	$ 1,050.57		

Figure 2.6   RightChain Practices Assessment

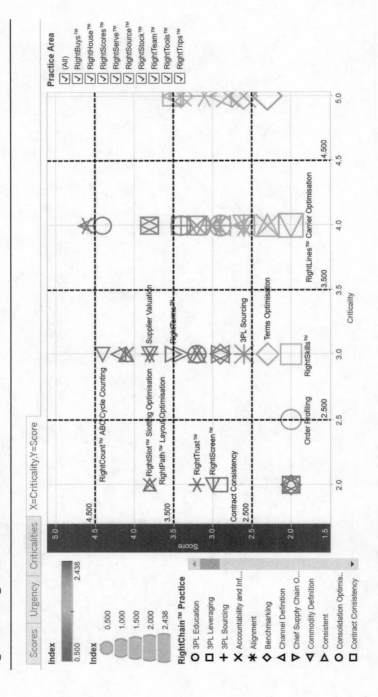

RightChain Performance Assessment

The RightChain Performance Assessment compares a company's current supply chain performance with RightChain targets for each RightChain metric. The targets are developed using three inputs—current performance, the percent improvement available from the RightChain practices that have yet to be implemented, and any reliable benchmarking information. An example RightChain Performance Assessment is shown in Figure 2.7.

RightChain Financial Assessment

The RightChain Financial Opportunities Assessment converts the RightChain Performance Gap Analysis into financials by computing the financial impact of the gap closures. An example is provided in Figure 2.8.

Supply Chain Development Planning

In supply chain development planning we tie the justifiable investment to a schedule of strategic supply chain initiatives typically playing out over a period of 6 to 24 months. An example supply chain development plan completed for a large aerospace company is illustrated in Figure 2.9.

Figure 2.7   RightChain Performance Assessment

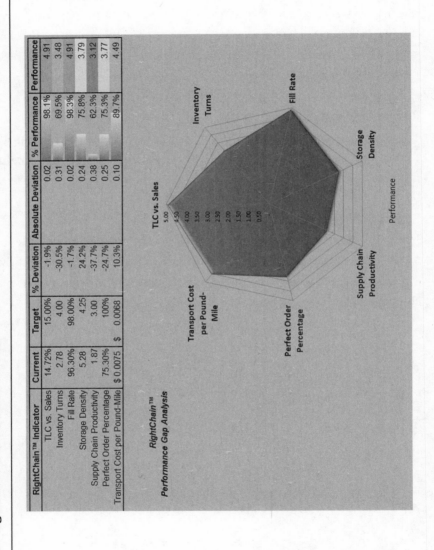

RightChain™ Indicator	Current	Target	% Deviation	Absolute Deviation	% Performance	Performance
TLC vs. Sales	14.72%	15.00%	-1.9%	0.02	98.1%	4.91
Inventory Turns	2.78	4.00	-30.5%	0.31	69.5%	3.48
Fill Rate	96.30%	98.00%	-1.7%	0.02	98.3%	4.91
Storage Density	5.28	4.25	24.2%	0.24	75.8%	3.79
Supply Chain Productivity	1.87	3.00	-37.7%	0.38	62.3%	3.12
Perfect Order Percentage	75.30%	100%	-24.7%	0.25	75.3%	3.77
Transport Cost per Pound-Mile	$ 0.0075	$ 0.0068	10.3%	0.10	89.7%	4.49

RightChain™
Performance Gap Analysis

Figure 2.8   RightChain Financial Opportunities Assessment

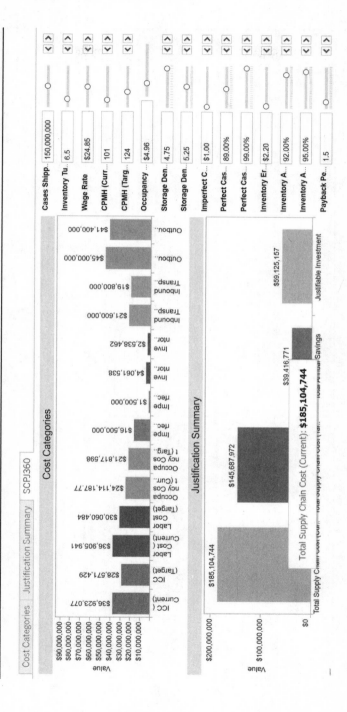

Figure 2.9 RightChain Development Plan

VALUE CHAIN	Value Chain Activity	Initiatives	Baseline Year 1	Intermediate Year 2	Advanced Year 3	World-Class Year 4
MISSION	Metrics & Targets	Connectivity	Silo	Spanning	Integrated	Predictive
		Finance	Traditional	Fiscal Logistics	Financial Engineering	VCROIC
		Quality	CSL, OTD	CSL II, OTD II	CSL III, OTD III	Perfect Delivery %
	Service Policies & Contracts	Cust Svc Policy	Ad-Hoc	ABC	ABC-ABC	Menu Based
		Contracting	One by One	Informal Coordination	Terms Optimization	Timing Optimization
SUPPLY	Inventory Optimization	Planning	SIOP	FLIOPS	SCIOPS	CPFR
		Lot Sizing	MOQ	EOQ	ELQ	EVCQ
		Deployment	Reactive	Proactive	Stage Optimization	Stage-Place Optimization
	Sourcing & Supplier Management	Costing	First Cost	Best Cost	Optimized Price	Risk Adjusted Cost
		Readiness	Readiness Book	Supply Simulation	Capacity Optimization	Predictive Readiness
LOGISTICS	Transportation & Material Flow / Whing, Kitting, & Material Handling	Material Flow	Decentralized	Logistics Centers	Regional Logistics Centers	Global Logistics Centers
		Packaging	Container by Container	Container Optimization	Flow Optimization	Design for VC
INFRASTRUCTUE	Outsourcing	Relationships	One-Off	BU Optimization	Corporate Optimization	Global Contract Optimization
	Value Chain Information Systems	Visualization	RYG Spreadsheets	Command Centers	Virtual Command Centers	Mobile Alerts
		Data Warehousing	Ad-Hoc, Dis-Integrated	Integrated Database	Integrated Portal	Data Mining
ADMINISTRATION	Security, Compliance & Risk	Risk	Qualitative/Subjective	Risk Assessment	Risk Valuation	Risk Optimization
	Organization & Culture	Integration	One Process	One Division	One BU	One Company
		Education	Course by Course	Value Chain University	PPS University	ABC University
		Units	800	900	1000	1100
		COGS/Unit	$ 5,000,000	$ 4,800,000	$ 4,500,000	$ 4,200,000
		COGS	$ 4,000,000,000	$ 4,320,000,000	$ 4,500,000,000	$ 4,620,000,000
		Turns	3.5	4	4.5	5
		AIV	$ 1,142,857,143	$ 1,080,000,000	$ 1,000,000,000	$ 924,000,000
		EBIT %	25%	30%	35%	40%
		EBIT/AIV	1.00	1.10	1.20	1.30
		CSL	90.0%	92.5%	95.0%	97.5%
		VCC/PD	$ 500,000	$ 444,444	$ 400,000	$ 363,636

CHAPTER 3

RightServe
Supply Chain Service Strategy

"The king's favor is toward a wise servant."
—SOLOMON

3.1 Supply Chain Service Principles

Over the many years of helping our clients optimize their supply chains, we have observed nine core principles of supply chain service. These principles are well known by and distinguish world-class supply chain organizations from the rest of the pack.

1. Leaders serve!
2. Monetize disappointment!
3. Recover well!
4. Design, document, and communicate!
5. It's OK to say no!
6. One size doesn't fit!
7. Tell it like it is!
8. It's a person and a company!
9. Count the cost!

Leaders Serve!

One of the character traits of the most admired companies and individuals is servant leadership. Simply put, servant leaders put a priority on serving others above themselves. Not at the exclusion of themselves, but above themselves. For example, in our work with Honda, any difficult supply chain trade-off is made in favor of serving the customer. In our work with Disney, guest satisfaction is the trump card in any supply chain decision. At L.L. Bean, the hospitality of the people of Maine is so embedded in the L.L. Bean culture that the company itself has become the state's icon. At Tiffany's, the white glove treatment in their world-renowned stores carries over into their world-class distribution centers. It is not a coincidence that these organizations—Honda, Disney, L.L. Bean, and Tiffany—are some of the most admired organizations and successful supply chains in global industry.

At the same time, those leaders do not ignore their own interests or the interests of the other supply chain and business stakeholders. They weigh the cost of offering various forms and levels of service against the value provided. The cost could come in terms of expenses, morale, capital, complexity, and/or risk. Our RightServe methodology quantifies those trade-offs and assists organizations in developing supply chain service strategies that address the concerns of all major supply chain stakeholders—employees, customers, shareholders, and the community (Figure 3.1).

Leadership is good service!

Monetize Disappointment!

Failing to monetize it, most organizations underestimate the fiscal harm accruing from poor service. Consider the following aspects of customer behavior:

- Dissatisfied customers tell many more about dissatisfaction than satisfied customers tell about satisfaction.
- The large majority of dissatisfied customers don't complain; they just leave.

Figure 3.1   Supply chain stakeholders

- It is easier and easier for customers to leave and find other sources.
- The large majority of the reasons customers leave for a competitor have nothing to do with product. The reasons have to do with service.
- It is much more expensive, time consuming, and disruptive to attract and on-board new customers than it is to retain current customers.

Dissatisfaction is rooted in unmet expectations and under-performance. One of the most important aspects of supply chain service is developing a profitable service strategy that the supply chain can reasonably support and then setting, communicating, and meeting the associated service expectations.

Monetizing and avoiding disappointment is good service!

Recover Well!

I often ask our seminar attendees who they think are the most satisfied guests at Walt Disney World. The typical responses go something like this. "The ones who didn't have to wait in line." "The ones who go when the weather's good." "The ones who stay on property." While those guests may be satisfied, the most satisfied guests at Walt Disney World are those who had a dissatisfying experience.

That notion seemed strange to me until I took a turn working side-by-side with one of their retail managers. She explained that the Disney cast members are trained to spot disappointed guests. There are not many of them, so they stand out.

One day when I was shadowing the retail manager in one of their stores on Main Street USA, she noticed a little girl crying. The retail manager gently approached the little girl and knelt down next to her. She asked her why she was crying. She said that she had come all the way from Oklahoma to buy a Daisy Duck T-shirt, but she could not find one in her size. The manager looked through the shirts on the shelf and could not find one.

The manager thanked the little girl for pointing out that the shelf was empty and said that she would look in the back room. She gave the little girl a small Disney book to read while she was gone. A few minutes later the retail manager came back empty-handed. She knelt down again to tell the little girl that they did not have the shirts in the back room either, but that she would call the other stores at Walt Disney World to find one. She gave the little girl another Disney book and went to the phone.

The manager called three stores. The third store had the T-shirt in the little girl's size. A Disney courier brought the T-shirt to the store in a special package and presented it to the little girl compliments of Disney. That little girl and her parents will remember that act of service for the rest of their lives.

Recovery is good service!

Design, Document, and Communicate!

Unmet expectations are the undercurrent of poor service evaluations and perceptions. It is impossible to meet expectations that are not designed, documented, and communicated. Yet, most supply chain service expectations are not designed, documented, or communicated. The void is typically filled with the fog of war waged between sales and operations.

I ask our clients why they have not designed, documented, or communicated their supply chain service strategy. The typical responses are as follows. "We don't know how." "It's too complicated." "We've never had one before." Those clichés are code for an underlying lack of tools, education, process discipline, initiative, and accountability. My hope is that this book serves as an inspirational guidebook to world-class supply chain service—providing tools, examples, training, and even motivation to design, document, and communicate a supply chain service strategy.

Clear, reasonable, and communicated expectations are good service!

It's OK to Say No!

During one of our supply chain strategy seminars I made the statement, "The customer is not always right or king." One of the seminar attendees took quick and loud offense. She blurted out, "The customer is always right and king in our organization." I asked her who she worked with. She said that she was the chief supply chain officer for a large utility company. I asked her how they responded when customers failed to pay their utility bill. She said, "That's simple. We just cut their power off." I asked her if that was how they treated kings. She said, "No, that's how we treat repeat offenders." I said, "So not every customer is a king." That's the point. Not every customer is a king or right.

One of my favorite books of all time is *Boundaries*, written by Dr. John Townsend. The book teaches when and how to say "yes" and "no", how to manage expectations, and how to deal with the unreasonable expectations of others. Some customers have unreasonable expectations. If there was a book titled *Boundaries in Business*, it might have a section on supply chain service policy that includes weeding out and managing unreasonable customers.

A few years ago, I was teaching our RightServe methodology at 3M. Their culture is uniquely receptive to customer and SKU segmentation as well as to the discipline of supply chain service policy making and keeping. The notion of *Boundaries* resonated in their organization. Suddenly my book titled *Supply Chain Strategy* and *Boundaries* were prominently and oddly linked on Amazon's related purchases promotions.

I spent about six months as the interim head of supply chain for a major retailer. It was awful, and I was awful at it. I can influence, teach, consult, write, research, and encourage, but when it comes to managing a large group of people, I am not the guy. I would have never accepted the assignment, except that the chief supply chain officer resigned suddenly and the retailer's president was a friend of mine. Part of my assignment was to help them find my replacement. The president kept asking me, "Who are we looking for?" I said many times, "Someone who can say *no* to the unreasonable expectations of customers with authenticity, credibility, and kindness." Fortunately, we found their former head of logistics, who was working directly for their stores at the time. He is a man of integrity, wisdom, and kindness. He was the perfect fit and a great relief to me.

Boundaries are good service!

One Size Doesn't Fit!

I was at a client site recently on their annual Bonus Day. On Bonus Day the CEO announced their bonus amounts, gave a "state of the company" speech, and conducted a Q&A with employees. The assembly was in their gymnasium. There was a band, lots of decorations, a buffet lunch, and all the accoutrements that go along with a big corporate announcement.

After lunch, the CEO stood up to speak. He said, "I've got some good news. For the first quarter in our history, we made our fill rate target." (That target was 88 percent.) The band strikes up. Balloons drop. Confetti showers.

Once the ballyhoo died down, the CEO said, "Unfortunately, I have some bad news. There is no bonus to report this quarter. There is no profit."

Why do you think there was no profit? Fill rate and profitability are indissoluble.

After the Bonus Day "celebration" I met with the head of inventory planning. During the meeting, I asked how they incorporated their fill rate target in inventory planning. He said, "We just set that as the target for every item." I said, "Okay. Suppose you call Land's End and they don't have a medium white turtleneck shirt. Land's End being out of medium white turtleneck shirts is like what happened to us when we went to a Kentucky Fried Chicken and they did not have chicken. 88 percent availability on medium white turtleneck shirts ain't gonna cut it. That's the next click to L.L. Bean so fast it would make your head spin."

I then asked their inventory planning team to name one of their most obscure items. They immediately and unanimously called out the same item—paisley dog beds. I asked incredulously, "You mean you have an 88 percent fill rate target for paisley dog beds?" They said, "Oh yeah, the target is 88 percent for everything." The first thing I thought is that they should not even have paisley dog beds. I asked, "What is the forecast error on paisley dog beds?" They said, "It is so high we can't even calculate it." An 88 percent fill rate target for an unforecastable item is ludicrously risky and expensive.

Differentiation is good service!

Tell It Like It Is!

I was in Cleveland visiting one of our clients a few years ago. We were sitting in a conference room in their automated distribution center when several attendees' cell phones rang. After an awkward, silent pause in the meeting, several of those same people stepped out. The meeting was adjourned for an hour.

When the meeting restarted, I asked what the hubbub was about. They explained that one of the aisles in their ASRS had malfunctioned and that several of the day's orders were going to be delayed. Each of the people who had stepped out had been assigned to investigate and expedite a group of affected orders. In addition, they were to communicate the findings and updated ETAs to the affected customers. The communication included a phone call and e-mail apology for the hiccup, a rebate for the cost of the order, a credit for future orders, and an update on the adjusted arrival time for each order. Their transparent, comprehensive, and quick response to the few hiccups in their supply chain converted what could have been reputation damaging incidents into reputation enhancers. It turns out that how people and organizations handle their failures may have as much or even more impact on their reputation than their successes.

We have worked on a variety of Caterpillar projects over the years. I was in a Caterpillar distribution center a few years ago and noticed some new banners. One in particular caught my eye. The prominent banner read, "Integrity: The Power of Honesty" (Figure 3.2). I was a little skeptical until the distribution center manager explained their metrics scoreboard. I noticed that their customer fill rate numbers seemed a bit lower than Caterpillar's typical world-class performance. He explained that during their ERP installation their numbers had dropped. I said, "Aren't you afraid that when your customers visit your DC they will see the lower numbers?" He explained that honesty is a more important aspect of supply chain service than fill rate.

Honesty is good service!

It's a Person and a Company!

One of the challenging issues in drone warfare is the literal and personal distance between the trigger puller and the intended target. There is minimal impact to the drone operator of the strike itself.

The planners and executors of supply chain service can become so far removed from the impact of their decisions and actions that they become desensitized to poor service. On the other side of every supply chain decision and action is a person or group of people depending personally and

Figure 3.2   The power of honesty at Caterpillar

professionally on our authentic consideration of their needs and successful design and execution of our service offering.

I always encourage our team and they encourage me to remember that our clients are people first and corporations second. We work very hard to reference each person's name that we are serving and then the name of their company. There's Jim at Honda, Lynn at Disney, Rob at Pratt & Whitney, etc.

Personalization is good service!

Count the Cost!

Customers and sales want an infinite number of items to be 100 percent available, in 100 percent customizable packaging, delivered 100 percent on time, with 100 percent accuracy, in zero response time, and with zero accountability to themselves for cost or profit. If that really happened there would be a 100 percent chance of bankruptcy. Going out of business is not good service.

No corporation or individual has infinite resources. Allocating finite resources to the supply chain, counting the cost of doing so, and optimizing the service they provide is good service.

Counting the cost is good service!

3.2 Supply Chain Service Methodology

We developed the RightServe methodology (Figure 3.3) to help our clients optimize and implement profitable service offerings. The methodology advances through four steps. The first is RightSales, customer valuation and stratification, allowing us to prune and prioritize customers for service. The second is RightPrice, order valuation and stratification allowing us to prune, prioritize, and price orders for delivery. The third step is Right-Terms, crafting and implementing a supply chain service strategy with channels, strata, dimensions, and levels of service. The fourth and last step is RightScores, monitoring the supply chain's service performance and customers' satisfaction. This four-phase cycle should repeat at least quarterly and ideally be included within a monthly S&OP.

RightSales | Customer Optimization

Several years ago we developed a methodology and analytics to evaluate customers, similar to that used by stock analysts to evaluate stocks (Figure 3.4). The methodology and analytics incorporate three valuation components—business value, strategic value, and cost-to-serve.

Figure 3.3   RightServe methodology

Figure 3.4   RightServe customer valuation model

Business	Strategic	Cost-to-Serve
• Revenue	• Reputation	• Variability
• Margin	• Potential	• Compliance
• Profit	• Loyalty	• Physicality
• Net Income	• Innovation	• Payment
• Return	• Geography	• Complexity

Customer Business Valuation

We take the following factors (Table 3.1) into account when computing the business value of a customer: (1) Revenue, (2) Margin, (3) Profit, (4) Income, and (5) Return. Our table of customer business valuation factors follows. We use those data points to evaluate, rank, and stratify the customer base. Some examples follow.

Table 3.1   RightServe Business Valuation Factor Table

Revenue	Margin	Profit	Income	Return
Revenue	Margin	Profit	Net Income	Return on Invested Capital
Revenue Contribution	Margin Contribution	Profit Contribution	Net Income Contribution	Gross Margin Return on Inventory
Revenue Rank	Margin Rank	Profit Rank	Net Income Rank	
Revenue per Unit	Margin per Unit	Profit per Unit	Net Income per Unit	
	Margin % of Revenue	Profit % of Revenue	Net Income % of Revenue	
		Profit % of Margin	Net Income % of Margin	
			Net Income % of Profit	

Large Food Company Customer Business Valuation

We were recently retained by a large food company that was lagging their industry's net income norms. Their RightServe customer business valuation is illustrated in Figures 3.5 to 3.7.

Figure 3.5 is a classic ABCD stratification of customers based upon revenue, gross margin, operating income, and net income. In the RightServe methodology, the customers who contribute the first 50 percent of revenue, margin, profit, income, and/or return are stratified as A customers. The customers who contribute the next 30 percent are stratified as B customers. The customers who contribute the next 15 percent are stratified as C customers. The customers who contribute the last 5 percent are stratified as D customers.

The matrix also draws attention to any customers for which we are losing margin, income, and/or profit. In this case, our client was losing $670,000 in annual margin serving 20 D customers; $7,306,000 in annual profit serving 39 D customers; and $9,754,000 net income serving 43 D

Figure 3.5   RightSales Pareto matrix

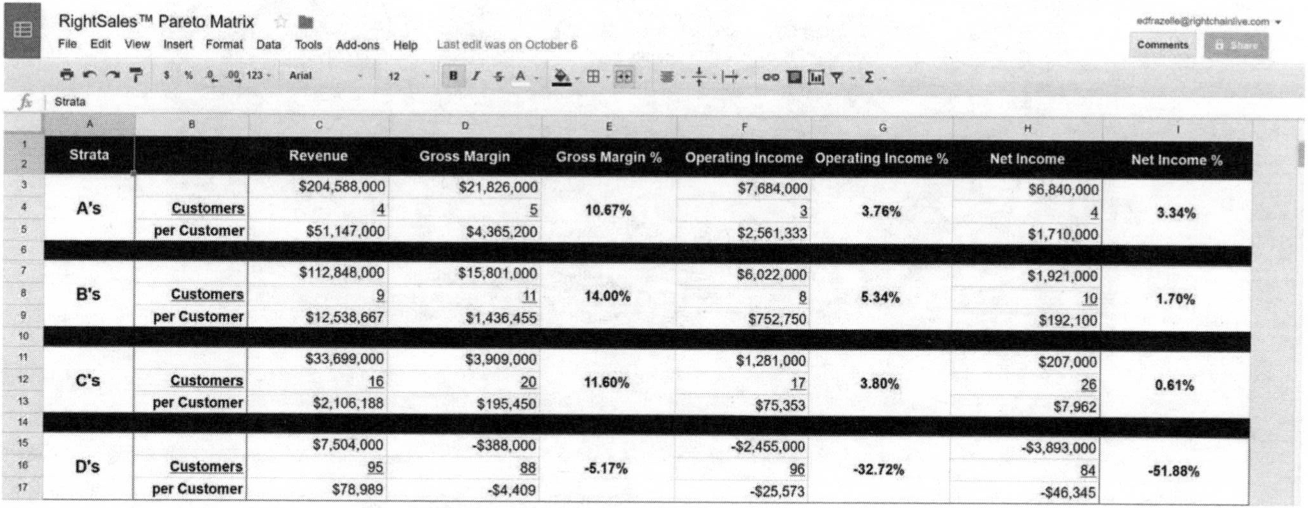

RightSales ™ Pareto Matrix
File   Edit   View   Insert   Format   Data   Tools   Add-ons   Help   Last edit was on October 6

softrachelle@rightchainlive.com
Comments   Share

Strata		Revenue	Gross Margin	Gross Margin %	Operating Income	Operating Income %	Net Income	Net Income %
A's		$204,588,000	$21,826,000	10.67%	$7,684,000	3.76%	$6,840,000	3.34%
	Customers	4	5		3		4	
	per Customer	$51,147,000	$4,365,200		$2,561,333		$1,710,000	
B's		$112,848,000	$15,801,000	14.00%	$6,022,000	5.34%	$1,921,000	1.70%
	Customers	9	11		8		10	
	per Customer	$12,538,667	$1,436,455		$752,750		$192,100	
C's		$33,699,000	$3,909,000	11.60%	$1,281,000	3.80%	$207,000	0.61%
	Customers	16	20		17		26	
	per Customer	$2,106,188	$195,450		$75,353		$7,962	
D's		$7,504,000	-$388,000	-5.17%	-$2,455,000	-32.72%	-$3,893,000	-51.88%
	Customers	95	88		96		84	
	per Customer	$78,989	-$4,409		-$25,573		-$46,345	

Figure 3.6 RightServe customer business valuation Pareto

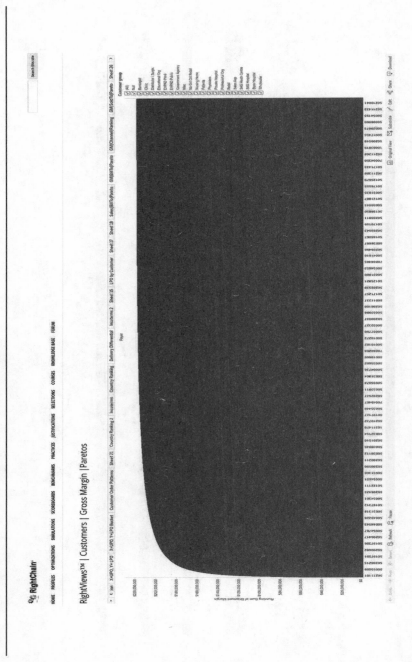

Figure 3.7   RightServe customer business valuation XYZ

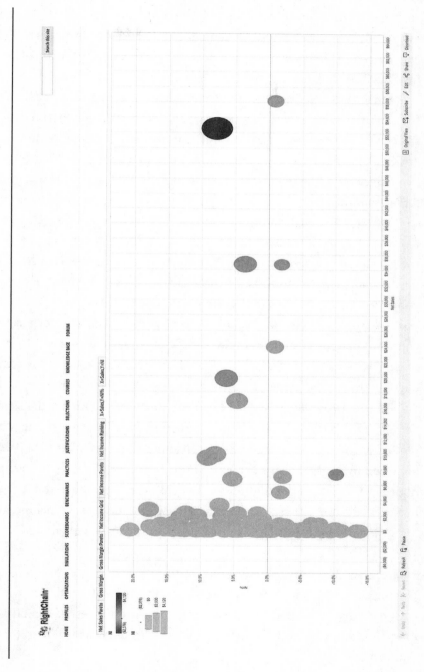

customers. Once those non-value-added customers were identified, their sales contracts were reviewed and quickly cancelled or renegotiated. Our client was quickly restored to their accustomed position at the top of their industry's net income benchmarks.

The RightServe Customer Business Valuation Pareto ranks customers from high to low in revenue, margin, profit, and net income and then plots the cumulative revenue, margin, profit, or net income at that point in the ranking. An example is in Figure 3.6, which ranks our client's customers by net income with the customer producing the highest net income at the far left and the customer producing the lowest net income at the far right.

As is typical with margin, profit, or net income Paretos, there are four distinct stratifications of customers corresponding to break points in the graph. The customers under the portion of the curve with a strongly positive slope, "A" customers, are those customers with high positive contribution. The customers under the portion of the curve with a slightly positive slope, "B" customers, are those customers with a slight positive contribution. The customers under the flat portion of the curve, "C" customers, are breakeven customers. The customers under the portion of the curve with negative slope, "D" customers, are fiscal liabilities.

A third helpful diagnostic in customer business valuation is the RightServe XYZ chart. An example is provided in Figure 3.7. Customers are plotted on an X (Revenue) and Y (Net Income) axis. Customer data points are sized by gross margin percent. Those customers with high revenue, high net income, and a high gross margin percentage have the highest business valuation. Those customers with low revenue, low net income, and low gross margin percentage receive the lowest business valuation.

Beverage Company Customer Business Valuation

During a recent engagement with a large beverage client we were provided with data that allowed us to compute the return-on-invested-capital and operating profit for each of their customers. The analysis is illustrated in Figure 3.8.

Figure 3.8   RightServe customer business valuation

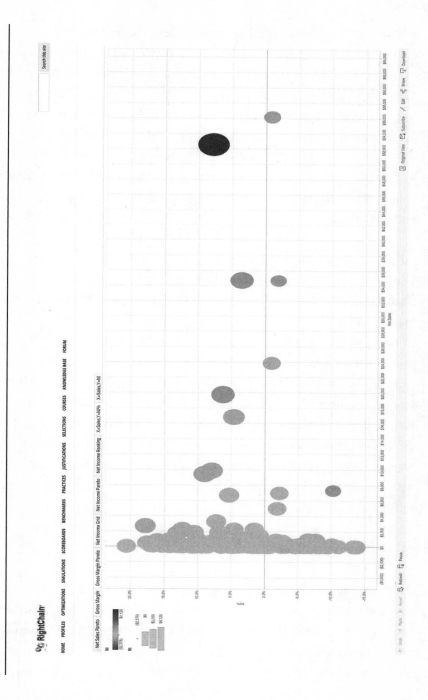

To their astonishment, they had over $100 million invested in serving customers with negative net income contributions (43 percent of the customer base), and over $140 million invested in customers yielding less than a 10 percent return on invested capital (their corporate threshold). They were also surprised to learn that 95 percent of the company's operating profit accrued from serving just 18 percent of their customer base.

These revelations shed a very alarming light on the company's policy to provide the same service offering to each of its customers, and motivated the development of a formal and segmented service optimization and offering.

Large Chemical Company Customer Business Valuation

One of our clients is a global chemical company. As chemists and chemical engineers, they were unfamiliar with the fiscal logistics of supply chain management. When their CFO became alarmed by a sudden downturn in their profitability, we were asked to assess the supply chain's role in the downturn. As we often find, our client had made no distinction in their service offering across their customer base. They were overserving many customers who took advantage of their one-size-fits-all approach to supply chain service strategy. For example, many customers negligently delayed receiving shipments and/or canceled orders well after their inventory had been produced. Using EBIT and shipping volumes (Figure 3.9), we developed a formal and distinct stratification of their customer base and subsequently tailored their supply chain service strategy.

Customer Strategic Value

Sales organizations are rarely initially fond of our valuations, rankings, and stratifications. Since their compensation is typically based on commission, any threat to potential service levels is met with strong cynical resistance. When our rankings highlight customers they are losing money serving, the typical pushback reaction is to claim that those are "strategic" customers. That may be true for some small subset of the unprofitable customers, but

Figure 3.9   RightServe customer business valuation and stratification

RightServe™ Business Valuation
File Edit View Insert Format Data Tools Add-ons Help   All changes saved in Drive

Customer	EBIT	EBIT Rank	Pounds	Pound Rank	EBIT/Pound	EBIT/Pound Rank	EBIT %	EBIT% Rank	Rank Sum	Value Rank	MVC	ABCD
LanChem	$4,440	1.0	13,147	1	$0.34	9	20.9%	9	20	40	1	A
Sun Plastics	$2,361	2.0	7,162	3	$0.33	12	21.0%	8	25	39	2	A
HyperChem	$896	6.0	2,656	12	$0.34	10	21.1%	5	33	38	3	A
Dip Integrated	$1,184	4.0	4,391	5	$0.27	16	18.7%	13	38	37	4	A
USA Hydro	$943	5.0	2,770	11	$0.34	8	17.7%	17	41	35	5	A
Flexicon	$531	11.0	586	28	$0.91	1	38.6%	1	41	35	5	A
AR Films	$694	9.0	2,092	13	$0.33	11	20.0%	11	44	34	7	A
Shipco	$850	7.0	3,683	7	$0.23	21	19.2%	12	47	33	8	A
Spectra	$359	14.0	959	22	$0.37	5	20.2%	10	51	32	9	A
Inspire	$1,722	3.0	10,938	2	$0.16	24	9.8%	26	55	29	10	A
Transyl	$845	8.0	3,558	8	$0.24	20	14.7%	19	55	29	10	A
Wypsyl	$252	18.0	409	33	$0.61	2	32.3%	2	55	29	10	A
SolChem	$277	16.0	882	23	$0.31	14	21.1%	6	59	28	13	B
Lorex	$649	10.0	3,968	6	$0.16	23	11.8%	23	62	27	14	B
ARPlastics	$294	15.0	966	21	$0.30	15	18.0%	16	67	26	15	B
Allcon	$474	12.0	3,071	10	$0.15	25	12.8%	22	69	24	16	B
Crowns	$107	27.0	233	36	$0.46	3	24.8%	3	69	24	16	B
Plasticon	$195	19.0	620	27	$0.31	13	18.4%	15	74	23	18	B
MX1	$80	29.0	220	37	$0.36	6	21.5%	4	76	22	19	B
BMS	$412	13.0	4,475	4	$0.09	32	5.8%	30	79	21	20	B
MXPrint	$70	32.0	176	38	$0.40	4	21.0%	7	81	20	21	C
D3 Films	$101	28.0	295	35	$0.34	7	18.5%	14	84	19	22	C
Glastyl	$183	20.0	1,220	19	$0.15	26	11.5%	24	89	17	23	C
ProFilms	$124	25.0	483	29	$0.26	17	16.5%	18	89	17	23	C
APK	$261	17.0	3,105	9	$0.08	33	5.5%	32	91	16	25	C
SUVCR	$130	23.0	701	26	$0.19	22	9.9%	25	96	15	26	C
ExPrint	$165	21.0	1,735	14	$0.10	31	5.7%	31	97	14	27	C
SR2 Films	$139	22.0	1,229	18	$0.11	29	6.8%	29	98	12	28	C
Reflex Nitro	$108	26.0	431	32	$0.25	19	13.8%	21	98	12	28	C

via our strategic valuation (Figure 3.10) we have a means for comparing the strategic *and* business value of a customer.

Strategic is a business buzzword that is often left undefined and available for loose and vague interpretation. As a part of assisting our clients in developing a formal evaluation of their customers, we consider a variety of factors in determining the strategic value of each customer. Those factors include but are not limited to (1) purchasing potential, (2) growth potential, (3) number of channels, (4) reputation, (5) innovation, (6) marketplace importance, and (7) off-season activity. An example customer strategic value evaluation for a large plastics company is shown in Figure 3.11.

Figure 3.10   Strategic customer valuation criteria

Strategic Valuation Criteria	Definition	Warehouse	Distributor	Club	Wholesale	International	Average
Purchasing Potential	Purchasing Potential = Sales Channel VP's estimated 12 month potential dollar sales for this specific customer when fully developed with products currently offered for sale by the company	3	3	3	4	5	3.60
Growth Potential	Growth Potential = Estimated percentage growth potential for the customer over the next 5 years	5	5	5	2	5	4.40
Channels	Channels = Number of Sales Channels for which this customer is currently actively purchasing product.	5	2	5	5	5	4.40
Relationship Life Cycle	Relationship Life Cycle = Indifferent (1) to SCBNA occasionally purchases, Moderate Interest (2) to SCBNA regularly purchases with minimal support, Active Interest (3) to SCBNA regularly purchases some products with consistent support for promotions etc, Engaged Interest (4) regularly purchases most products offered and consistently supports promotional and new product offers; Loyal Customer (5) in the past and predicted to be so in the future not only actively purchases products offered and consistently supports products but favors SCBNA to the competition. Customer participates in new product development with follow-through on purchase and actively solicits and or develops promotional opportunities.	1	5	2	5	5	3.60
Innovation	Innovation - Assign a rating of 1-5 (highest) indicating the degree of innovation demonstrated by the customer. Based on participation in new SCBNA Product development with follow-through on purchase and actively solicitation and or develops promotional opportunities OR is an innovator in their Business Segment setting the bar for which their competitors reach.	5	2	5	4	1	3.40
Branded vs. Private Label	Branded vs. Private Label - 1 = Customer only buys only Private Label Products, 2 = Customer Buys Private Label & Branded Products, 3 = Customer purchases only SCBNA Branded Product	5	3	5	5	5	4.60
Loyalty	Loyalty - On a scale of 1-5 (highest) rate the customer in terms of how recently they have purchased, how frequently they purchase and the length of time that they have purchased SCBNA products.	4	5	5	2	5	4.20
Geographic	Geographic - Rate this customer's geographic location on a scale of 1-5 (Highest) in importance to your sales efforts. Example - new targeted market area, location projected to have significant population growth in the next 5 years, etc.	1	5	4	5	2	3.40
Marketplace Importance	Marketplace Importance - rate this customer's importance in the marketplace on a scale of 1-5 (Highest).	3	5	1	5	4	3.60
% of SKUs Purchased that are Strategic SKUs	% of SKUs Purchased that are Strategic SKUs - Number of SKUs purchased by this Customer that are defined by the Sales Channel VP to be Strategic divided by total number of SKUs purchased	5	3	5	3	5	4.20
Off-Season Activity	Off-Season Activity = Customer's % of units purchased during the periods deemed to be "Off-Season" for specific SKU groups.	5	5	3	5	5	4.60

Figure 3.11 Customer strategic valuation for a large plastics company

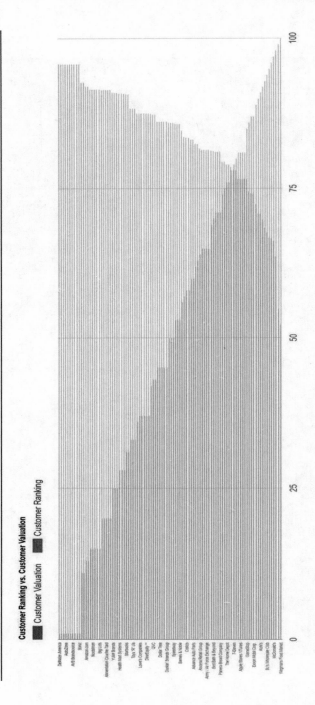

Cost-to-Serve

"Cost-to-serve" is another business buzzword that is rarely formally defined. Since any monetized cost of serving customers is captured in our business valuation, we use the phraseology "cost-to-serve" as a reference to the general difficulty in serving customers. The three factors contributing to that difficulty include (1) compliance, (2) physicality, and (3) variability. Compliance cost-to-serve factors include noncompliance penalties, payment terms, payment history, inventory commitments, and return rates. Physicality cost-to-serve factors include packaging requirements, handling unit requirements, and accessibility of delivery locations. Variability cost-to-serve factors include the frequency of change orders, order size variability, order timing variability, demand notice, and demand forecastability. An example cost-to-serve analysis for a large consumer products company is presented in Figures 3.12 and 3.13.

Figure 3.12   Components of a cost-to-serve analysis

Figure 3.13 RightServe cost-to-serve computation matrix

Cost-to-Serve Valuation Criteria	Definition	Warehouse	Distributor	Club	Wholesale	International	AVERAGE
Time Between Orders	Time Between Orders = 365 days divided by total number of orders during the last 12 months.	2	4	4	4	4	3.60
Forecastability	Forecastability = Average Forecast Accuracy at the Customer Level since January 04.	4	0	4	4	4	3.20
Re-Distribution Activity	Re-Distribution Activity = Does the customer re-distribute SCBNA products? (Shelf-life requirements?)	4	4	4	3	4	3.80
Average Order Size	Average Order Size = Last 12 months case sales divided by number of orders placed in the last 12 months.	4	1	4	4	4	3.40
Order Size Variability	Order Size Variability = % variability in customer's order size based on lowest cost order multiples during a 12 month period.	4	4	4	4	4	4.00
Dock Delays	Dock Delays = Average time for unloading at customer's location	5	4	4	4	4	4.20
Seasonality	Seasonality = % of annual volume that falls in Sep to Dec	4	4	2	4	3	3.40
Complementary Seasonality	Complementary Seasonality = % of annual volume that falls in Jan to May	4	4	4	4	4	4.00
% Change Orders	% Change Orders = Customer's number of changed orders divided by the total number of orders placed.	4	4	4	4	2	3.60
EDI vs. Not	EDI vs. Not = Does the customer utilize EDI for order processing.	4	4	2	4	4	3.60
VMI vs. Not	VMI vs. Not = Does SCBNA manage the customer's DC inventory & order placement process	2	4	4	4	4	3.60
Payment History	Payment History = Average number of days between order shipment and receipt of payment	4	4	1	4	4	3.40
Terms of Payment	Terms of Payment - What are the payment terms for this customer?	4	3	4	4	4	3.80
Invalid Deduction Rate	Deductions = last 12 months dollar value of this customer's deductions divided by the last 12 month's dollar value of customer's purchases	4	4	4	4	2	3.60
COA Requirements	COA Requirements - Does this customer require a COA on finished goods?	4	4	4	2	4	3.60
Return Rate	Returns = last 12 months dollar value of this customer's returns divided by the last 12 month's dollar value of customer's purchases	4	4	4	4	4	4.00
Service Penalties	Service Penalties - Does this customer impose service failure penalties or cause service penalties in other areas?	1	4	4	4	4	3.40
Inventory/Deployment Commitments	Inventory Commitments - Does this customer mandate any specific inventory commitments and/or deployment?	4	4	4	4	4	4.00
Pallet/Layer/Case Pick	Pallet/Layer/Case Pick = Percentage of customer's case sales that are Pallet, Layer and Case picked. (3 measures)	3	4	4	4	4	3.80
Plant Direct/Pickup	Plant Direct / Pick-up - Percentage of Customer's Sales that are Shipped Plant Direct and Percentage of Customer's Sales that are Picked-up at Plant (2 measures)	4	4	4	4	0	3.20

Most Valuable Customer

Based on those myriad business, strategic, and cost-to-serve factors, our methodology computes a Most Valuable Customer ranking. We use that ranking to stratify customers into A, B, C, and D strata for means of optimizing supply chain service. An example Most Valuable Customer ranking and subsequent stratification is shown in Figure 3.14.

The notion that some customers may be less valuable than others nearly always meets with resistance. Some of the resistance is denial and false hope—denying there is a difference and falsely hoping everything works out in the end. Some of the resistance is sentimental. However, this evaluation is not a judgment of human worth, but an assessment of how each customer interacts with our business. Some of the resistance is inertial. Most customers have never been evaluated, and doing so requires energy. Optimizing service based on facts requires even more energy.

Avoiding an evaluation is equivalent to making an evaluation that all the customers are of equal value and should be allocated equal service resources. When I make this point in a seminar, the popular retort is that every customer should be treated like an A customer. That typically translates to A customers being underserved and C customers being overserved.

Another question I get is, "What if a C customer finds out they are a C customer?" First, we do not have to let anyone know their strata. Second, if they find out, we will gladly work with them to help them become an A customer.

Customer—SKU Stratification

With sufficient data and time, we combine customer and SKU analysis into a Customer-SKU stratification. The Customer-SKU stratification is a joint distribution revealing the amount of revenue, margin, profit, net income, and/or volume in 16 business strata composed of ABCD customers and ABCD SKUs.

An example Customer-SKU stratification is provided in Figure 3.15. The size of the square in a cell represents the revenue, margin, profit, net

Figure 3.14 Most Valuable Customer ranking and stratification

RightServe™ Customer Valuation
File Edit View Insert Format Data Tools Add-ons Help All changes saved in Drive

fx Customer

	A	B	C	D	E	F	G	H	I	J	K	L	M
1	Customer	EBIT	EBIT Rank	Pounds	Pound Rank	EBIT/Pound	EBIT per Lb Rank	EBIT %	EBIT% Rank	Rank Sum	Value Rank	MVC	ABCD
2	YLUAY	$ 4,440	1.0	13,147	1	$ 0.34	9	20.9%	9	20	40	1	A
3	RLNLCL	$ 2,361	2.0	7,162	3	$ 0.33	12	21.0%	8	25	39	2	A
4	INTERNILM	$ 896	6.0	2,656	12	$ 0.34	10	21.1%	5	33	38	3	A
5	UUPLNT	$ 1,184	4.0	4,391	5	$ 0.27	16	18.7%	13	38	37	4	A
6	PRINTPACY - VIRGINIA	$ 943	5.0	2,770	11	$ 0.34	8	17.7%	17	41	35	5	A
7	NLEL PRLUUCTR	$ 531	11.0	586	28	$ 0.91	1	38.6%	1	41	35	5	A
8	C P NILMR	$ 694	9.0	2,092	13	$ 0.33	11	20.0%	11	44	34	7	A
9	MEAUTERT VACL	$ 850	7.0	3,683	7	$ 0.23	21	19.2%	12	47	33	8	A
10	RPECTRATEY	$ 359	14.0	959	22	$ 0.37	5	20.2%	10	51	32	9	A
11	RYC LIMITEU - RUTLN	$ 1,722	3.0	10,938	2	$ 0.16	24	9.8%	26	55	29	10	A
12	TRANRILTRAP	$ 845	8.0	3,558	8	$ 0.24	20	14.7%	19	55	29	10	A
13	TAVENRLNT	$ 252	18.0	409	33	$ 0.61	2	32.3%	2	55	29	10	A
14	RLLIANT	$ 277	16.0	882	23	$ 0.31	14	21.1%	6	59	28	13	B
15	LLPAREL	$ 649	10.0	3,968	6	$ 0.16	23	11.8%	23	62	27	14	B
16	MULTI-PLARTICR	$ 294	15.0	966	21	$ 0.30	15	18.0%	16	67	26	15	B
17	AVERY	$ 474	12.0	3,071	10	$ 0.15	25	12.8%	22	69	24	16	B
18	CRLTN	$ 107	27.0	233	36	$ 0.46	3	24.8%	3	69	24	16	B
19	PLARTIC RUPPLIERR	$ 195	19.0	620	27	$ 0.31	13	18.4%	15	74	23	18	B
20	MPI	$ 80	29.0	220	37	$ 0.36	6	21.5%	4	76	22	19	B
21	BEMIR	$ 412	13.0	4,475	4	$ 0.09	32	5.8%	30	79	21	20	B
22	MILPRINT	$ 70	32.0	176	38	$ 0.40	4	21.0%	7	81	20	21	C
23	AUNILM	$ 101	28.0	295	35	$ 0.34	7	18.5%	14	84	19	22	C
24	GLARTEEL	$ 183	20.0	1,220	19	$ 0.15	26	11.5%	24	89	17	23	C
25	PRLTECT-ALL	$ 124	25.0	483	29	$ 0.26	17	16.5%	18	89	17	23	C
26	ALCAN PYG	$ 261	17.0	3,105	9	$ 0.08	33	5.5%	32	91	16	25	C
27	RLEEVECL	$ 130	23.0	701	26	$ 0.19	22	9.9%	25	96	15	26	C
28	ELLPACY	$ 165	21.0	1,735	14	$ 0.10	31	5.7%	31	97	14	27	C
29	RMP	$ 139	22.0	1,229	18	$ 0.11	29	6.8%	29	98	12	28	C
30	RENLELITE	$ 108	26.0	431	32	$ 0.25	19	13.8%	21	98	12	28	C

Figure 3.15   RightSales customer-SKU stratification

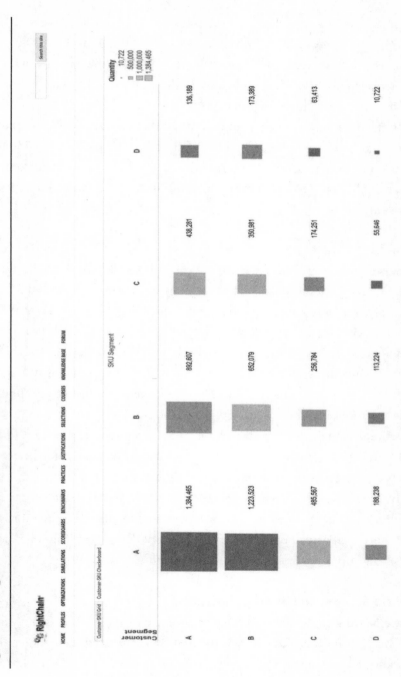

income, or volume. As is nearly always the case, a majority of the revenue, margin, profit, net income, and volume accrues from A customers buying A items. There are typically few customers or SKUs in that strata, but there is intense competition for that business. The least revenue, margin, profit, net income, and volume accrue from D customers buying D items. There are typically many customers and SKUs in that strata, and the competition is glad we operate in that strata. That said, is it logical to provide the same service offering for A customers buying A SKUs as for D customers buying D SKUs? No! Yet, most organizations offer the same service level across all strata.

RightPrice I Order Valuation

Orders connect customers and SKUs. And, just like a minority of customers and SKUs are responsible for a majority of margin and profitability, a minority of orders are responsible for a majority of the profit. Identifying the order characteristics that are most profitable is a key step in order valuation, order management, and supply chain service policy construction. The supply chain service policy should not only facilitate our ability to offer high levels of supply chain service, but also steer customers to profitable order patterns. We call that steering *order shaping*.

A recent RightPrice analysis for a large frozen food company is illustrated in Figure 3.16. In the analysis, we found a strong correlation between the portion of a pallet ordered and the profitability on the order. Essentially, if our client had to break a pallet, they lost money on the order. To counter, our client began offering steeper discounts for full pallet orders and more expensive premiums on less than pallet orders. That relatively simple pricing adjustment put $4 million on their bottom line.

RightTerms I Service Terms Optimization

I have heard it said, "Either manage customers or they will manage you." The supply chain service policy is the first step in proactive customer and demand management. The supply chain service policy is like a contract

Figure 3.16   RightPrice order optimization for a large food company

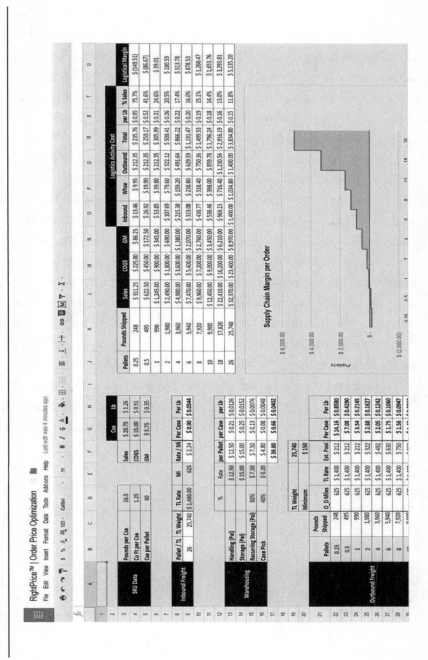

between the supply chain organization and the customers and business it serves. It defines the service targets for each supply chain channel and customer/SKU strata. It sets the service requirements for each supply chain activity including inventory management, sourcing, transportation, and warehousing. As such, the supply chain service policy is the foundation for supply chain planning. Nonetheless, most organizations operate without a supply chain service policy.

Supply chain service policies typically reflect the culture and supply chain sophistication of an organization. We characterize supply chain service policies four ways. There is the ad hoc approach where there practically is no service policy. The typical service policy stated in those organizations goes something like, "We just do whatever the customer wants." Next is what we call "well-defined exuberance" where the service policy is stated but not quantified. A typical service quote in those organizations might be, "Our service rolls our customers' socks down." Another approach is "one-size-fits-all," where there is a stated and quantified policy but no segmentation. There you might hear, "We will provide 100 percent availability for 100 percent of our SKUs for 100 percent of our customers 100 percent of the time and make our customers so excited about us that they will tell their friends and neighbors." Last is what we call a "mature" approach where the service policy is stated, quantified, differentiated within channels, and stratified by customer and SKU.

Supply Chain Service Policy Components

A mature supply chain service policy is comprised of the following four components (Figure 3.17):

- Service Channels
- Service Strata
- Service Dimensions
- Service Levels

Figure 3.17   Components of a supply chain service strategy

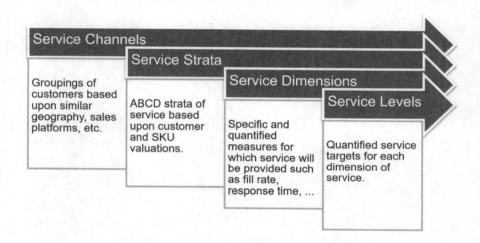

An example supply chain service strategy constructed for a large food company is provided in Figure 3.18.

Service Channels

Service channels are distinguished from one another by their geography, handling units, business purpose, customer base, and format. For example, Coca-Cola serves five major channels—restaurants, grocery stores, convenience stores, vending machines, and institutions such as schools and public facilities. One of our retail clients, Payless Shoes, serves three major channels—standalone retail stores, shopping mall retail stores, and end consumers via e-commerce. It is critical to differentiate service strategy by channel because the supply chain culture, competitive environment, physical conditions, security, and logistics infrastructure are unique in each service channel.

Figure 3.18   Example supply chain service strategy

RightServe™ Customer Service Optimization System™	Customer Class	SKU Class	Shipment Preparation Time *Internal Prep Time*	Delivery Frequency *Time Between Deliveries*	Order Cutoff Time *Latest Time for Order Placement*	Fill Rate *Inventory Availability and Allocation Rules*
Channel I	A	A	Same Day Pickup- 9:00 AM	Twice Daily	10:00 PM	99.5% – Allocation
		B	Next Day – 12:00 PM	Daily	9:00 PM	98% – Allocation
		C	72 Hours	Weekly	8:00 PM	96% – Allocation
	B	A	Next Day – 12:00 PM	Daily	9:00 PM	99% – Right of Refusal
		B	Two–Day – 12:00 PM	Weekly	7:00 PM	94% – Right of Refusal
		C	Leadtime by SKU	Monthly	5:00 PM	91% – Right of Refusal
	C	A	Two–Day – 12:00 PM	Weekly	5:00 PM	Delayed Acknowledgement
		B	72 Hours	Monthly	3:00 PM	Delayed Acknowledgement
		C	One Week	Monthly	3:00 PM	Delayed Acknowledgement
Channel II	A	A	Next Day – 12:00 PM	Daily	7:00 PM	97.5% – Allocation
		B	Next Day – 12:00 PM	Daily	7:00 PM	93% – Allocation
		C	Two–Day – 12:00 PM	Weekly	6:00 PM	84% – Allocation
	B	A	72 Hours	Weekly	5:00 PM	94% – Right of Refusal
		B	72 Hours	Monthly	6:00 PM	89% – Right of Refusal
		C	One Week	Monthly	7:00 PM	77% – Right of Refusal
	C	A	One Week	Monthly	4:00 PM	Delayed Acknowledgement
		B	Leadtime by SKU	Monthly	5:00 PM	Delayed Acknowledgement
		C	Leadtime by SKU	Monthly	6:00 PM	Delayed Acknowledgement

Service Strata

The mantra for success in real estate is "Location, Location, Location." We say the mantra for success in supply chain service is "Segmentation, Segmentation, Segmentation." Our methodology segments customers within channels based upon the value they bring to the business. We typically stratify the customer base into A, B, C, and D segments and differentiate service offerings accordingly.

This notion of stratification may or may not resonate within our client's culture. The organization psychology challenge is that by their very nature, stratification and service differentiation yield disappointment and conflict somewhere in the supply chain. Our human nature avoids conflict and disappointing anyone.

The very most mature supply chain organizations have learned how to deal with both in healthy ways. The supply chain service policy is a tool in their arsenal.

Service Dimensions

A supply chain service policy is like a contract between the supply chain organization and the customers it serves. Accordingly, the service policy should address the critical aspects of supply chain performance. Those include fill rate, response time, returns policy, value-added services, minimum order quantities, consolidation, and so on. We call those dimensions of service.

Service Levels

Our methodology determines an optimal performance target for each dimension of service, taking into account the financial and service implications of each. We call those optimal performance targets "levels of service." We employ our RightChain algorithms to determine the optimal level of service for each service dimension within each segment within each channel.

High-Tech Service Parts Supply Chain Service Strategy

We were recently engaged by a global provider of semiconductor machinery and parts. Their business, like most in Silicon Valley, is subject to wild business cycle swings. At the end of the business rope, their supply chain suffered amplified swings. Their supply chain was continually out of phase with the business cycle, jerked around feverishly to speed up or slow down based upon the timing of the business waves. Those waves drowned multiple chief supply chain officers.

We were retained by their COO to help them establish some steadying forces, and to devise a means of keeping their supply chain in phase with their business. One of the most steadying forces and phase-syncing mechanisms we have developed is the RightChain service strategy. The example in Figure 3.19 was developed for their service parts business.

Note that this particular supply chain service strategy differentiates ABC customers and ABC SKUs, yielding nine service strata. Fill rate targets range from 99 percent for A items going to A customers to 50 percent for C items going to C customers. Response times range from a low of 24 hours for A items going to A customers to a high of 96 hours for C items going to C customers. Returns permissions range from a high of 100 percent for A items going to A customers to a low of 0 percent for C items going to C

Figure 3.19   RightServe strategy for a large semiconductor company

Service Segment	Customer-Item Class	Fill Rate	Response Time (Hours)	Returns Policy	Value Added Services	Minimum Order Quantity	Consolidation
I	A - A	99.0%	24	100%	Custom	None	Custom
II	A - B	95%	24	100%	Custom	None	Custom
III	A - C	85%	48	100%	Custom	None	Custom
IV	B - A	97%	24	50%	Limited	1000+	Partial
V	B - B	90%	48	50%	Limited	500+	Partial
VI	B - C	80%	72	0%	None	100+	Partial
VII	C - A	90%	48	50%	None	5000+	Partial
VIII	C - B	75%	72	0%	None	1000+	Partial
IX	C - C	50%	96	0%	None	500+	Partial

customers. Value-added services range from custom for A items going to A customers to none for C items going to C customers. Minimum order quantities range from zero for A items going to A customers to 1,000 for C items going to C customers. Consolidation options range from full customization for A items going to A customers to partial for C items going to C customers.

Frozen Food Supply Chain Service Strategy

One of our clients is a large frozen food producer and distributor. As such, they move product through a wide variety of supply chain channels including mass merchants, traditional grocery stores, drugstores, institutions, food distributors, and even home delivery. Yet, they had not differentiated their supply chain service strategy across those channels. It was a classic one-size-fits-all approach to supply chain strategy.

We were retained to help them craft a supply chain strategy optimized and differentiated by channel and customer strata while identifying channel synergies where possible. The resulting supply chain service strategy is illustrated in Figure 3.20.

Consumer Products Supply Chain Service Strategy

One of our clients is a global provider of consumer products. Their research, development, and product innovation are world renowned. Unfortunately, their supply chain innovation was not keeping pace with their product innovation. The disconnect was creating product shortages and supply chain costs well above their industry's norms.

We were retained to develop and implement a methodology and tool set that would help their supply chain keep pace with their product and marketplace innovation. After a rigorous weeding out of their underperforming SKUs, we worked with them to craft a supply chain service strategy that allowed them to work collaboratively with product and marketplace development and maintain profitability. The strategy is illustrated in Figure 3.21.

Their channels include distributors, customer direct, and retail. ABCD customer strata are distinguished for distributors and customer direct. The

Figure 3.20   RightServe strategy for a frozen food company

RightTerms™ | Supply Chain Service Terms Optimization ☆
File Edit View Insert Format Data Tools Add-ons Help   Last edit was seconds ago

CHANNEL	Customer Strata	SKU Strata	Shipment Preparation Time (Warehouse Order Cycle Time)	Response Time (Hours to Pick and Deliver)	Delivery Frequency (Time Between Deliveries)	Order Cutoff Time (Hours to Pick and Deliver)	Fill Rate (Inventory Availability)	Returns Allowance	Palletization	Labelling	Minimum Order Quantity	Change Orders
Mass Merchants	A	A	1 hour	1 day	On-Demand	End of Business Day	Never Short on All SKUs	Yes - Unconditional	Custom - Complimentary	Custom	RFID	None
		B	4 hours	3 days	Daily - 5 Days per Week	End of Business Day	Substitution	Yes - Unconditional	Case Pick - Comp	Custom	RFID	None
		C	8 hours	1 day	Daily - 5 Days per Week	End of Business Day	Right of Refusal	Yes - Within Date Code	No	Custom	RFID	None
	B	A	4 hours	2 days	Pool Schedule	12:00:00 PM	Delayed Acknowledgement	Yes - Within Date Code	Rainbow	Custom	RFID	None
		B	8 hours	2 days	Pool Schedule	12:00:00 PM	Delayed Acknowledgement	Yes - Within Date Code	Rainbow	Custom	RFID	None
		C	12 hours	4 days	Pool Schedule	9:00 AM for Next Day	Delayed Acknowledgement	No	Rainbow	Custom	RFID	None
	C	A	24 hours	4 days	Pool Schedule	9:00 AM for Next Day	Delayed Acknowledgement	No	Premium	Custom	RFID	None
		B	24 hours	4 days	Pool Schedule	9:00 AM for Next Day	Delayed Acknowledgement	No	Premium	Custom	RFID	None
		C	48 hours	4 days	Pool Schedule	9:00 AM for Next Day	Delayed Acknowledgement	No	Premium	Custom	RFID	None
Traditional Grocery	A	A	4 hours	1 day	Daily - 7 Days per Week	12:00:00 PM	Allocation	Yes - Unconditional	Custom - Complimentary	Custom	RFID	None
		B	24 hours	2 days	Daily - 6 Days per Week	12:00:00 PM	Substitution	Yes - Unconditional	Custom - Complimentary	Custom	RFID	None
		C	24 hours	2 days	Daily - 5 Days per Week	12:00:00 PM	Delayed Acknowledgement	Performance Based	Custom - Premium Charge	Custom	RFID	None
	B	A	12 hours	2 days	Daily - 6 Days per Week	9:00 AM for Next Day	Allocation	Performance Based	Standard Palletization - Complimentary	Custom	Case - RFID	None
		B	24 hours	2 days	Weekly	9:00 AM for Next Day	Substitution	Performance Based	Standard Palletization - Complimentary	Custom	RFID	None
		C	48 hours	4 days	Weekly	9:00 AM for Next Day	Delayed Acknowledgement	No	Standard Palletization - Complimentary	Custom	RFID	None
	C	A	24 hours	3 days	Monthly	9:00 AM for Next Day	Right of Refusal	No	No	Custom	RFID	None
		B	48 hours	3 days	Monthly	9:00 AM for Next Day	Substitution	No	No	Custom	RFID	None
		C	72 hours	4 days	Monthly	9:00 AM for Next Day	Delayed Acknowledgement	No	No	Custom	RFID	None
Drug Stores	A	A	24 hours	2 days	Daily - 5 Days per Week	Same Day	Right of Refusal	Yes - Within Date Code	Rainbow	Custom	RFID	None
		B	48 hours	2 days	Daily - 5 Days per Week	Same Day	Delayed Acknowledgement	Yes - Within Return Allowance	Layers - Comp	Custom	RFID	None
		C	72 hours	2 days	Weekly	Same Day	Delayed Acknowledgement	Yes - Within Return Allowance	Layers - Premium	Custom	RFID	None
	B	A	48 hours	3 days	Pool Schedule	Same Day	Right of Refusal	Yes - Within Return Allowance	Standard Palletization - Premium	Custom	RFID	None
		B	48 hours	3 days	Pool Schedule	Same Day	Right of Refusal	Yes - Within Return Allowance	Standard Palletization - Premium	Custom	RFID	None
		C	72 hours	3 days	Pool Schedule	Same Day	Right of Refusal	Yes - Within Return Allowance	Standard Palletization - Premium	Custom	RFID	None
	C	A	72 hours	4 days	Monthly	Same Day	Delayed Acknowledgement	No	No	Custom	RFID	None
		B	72 hours	4 days	Monthly	Same Day	Delayed Acknowledgement	No	No	Custom	RFID	None
		C	72 hours	4 days	Monthly	Same Day	Delayed Acknowledgement	No	No	Custom	RFID	None

Figure 3.21   RightServe strategy for a large CPG

CHANNEL	CUSTOMER CLASS	SKU CLASS	SERVICE LEVEL						PLANNING TYPE
			% OTIF	PA	SHIPPING FREQUENCY	RETURN POLICY	VALUE ADDED SERVICES	SAFETY STOCK	
DISTRIBUTORS	A	A	95%	97%	3 TIMES A WEEK	ONLY STOCKABLE ITEMS SOLD LESS THAN 6 MONTHS AGO	CUSTOM	25 DAYS	COLLABORATIVE LEVEL 3
		B	93%	95%				27 DAYS	
		C	90%	92%				38 DAYS	
		D	88%	90%				59 DAYS	
	B	A	93%	95%	TWICE A WEEK	ONLY STOCKABLE ITEMS SOLD LESS THAN 6 MONTHS AGO	LIMITED	25 DAYS	STATISTICAL FORECAST
		B	90%	92%				27 DAYS	
		C	88%	90%				38 DAYS	
		D	85%	87%				59 DAYS	
	C	A	90%	92%	ONCE A WEEK	ONLY STOCKABLE ITEMS SOLD LESS THAN 6 MONTHS AGO	LIMITED	25 DAYS	STATISTICAL FORECAST
		B	88%	90%				27 DAYS	
		C	85%	87%				38 DAYS	
		D	82%	84%				59 DAYS	
	D	A	85%	87%	ONCE A WEEK	ONLY STOCKABLE ITEMS SOLD LESS THAN 6 MONTHS AGO	LIMITED	25 DAYS	STATISTICAL FORECAST
		B	83%	85%				27 DAYS	
		C	80%	82%				38 DAYS	
		D	80%	82%				59 DAYS	
CUSTOMERS	A	A	98%	100%	5 TIMES A WEEK	ONLY STOCKABLE ITEMS SOLD LESS THAN 6 MONTHS AGO	CUSTOM	25 DAYS	COLLABORATIVE LEVEL 2
		B	96%	98%				27 DAYS	
		C	94%	96%				38 DAYS	
		D	92%	94%				59 DAYS	
	B	A	96%	98%	3 TIMES A WEEK	ONLY STOCKABLE ITEMS SOLD LESS THAN 6 MONTHS AGO	LIMITED	25 DAYS	STATISTICAL FORECAST
		B	94%	96%				27 DAYS	
		C	92%	94%				38 DAYS	
		D	90%	92%				59 DAYS	
	C	A	96%	98%	TWICE A WEEK	ONLY STOCKABLE ITEMS SOLD LESS THAN 6 MONTHS AGO	LIMITED	25 DAYS	STATISTICAL FORECAST
		B	94%	96%				27 DAYS	
		C	92%	94%				38 DAYS	
		D	90%	92%				59 DAYS	
	D	A	96%	98%	ONCE A WEEK	ONLY STOCKABLE ITEMS SOLD LESS THAN 6 MONTHS AGO	LIMITED	25 DAYS	STATISTICAL FORECAST
		B	94%	96%				27 DAYS	
		C	92%	94%				38 DAYS	
		D	90%	92%				59 DAYS	
RETAILERS	A	A	95%	97%	TWICE A WEEK	ONLY STOCKABLE ITEMS SOLD LESS THAN 6 MONTHS AGO	CUSTOM	VIRTUAL WAREHOUSE	COLLABORATIVE LEVEL 1
		B	95%	97%					
		C	95%	97%					
		D	95%	97%					

strategy specifies targets for fill rate, on-time shipping, shipping frequencies, returns policies, value-added service offerings, and safety stock levels. The strategy even specifies tailored supply chain planning models. It is one of the most comprehensive and effective supply chain service strategies operating in global industry.

RightScores I Service Performance Optimization

Once the supply chain service policy has been developed and implemented, the next step is to monitor how well the supply chain lives up to its promises. As we will discuss in a bit, the dimensions of service the supply chain is most ably prepared to impact are inventory availability, response time, delivery frequency, and delivery timing. The byproduct metrics become fill rate and on-time delivery. Joined together they are on-time-in-full, or OTIF. If we add order accuracy to the mix we get on time, in full, and accurate; commonly known as the perfect order percentage (Table 3.2).

Table 3.2　RightServe Scoreboard

Measure	Previous	Current	Competition	Satisfaction
Fill Rate	98.6%	99.1%	99.3%	−0.2
On Time	93.4%	92.8%	92.3%	+0.3
OTIF	92.1%	91.9%	91.7%	−0.1
Accuracy	97.7%	98.2%	98.4%	−0.1
Perfect Order Percentage	82.9%	83.0%	82.7%	0

Not only should we be concerned with how we are doing relative to our past performance, but also relative to our competition. We call that monitoring service competitiveness analysis (Figure 3.22). We should be particularly concerned with the dimensions of service that are especially important to the customer, and where our performance relative to the competition is low. In the example, inventory availability and DC locations are our two supply chain service vulnerabilities. Guess what the focus of the next supply chain planning meeting will be?

Figure 3.22   Service competitiveness analysis

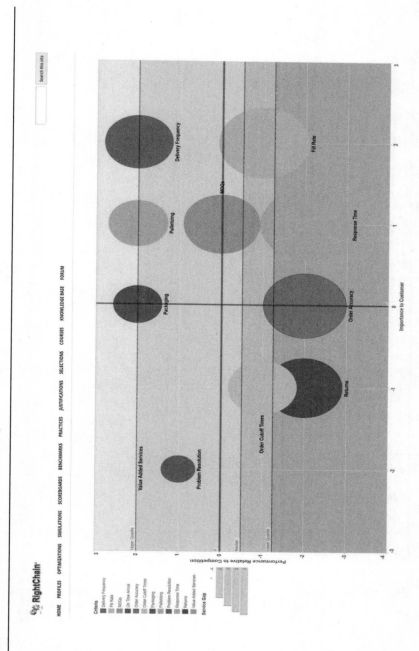

CHAPTER 4

RightStock
Inventory Strategy

*"In the house of the wise are stores of choice food
and oil, but a foolish man devours all he has."*
—SOLOMON

I developed the RightStock (Figure 4.1) inventory strategy model as a part of our RightChain framework to help professionals work through the financial, service, and operational complexities of inventory decision making. The model is based on 30-plus years of consulting, research, and development in inventory and supply chain strategy.

RightStock is quantitative, logical, and methodical. It is not a philosophy unless you call not having a philosophy a philosophy, or unless you call objectively putting numbers to decisions a philosophy. The model is also unique in that it works from the SKU level up. We begin by determining optimal SKU-level inventory strategies. We aggregate those into category, business unit, and/or geographical inventory strategies.

RightStock is a seven-step journey designed to optimize (not minimize) inventory levels. The optimal inventory level is the level that yields the optimal financial and service performance simultaneously. The first step in the journey is SKU optimization (RightSKUs), the search for the portfolio

Figure 4.1   RightStock inventory model

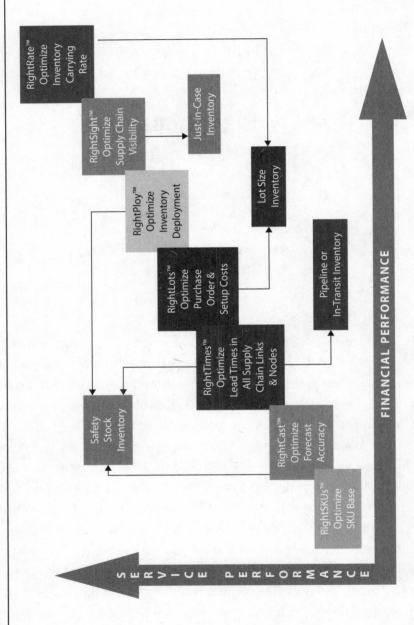

that balances financial performance with customer needs for service and variety. The second step is forecast optimization (RightCast), establishing forecast accuracies that improve decision making across the entire supply chain. Next is lead time optimization (RightTimes), the computation and implementation of lead times that balance purchase prices, transportation costs, and inventory levels. Step four is lot size optimization (RightLots), establishing lot sizes across the supply chain that balance inventory carrying costs with manufacturing setup and procurement purchase order costs. The fifth step is deployment optimization (RightPloy), defining the inventory allocation to facilities that optimizes inventory carrying costs, redeployment costs, and response times to customers. The sixth step is visibility optimization (RightSight), defining and implementing the level and form of inventory visibility that yields the highest return on investment. The final step is inventory carrying rate optimization (RightRate), measuring and then optimizing the opportunity cost of capital, storage and handling, loss and damage, obsolescence and markdowns, and insurance and taxes.

RightSKUs | SKU Valuation

SKU valuation, sometimes referred to as SKU rationalization or SKU portfolio management, is one of the first, best, and most important steps in inventory strategy development. When we begin client projects, we typically find that about a third of the SKUs are profitable, about a third are breaking even, and about a third are losing money; yet the service policy for each of those SKU valuation strata is nearly always the same. The service policy differentiation across those strata is a critical component of business and supply chain strategy, and may require eliminating the extremely unprofitable SKUs. When clients push back on the elimination of even extremely unprofitable SKUs sold only to extremely unprofitable customers I remind them that:

- The forecast accuracy for a SKU you don't have is perfect.
- The lead time for a SKU you don't have is zero.

- The inventory investment in a SKU you don't have is zero.
- The cube occupied by a SKU you don't have is zero.
- The length of the pick line for a SKU you don't have is zero.
- The planning time required for a SKU you don't have is zero.
- The cost to produce a SKU you don't have is zero.
- The transportation cost for a SKU you don't have is zero.

Rare is the company that is immune to the Pareto phenomenon, the fact that a majority of sales, margin, and profit come from a minority of the SKUs. Some examples of the SKU Pareto phenomenon and SKU optimization from recent client engagements across a range of industries follow.

Biotechnology SKU Valuation

A RightSKUs analysis from a biotechnology company is illustrated in Figure 4.2. The top-selling 5 percent of the SKUs yield the first 67 percent of revenue; 10 percent yield 81 percent; and 20 percent yield 92 percent.

Industrial Distributor SKU Valuation

Another example is in Figure 4.3. The example is from a large industrial distributor. Note that just 427 (8.8 percent) of their SKUs yield 99 percent of their revenue. Unfortunately, 34.7 percent of their inventory investment, $8,732,685, was tied up in the SKUs that yielded the last 1 percent of their revenue. Worse yet, over $18 million worth of new product was on order for those same 1 percent.

Beverage Company SKU Valuation

Another example of the phenomenon is illustrated in Figure 4.4. The figure is a deliverable from a recent client engagement focused on SKU strategy in the food and beverage industry. Note that just 28 percent of the SKUs yield the first 90 percent of total operating profit. Just 39 percent of the SKUs yield the first 95 percent of operating profit. On the other end of the

Figure 4.2   Pareto's Law at work in biotech SKU revenue

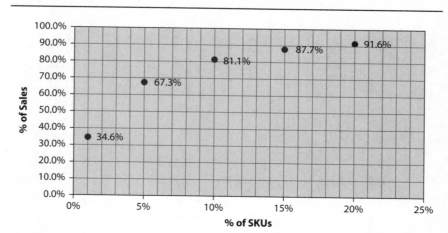

Figure 4.3   RightSKUs analysis for an industrial distributor

	% of Revenue	No. of SKUs	% of SKUs	On Hand $s	% On Hand $s	On Order $s	% On Order $s
A	50%	38	0.8%	$ 4,039,410	16.0%	$49,172,393	52.5%
B	80%	143	3.0%	$ 4,062,673	16.1%	$12,720,699	13.6%
C	90%	153	3.2%	$ 2,866,522	11.4%	$5,676,796	6.1%
D	95%	165	3.4%	$ 2,531,909	10.1%	$4,370,671	4.7%
E	99%	427	8.8%	$ 2,942,393	11.7%	$2,929,997	3.1%
F	Remainder	3,901	80.8%	$ 8,732,685	34.7%	$18,755,643	20.0%

spectrum, 28 percent of the SKUs yield return on invested capital lower than the corporate threshold of 10 percent.

As with many organizations, their false hope was that more SKUs would translate to more sales and profit. In Figure 4.5 you can see that the introduction of new SKUs did not yield more sales, but spread the same sales over more SKUs. Maintaining sales may seem like a victory; however, the introduction of the additional SKUs and their related complexity

Figure 4.4 RightSKUs analysis in the food and beverage industry

Operating Profit	SKUs	% SKUs	Cum SKUs	Cum% SKUs	Inventory $s	Cum Inv$s	Total Supply Chain Cost
Negative	49	12.66%	49	12.66%	$ 1,565,462	$ 1,565,462	$ 29,540,720
0% to 5%	22	5.68%	71	18.35%	$ 1,457,217	$ 3,022,678	$ 33,483,000
6% to 10%	15	3.88%	86	22.22%	$ 1,317,098	$ 4,339,776	$ 38,401,000
11% to 15%	32	8.27%	118	30.49%	$ 2,524,189	$ 6,863,965	$ 42,000,000
16% to 20%	43	11.11%	161	41.60%	$ 2,793,378	$ 9,657,343	$ 21,339,333
21% to 30%	95	24.55%	256	66.15%	$ 12,272,727	$ 21,930,070	$ 34,888,211

IVA	SKUs	% SKUs	Cum SKUs	Cum% SKUs	Inventory $s	Cum Inv$s	Total Supply Chain Cost
Negative	26	6.72%	26	6.72%	$ 270,497	$ 270,497	$ 27,991,299
$0 to $1,000	25	6.46%	51	13.18%	$ 224,322	$ 494,818	$ 31,099,543
$1,000 to $5,000	30	7.75%	81	20.93%	$ 374,084	$ 868,902	$ 33,099,798
$5,000 to $10,000	24	6.20%	105	27.13%	$ 366,336	$ 1,235,238	$ 41,222,908
$10,000 to $25,000	47	12.14%	152	39.28%	$ 1,680,720	$ 2,915,958	$ 52,772,939

GMROI	SKUs	% SKUs	Cum SKUs	Cum% SKUs	Inventory $s	Cum Inv$s	Total Supply Chain Cost
Negative	5	1.29%	5	1.29%	$ 82,853	$ 82,853	$ 27,991,299
0's	45	11.63%	50	12.92%	$ 2,420,399	$ 2,503,252	$ 31,099,543
1's	14	3.62%	64	16.54%	$ 1,839,287	$ 4,342,538	$ 33,099,798
2's	26	6.72%	90	23.26%	$ 2,890,469	$ 7,233,007	$ 41,222,908
3's	9	2.33%	99	25.58%	$ 602,301	$ 7,835,308	$ 52,772,939
4's	11	2.84%	110	28.42%	$ 411,224	$ 8,246,531	$ 28,882,221
5's	19	4.91%	129	33.33%	$ 1,517,483	$ 9,764,014	$ 17,333,119

ROIC	SKUs	% SKUs	Cum SKUs	Cum% SKUs	Inventory $s	Cum Inv$s	Total Supply Chain Cost
Negative	49	12.7%	49	12.7%	$ 1,565,462	$ 1,565,462	$ 29,540,720
0% to 5%	42	10.9%	91	23.5%	$ 3,027,972	$ 4,593,434	$ 25,342,000
6% to 10%	30	7.8%	121	31.3%	$ 4,404,671	$ 8,998,105	$ 60,285,000

Figure 4.5   Case volume vs. SKU proliferation

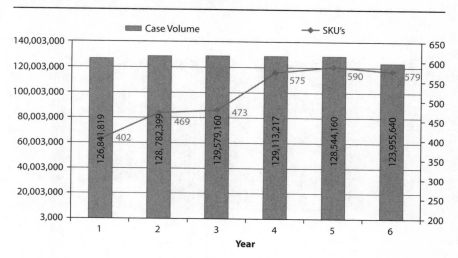

works against supply chain, inventory, and profit performance. In this case, inventory investment grew from $51 million to $69 million; a 35 percent increase in inventory investment coming with a 44 percent increase in the number of SKUs (Figure 4.6). To make matters worse, by spreading the same demand over more SKUs, forecast accuracy declined, resulting in significantly higher out-of-stock levels, growing from a low of 2 percent to a high of 7 percent, a 250 percent increase in out-of-stock rates (Figure 4.7)!

The additional warehousing space, warehouse congestion, longer pick lines, increased planning cycles, and shorter run lengths all resulted in a 27 percent increase in total supply chain cost. Total supply chain cost per case increased from $2.56 to $3.26 (Figure 4.8). Turning back the clock to the good old days of $2.56 per case was worth more than $50,000,000 per year in supply chain cost savings. Lastly, without an increase in sales, with higher inventory levels and reduced gross margins due to higher supply chain costs, GMROI declined from a high of 1,143 percent to a low of 848 percent, a 26 percent decline (Figure 4.9).

Figure 4.6   Inventory investment vs. SKU proliferation

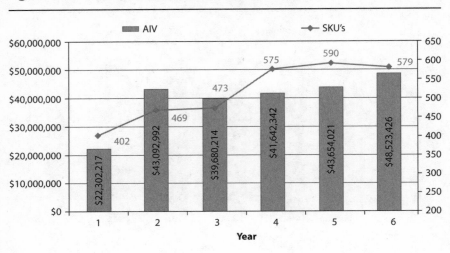

Figure 4.7   Out-of-stocks vs. SKU proliferation

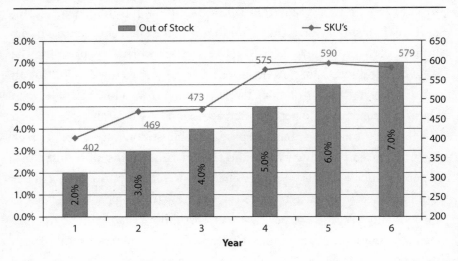

Figure 4.8   Supply chain cost per unit vs. SKU proliferation

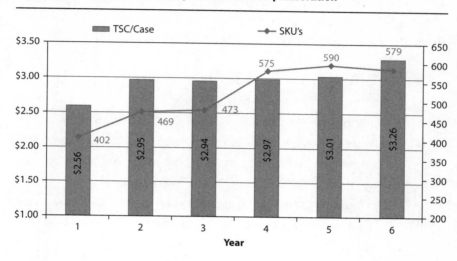

Figure 4.9   Gross margin return on inventory vs. SKU proliferation

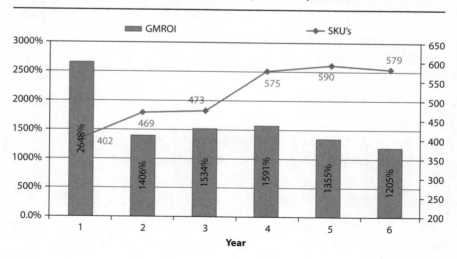

But It's Just a SKU

The impact of a single SKU working in a supply chain is greatly underestimated. In this client example we established that each "little" SKU was:

- **Ordered 1,934,000 times per year.** There were 1,212,000,000 SKU-orders in a year costing $30,000,000 or $.04 per SKU-order. Removing one SKU would potentially save $60,000.
- **Delivered 1,815,358 times per year.** There were 907,679,000 SKU-deliveries in a year costing $91,000,000 or $.10 per SKU-delivery. Removing one SKU would potentially save $182,000.
- **Merchandised 1,063,463 times per year.** There were 500,908,801 SKU-pulls in a year costing $55,246,000 or $.09 per SKU-pull. Removing one SKU would potentially save $110,000.
- **Picked in warehouses 120,000 times per year.** There were 12,000,000 SKU-picks in a year costing $65,000,000 or $5.42 per SKU-pick. Removing one SKU would potentially save $130,000.
- **Made or bought 60,000 times per year.** There were 6,000,000 SKU-lots in a year, costing $47,000,000 per year.
- **Handled in some way 7,000,000 times per year.** Removing one SKU could potentially save up to $480,000 per year; 10 SKUs $4,800,000 per year; 100 SKUs $48,000,000 per year!

This is obviously an extreme example of the power of pruning, but the point is the same; when it comes to SKUs, less is usually more.

RightSKUs Methodology

One of our major CPG industry clients recently brought to our attention that in the three years we had been working with them the most effective initiative we had put in place was RightSKUs. That initiative had reduced their total SKU base from 3,000 to 2,000 (a 33 percent reduction), and over that time their gross margin return on inventory, fill rate, and market share had increased substantially. The overall EBIT increase was in the multimillions.

Many organizations have initiated similar kinds of SKU rationalization projects. Many of those projects have died on the vine. The only means we have found to successfully carry out a pruning project is to follow a facilitated methodology and to make the project a process. We have developed a formal methodology for SKU rationalization called RightSKUs. Through the RightSKUs methodology we develop formal criteria for evaluating the value of a SKU. The project team assigns weights to each criterion, and all SKUs are given a valuation ranking. That ranking is used and updated in an ongoing process and series of RightChain meetings that institutionalize the pruning process. An example of a recent SKU valuation for a major plastics company is presented in Figure 4.10. In this particular analysis we included pounds sold, EBIT, EBIT per pound, and EBIT percent in the most valuable SKU rankings. D SKUs were pruned.

High-Tech SKU Valuation

We were recently approached by a global provider of high-tech components. They challenged us to optimize the supply chain for a large but mature and slowly declining business unit. We began with the net income SKU optimization illustrated in Figure 4.11. As mentioned earlier, SKUs fall into great (high positive contribution), good (positive contribution to net income), bad (breakeven), and ugly (negative net income) strata. The "ugly" strata is so ugly in this case that the overall business case is a net loser, further raising the urgency to identify, purge, and restrategize the ugly SKUs. In this case an aggressive SKU purging and centralized stocking strategy was implemented, netting our client more than $20,000,000 in annual savings.

Figure 4.10   Most valuable SKU analysis for a plastics company

SKU	EBIT ($000s)	EBIT Rank	Pounds (000s)	Pounds Rank	EBIT/Pound	EBIT/Pound Rank	EBIT%	EBIT% Rank	Rank Sum	Value Rank	MVSKU	ABCD
3097001	$ 4,440	1.0	13,147	1	$ 0.34	1	20.9%	9	20	40	1	A
3022012	$ 2,361	2.0	7,162	3	$ 0.33	12	21.0%	8	25	39	2	A
3022022	$ 896	6.0	2,656	12	$ 0.34	10	21.1%	5	33	38	3	A
3092001	$ 1,184	4.0	4,391	5	$ 0.27	16	18.7%	13	38	37	4	A
3092002	$ 943	5.0	2,770	11	$ 0.34	8	17.7%	17	41	35	5	A
3092003	$ 531	11.0	586	28	$ 0.91	1	38.6%	1	41	35	5	A
3092031	$ 694	9.0	2,092	13	$ 0.33	11	20.0%	11	44	34	7	A
3022068	$ 850	7.0	3,683	7	$ 0.23	21	19.2%	12	47	33	8	A
3022195	$ 359	14.0	959	22	$ 0.37	5	20.2%	10	51	32	9	A
3022240	$ 1,722	3.0	10,938	2	$ 0.16	24	9.8%	26	55	29	10	A
3092007	$ 845	8.0	3,558	8	$ 0.24	20	14.7%	19	55	29	10	A
3032111	$ 252	18.0	409	33	$ 0.61	2	32.3%	2	55	29	10	A
3032259	$ 277	16.0	882	23	$ 0.31	14	21.1%	6	59	28	13	B
3061001	$ 649	10.0	3,968	6	$ 0.16	23	11.8%	23	62	27	14	B
3061006	$ 294	15.0	966	21	$ 0.30	15	18.0%	16	67	26	15	B
3061010	$ 474	12.0	3,071	10	$ 0.15	25	12.8%	22	69	24	16	B
3061012	$ 107	27.0	233	36	$ 0.46	3	24.8%	3	69	24	16	B
3061014	$ 195	19.0	620	27	$ 0.31	13	18.4%	15	74	23	18	B
3061016	$ 80	29.0	220	37	$ 0.36	6	21.5%	4	76	22	19	B
3061023	$ 412	13.0	4,475	4	$ 0.09	32	5.8%	30	79	21	20	B
3061006	$ 70	32.0	176	38	$ 0.40	4	21.0%	7	81	20	21	C
3061011	$ 101	28.0	295	35	$ 0.34	7	18.5%	14	84	19	22	C
3061012	$ 183	20.0	1,220	19	$ 0.15	26	11.5%	24	89	17	23	C
3061014	$ 124	25.0	483	29	$ 0.26	17	16.5%	18	89	17	23	C
3061016	$ 261	17.0	3,105	9	$ 0.08	33	5.5%	32	91	16	25	C
3061026	$ 130	23.0	701	26	$ 0.19	22	9.9%	25	96	15	26	C
3061031	$ 165	21.0	1,735	14	$ 0.10	31	5.7%	31	97	14	27	C
3061034	$ 139	22.0	1,229	18	$ 0.11	29	6.8%	29	98	12	28	C
3061051	$ 108	26.0	431	32	$ 0.25	19	13.8%	21	98	12	28	C
3061052	$ 129	24.0	1,117	20	$ 0.12	28	7.7%	28	100	11	30	C
3061055	$ 78	30.0	1,327	15	$ 0.06	34	4.2%	34	113	10	31	D
3051031	$ 9	36.0	37	40	$ 0.26	18	14.6%	20	114	9	32	D
3094005	$ 73	31.0	726	25	$ 0.10	30	5.4%	33	119	7	33	D
3051040	$ 55	33.0	1,303	16	$ 0.04	35	3.3%	35	199	7	33	D
3061008	$ 11	35.0	83	39	$ 0.13	27	8.4%	27	128	6	35	D
3061010	$ (23)	39.0	1,254	17	$ (0.02)	39	-1.5%	39	134	5	36	D
3061012	$ 9	37.0	753	24	$ 0.01	37	0.8%	37	135	4	37	D
3061014	$ 12	34.0	473	31	$ 0.03	36	1.3%	36	137	3	38	D
3061016	$ (3)	38.0	385	34	$ (0.01)	38	-0.5%	38	148	2	39	D
3061031	$ (170)	40.0	475	30	$ (0.36)	40	-31.5%	40	150	1	40	D

Figure 4.11   RightSKUs net income Pareto

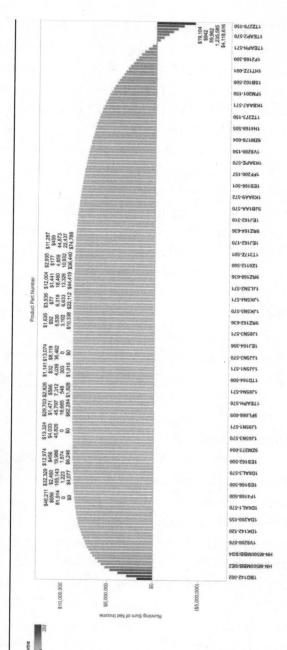

Most Valuable SKU Rankings

As we do with customers, we rank SKUs based on their overall value contribution to the business using business, strategic, and cost-to-serve factors. Accordingly, those SKUs providing the most value to the business are A SKUs, the next most valuable are B SKUs, the next most are C SKUs, and the least and often negative valued are D SKUs.

As was the case with customer valuations, there is often strong resistance from the sales organization to SKU valuation. However, we have yet to find a client where SKU proliferation helped sales, margin, profit, market share, or inventory availability. In my experience, very few organizations understand the underlying cost of supply chain complexity introduced by each new SKU. The SKU valuation and corresponding most and least valuable SKU rankings improve this understanding.

Step by Step

As stated earlier, pruning is painful, and you probably know from your personal life when you'v e had to cut out certain activities or certain relationships that are not profitable or are even harmful. It comes up in supply chain strategy when someone in marketing and/or product development has to face the fact that their SKU is no longer profitable. Simplification is rarely easy, or popular. It challenges the status quo. It is in vogue in many organizations to boast about the complexity of their work, even if the complexity is non-value-added and self-inflicted. At the same time, simplification is profitable and one of the key common denominators of successful supply chain organizations.

Instead of radically cutting back in the beginning, our clients have had success in piloting and implementing SKU optimization incrementally. An example incremental SKU optimization from the CPG industry is provided in Figure 4.12. The program yielded a $7,000,000 increase in profitability.

Once the ideal portfolio has been developed, diligence is required to maintain it. With one retail client we made a simple rule that every new SKU introduction had to be presented with the SKU that would be pruned as a result.

Figure 4.12   Incremental RightSKUs implementation

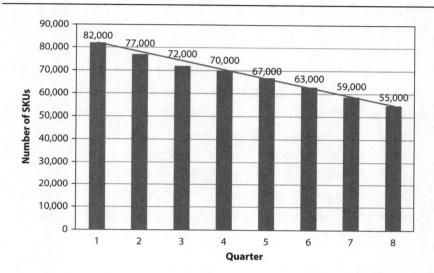

4.2 Forecast Optimization

A few years ago we assisted a major sporting goods company with their inventory strategy. Based on my observations of their inventory and supply chain I made a strong recommendation to them to implement forecasting. The CIO interrupted my presentation and strongly disagreed. He said, "We are not going to do forecasting!" I was taken aback by the interruption and the forcefulness of his rebuke. I asked him, "Why are you not going to forecast?" He said, "Because the forecast will be wrong." I wanted to say, "Duhhhh." But I restrained myself and said. "You are right. There is only one source of perfect forecasting whom I know, but He does not work for most supply chains. However, wouldn't you like to know how far off your forecast is, in what direction, and if it is getting better or worse?"

The CIO's strong reaction to my recommendation that they implement forecasting may sound unusual. Unfortunately, I don't find it that far from the norm. Most organizations either don't forecast at all, forecast at such a high level that it is practically irrelevant for inventory planning purposes, and/or don't hold anybody accountable for it, which is tantamount to not forecasting at all.

Forecasting plays a pivotal and vital role in determining required inventory levels. Forecasting also influences nearly every supply chain decision. As a result, the degree to which forecasting is in error foreshadows the error in all supply chain decision making.

Even a small improvement in forecast accuracy can yield significant inventory savings. In a recent project with a major engine manufacturer we found that every 10 percent improvement in forecast accuracy yielded a 5 percent reduction in inventory (Figure 4.13). In that particular case the reduction was worth more than $5,000,000 in safety stock inventory.

RightCast Simulation

A simulation of the benefits of forecast optimization for a single SKU for a large toy company is presented here.

Suppose we implement a few RightCast practices like forecast bias identification and minimization, individual accountability and dedication to forecast accuracy, back casting, and rapid error correction. In this case those practices helped reduce forecast error from 140 percent to 80 percent (Figure 4.14). What's the ripple effect (Figure 4.15)?

As you would expect, less safety stock inventory is required to support the same target fill rate of 92 percent. In this case safety stock inventory value (SSIV) declines from $60,630 to $34,646; a savings of $25,984. Average inventory value (AIV) declines by that same amount. The resulting inventory carrying cost declines from $42,632 to $30,680; a savings of $11,953 per year. Inventory turn rate increases from 1.24 to 1.72; an increase of 39 percent. GMROI increases from 144 percent to 200 percent; a 39 percent increase. Inventory value added (IVA) increases from $90,768 to $102,721; a 13 percent increase. Inventory Policy Cost (IPC) declines from $49,112 to $37,160; a 24 percent decrease.

Figure 4.13   Forecast accuracy and inventory savings

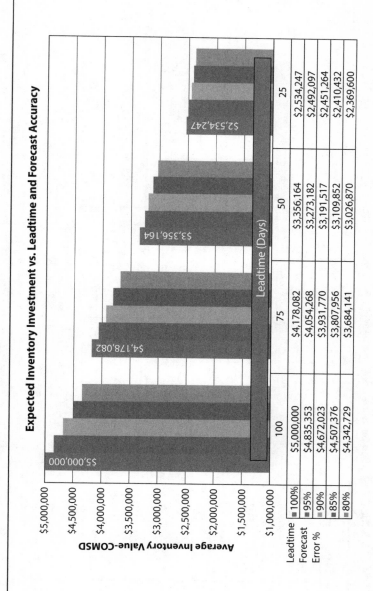

Expected Inventory Investment vs. Leadtime and Forecast Accuracy

Leadtime		100	75	50	25
Forecast Error %	100%	$5,000,000	$4,178,082	$3,356,164	$2,534,247
	95%	$4,835,353	$4,054,268	$3,273,182	$2,492,097
	90%	$4,672,023	$3,931,770	$3,191,517	$2,451,264
	85%	$4,507,376	$3,807,956	$3,109,852	$2,410,432
	80%	$4,342,729	$3,684,141	$3,026,870	$2,369,600

Figure 4.14   RightCast simulation for a large toy company

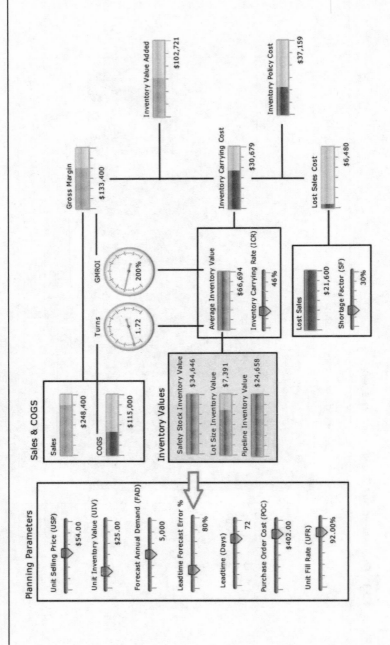

Figure 4.15   RightCast simulation results for a large toy company

	Baseline	RightCast™	Improvement	%
Unit Selling Price (USP)	$ 54.00	$ 54.00		
− Unit Inventory Value (UIV)	$ 25.00	$ 25.00		
Unit Gross Margin (UGM)	$ 29.00	$ 29.00		
× Forecast Annual Demand (FAD)	5,000	5,000		
Gross Margin Potential (GMP)	$ 145,000.00	$ 145,000.00		
× Unit Fill Rate (UFR)	92.00%	92.00%		
Gross Margin (GM)	$ 133,400.00	$ 133,400.00		
Leadtime Forecast Error % (LFEP)	**140%**	**80%**	60%	43%
Leadtime (Days)	72	72		
Purchase Order Cost (POC)	$ 402.00	$ 402.00		
Safety Stock Inventory Value (SSIV)	**$ 60,630**	**$ 34,646**	$ 25,984	43%
+ Lot Size Inventory Value (LSIV)	$ 7,391	$ 7,391		
+ Pipeline Inventory Value (PIV)	$ 24,658	$ 24,658		
Average Inventory Value (AIV)	**$ 92,679**	**$ 66,695**	$ 25,984	28%
× Inventory Carrying Rate (ICR)	46%	46%		
Inventory Carrying Cost (ICC)	**$ 42,632**	**$ 30,680**	$ 11,953	28%
Inventory Turn Rate (ITR)	**1.24**	**1.72**	0.48	39%
GMROI	**144%**	**200%**	56%	39%
Inventory Value Added™	**$ 90,768**	**$ 102,721**	$ 11,953	13%
Lost Sales (LS)	$ 21,600	$ 21,601		
Shortage Factor (SF)	30%	30%		
Lost Sales Cost (LSC)	$ 6,480	$ 6,480		
Inventory Policy Cost (IPC)	**$ 49,112**	**$ 37,160**	$ 11,953	24%

Is a 43 percent reduction in inventory investment, a 39 percent increase in inventory turns, an increase in GMROI from 144 percent to 200 percent, a 13 percent increase in inventory value added, and a 24 percent decrease in inventory policy cost worth the effort? Most likely. In fact, we have yet to conduct a project where there was not an overwhelming business case for pursuing a RightCast initiative.

4.3 Lead Time Optimization

There is a near maniacal emphasis on lead time reduction in many organizations. A few years ago we completed a supply chain benchmarking
project with a large company in the computing industry. I met a group
of engineers there unlike any I had ever met, the velocity engineering
group. I asked what they did. They shared that their entire purpose was
to reduce cycle times in all the processes in the company. They all spoke
like auctioneers and lived in their own secretive subculture, kind of like
a secret society of cycle time ninjas. They are not the kind of people I
want to hang out with, but they were very effective at taking time out of
processes.

Another client recently called and asked how they could reduce their
cycle time in aircraft engine repair. I asked them how long it currently
takes them. They said it required seven days—including the round trip to
Europe. Given how short the cycle time already was, I was stunned that
they were even asking. They insisted I consider the question. I asked them
what the cycle time was before it had been reduced to seven days. They
said it had been 21 days. I asked them how they condensed the cycle time
to seven days. They said they value stream mapped the process into daily
buckets and found opportunities to work activities in parallel and to eliminate wasted time. I encouraged them to repeat the process, but to use
hourly buckets and to look specifically at which days in the week and hours
in a day each activity would be performed. They took my suggestion and
are now working the international process in 4.5 days.

Lead time plays a primary role in the inventory required to support
a supply chain strategy. It contributes directly to pipeline inventory and
safety stock inventory.

In safety stock inventory, lead time has a multiplicative effect. My
friend at Honda, Chuck Hamilton, uses a golf analogy to explain the effect.
If a golfer hits a ball 100 yards off the tee with the face off center by 10
percent, the ball is only 10 yards off center at the end of its flight, and still

in the fairway. If a golfer hits a ball 200 yards off the tee with the face off center by 10 percent, the ball is 20 yards off center at the end of its flight, and barely in the fairway. If a golfer hits a ball 300 yards off the tee with the face off center by 10 percent, the ball is off center by 30 yards at the end of its flight, in the rough, probably the deep rough. The longer the lead time, the greater the impact of forecast errors.

In a recent project with a large food company we found that every day of lead time reduction was worth approximately $5 million (Figure 4.16).

Given these results, the logical prevailing assumption is that shorter lead times are better. At the risk of being heretical, I would say that the right lead time is better. Many times customers, suppliers, and internal systems are not prepared to accommodate reduced lead times. Also, lead time reductions usually have a price tag. Some lead times are shortened by moving product more frequently by more expensive transportation modes (air vs. ocean, truck vs. rail, etc.). Some lead times are reduced by purchasing from local suppliers at a higher price. Some lead times are reduced via forward stocking nearer the point of consumption, requiring extra inventory. Some lead times are reduced by investing in material handling automation to speed product through warehouses, distribution centers, ports, and factories. Those investments must be weighed against the benefits associated with the lead time reductions they bring.

RightTimes Simulation

Determining the appropriate investment in lead time reduction is the purpose of RightTimes optimization and simulation. An example Right-Times simulation for a single SKU for a large toy company is presented in Figure 4.17. In the example a variety of lead time reduction options were under consideration including alternate transportation modes, alternate transportation schedules, near-sourcing, and receiving automation. Those options had the potential to reduce lead time from the baseline of 72 days to 40 days. What is the ripple effect (Figure 4.18)? How much could be justifiably invested in the options?

Figure 4.16 Inventory investment vs. days of leadtime

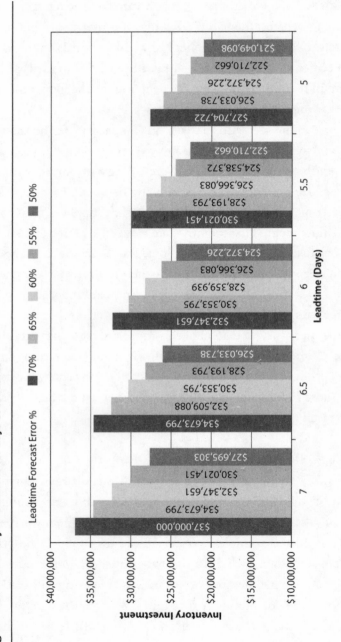

Figure 4.17   RightTimes lead time simulation for a large toy company

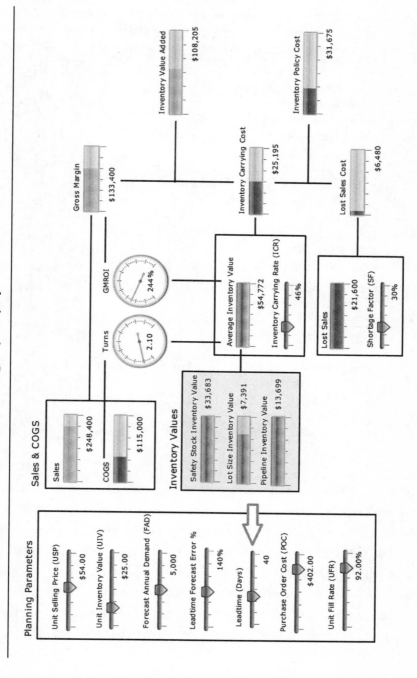

Figure 4.18   RightTimes simulation results for a large toy company

Factor	Baseline	RightTimes™	Improvement	%
Unit Selling Price (USP)	$ 54.00	$ 54.00		
− Unit Inventory Value (UIV)	$ 25.00	$ 25.00		
Unit Gross Margin (UGM)	$ 29.00	$ 29.00		
× Forecast Annual Demand (FAD)	5,000	5,000		
Gross Margin Potential (GMP)	$ 145,000.00	$ 145,000.00		
× Unit Fill Rate (UFR)	92.00%	92.00%		
Gross Margin (GM)	$ 133,400.00	$ 133,400.00		
Leadtime Forecast Error % (LFEP)	140%	140%		
Leadtime (Days)	**72**	**40**	32	44%
Purchase Order Cost (POC)	$ 402.00	$ 402.00		
Safety Stock Inventory Value (SSIV)	**$ 60,630**	**$ 33,683**	$ 26,947	44%
+ Lot Size Inventory Value (LSIV)	$ 7,391	$ 7,391		
+ Pipeline Inventory Value (PIV)	**$ 24,658**	**$ 13,699**		
Average Inventory Value (AIV)	**$ 92,679**	**$ 54,773**	$ 37,906	41%
× Inventory Carrying Rate (ICR)	46%	46%		
Inventory Carrying Cost (ICC)	**$ 42,632**	**$ 25,196**	$ 17,436	41%
Inventory Turn Rate (ITR)	**1.24**	**2.10**	0.86	69%
GMROI	**144%**	**244%**	100%	69%
Inventory Value Added™	**$ 90,768**	**$ 108,204**	$ 17,436	19%
Lost Sales (LS)	$ 21,600	$ 21,601		
Shortage Factor (SF)	30%	30%		
Lost Sales Cost (LSC)	$ 6,480	$ 6,480		
Inventory Policy Cost (IPC)	**$ 49,112**	**$ 31,676**	$ 17,436	36%

First, notice that safety stock inventory value drops from $60,330 to $33,683; a reduction of $26,947 or 44 percent. Pipeline inventory investment drops from $24,650 to $13,699; a reduction of $10,951 or 44 percent. Total inventory investment drops from $92,679 to $54,773; a reduction of $37,906 or 41 percent. Inventory carrying cost drops from $42,632 to $25,196; a reduction of $17,437 per year. Inventory turns increase from 1.24 to 2.10; a 69 percent increase. GMROI increases from 144 percent to 244 percent. Inventory value added increases from $90,768 to $108,204; a $17,437 increase or

19 percent. Inventory policy cost drops from $49,112 to $31,676; a reduction of $17,437 or 36 percent.

Is a 41 percent reduction in inventory investment, a 69 percent increase in inventory turns, a 100 percent increase in GMROI, a 19 percent increase in inventory value added, and a 36 percent reduction in inventory policy cost worth the investment? In this case those percentages, applied to the entire SKU base, yielded a $20,000,000 reduction in inventory, a $8,000,000 per year reduction in inventory carrying costs, turns increasing from 1.2 to 2.0, an increase in GMROI from 150 percent to 250 percent, and an increase in inventory value added of over $17,000,000. The investments in alternate transportation modes and routes, near-sourcing, and automated logistics and material handling systems required to accomplish the lead time reduction totaled approximately $4,500,000, yielding a payback against inventory carrying cost savings of 0.56 years.

4.4 Lot Size Optimization

To teach lot size optimization I like to use an example that is close to home. Suppose you live in Georgia and there is only one ATM machine in the state. The single ATM is located in a small, remote town in south Georgia. (Are there other kinds?) The ATM is only open during the last week of July. For whatever cash you need you endure a trip down heavily congested country roads through swarms of gnats in humidity so thick you will need an umbrella in heat so intense you will think you are in a sauna to stand in lines so long you will think you are at Disney World. One last thing. When you finally get your turn at the ATM, the fee to withdraw your money is $1,000. How much money will you withdraw? Yep. All of it. Even though while it is not in the bank, it is not earning interest. It is likely to get lost or stolen, and if you are like me you are much more likely to spend it.

The sum total of the hassle, pain, and literal withdrawal fee equate to the transaction cost. In general, the higher the transaction cost, the fewer times we want to experience the transaction.

In manufacturing and production contexts, the transaction cost related to lot sizing is the cost, hassle, and time of setting up or changing over a production line. The higher the cost, the longer the time, and the greater the hassle, the fewer times we want to execute the transaction. So, when we get the line set up, we should wisely run it for a while. The result may be a lot of inventory. (No wonder it's called a lot size.)

In the purchasing and procurement context, the cost related to the time, telecommunications, planning, and execution of a purchase order is the transaction cost. As was the case with production, the higher the cost, the longer the time, and the greater the hassle, the fewer times we want to execute the transaction. So, when it comes time to place a purchase order, we are going to order a lot.

Now, let's run the south Georgia ATM tape back and fast-forward to another time. Suppose there is an ATM machine within arm's reach wherever you are. It is open 7 x 24 x 365. There is no withdrawal fee. (Amazingly, it's free to access your own money.) Now, how much will you withdraw each time? Yes, just enough for the next few minutes or until some cash is needed.

In manufacturing, if it's free and requires no time to set up or change over a line, we can afford as many setups as we wish. Manufacturing lot size inventory in those cases should be virtually zero. In procurement, if it's cost and hassle free to place a purchase order, we can afford to place as many as we like. Procurement lot size inventory in those cases should be virtually zero.

Transaction costs should go a long way toward determining the size of the transaction. Unfortunately, not many supply chain organizations can tell you the true cost of their most important supply chain transactions; setup costs, changeover costs, purchase order cost, freight bill payment costs, transportation setup costs, and so on. As a result, lot sizing is often overlooked as an opportunity to improve inventory and supply chain performance. Lot sizing has become a lost science in supply chain optimization. Even the EOQ has been one of the babies thrown out with the bathwater.

In an attempt to reinstitute lot sizing in supply chain strategy, we developed and execute lot size deviation analyses as a part of most supply chain assessments. We typically find that lot sizes are off target in one direction or another by 100 percent to 300 percent. The example in Figure 4.19 is from a large food and beverage company. Note that 86.5 percent of the SKUs were undersized, to the tune of 50 percent of the optimal lot size. Once corrected, total supply chain costs were reduced by more than $10 million.

RightLots Simulation

Just as the prevailing trade press winds have blown toward lower and lower inventory, they have carried with them the move toward smaller and smaller lot sizes, highly flexible production cells, mixed model rapid changeovers, and lot sizes approaching one. In many cases and for many SKUs there is a high return on investment for reducing lot sizes, and in many cases there is not. Computing and implementing optimal lot sizes for manufacturing run lengths and purchasing lot sizes is the focus of Right-Lots—lot size optimization. An example lot size simulation is illustrated in Figures 4.20 and 4.21.

In the example, procurement process mapping, e-procurement, blanket ordering, and receiving automation were all under consideration. In combination those initiatives were estimated to reduce the purchase order cost from $402 per purchase order to $100 per purchase order. As you would expect, the optimal lot size inventory is significantly reduced, from $7,391 to $3,686, a 50 percent reduction in lot size inventory value. However, since lot size inventory represents only a small portion of total inventory in this case, the reduction in lot size inventory only yielded a 4 percent reduction in expected total inventory investment. The related percentage improvements to inventory carrying rate, turns, GMROI, inventory value

Figure 4.19   RightLots lot size deviation analysis

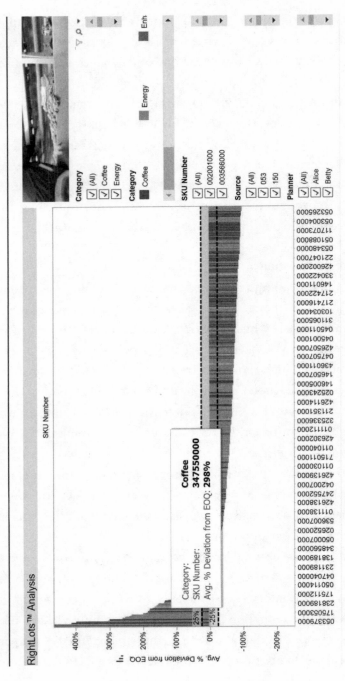

Figure 4.20 RightLots simulation for a large toy company

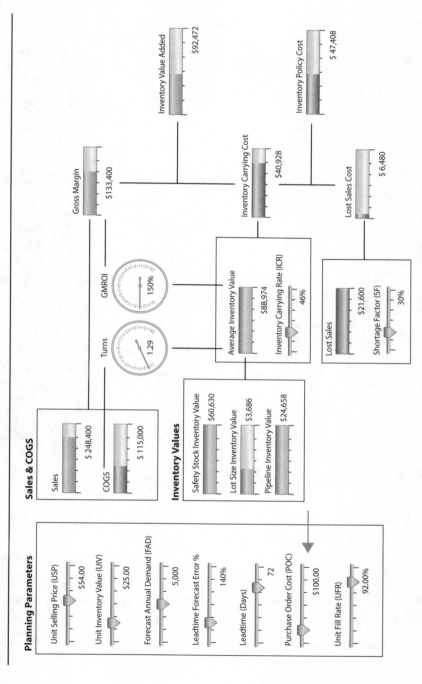

Figure 4.21   RightLots simulation results for a large toy company

Factor	Baseline	RightLot™	Improvement	%
Unit Selling Price (USP)	$ 54.00	$ 54.00		
− Unit Inventory Value (UIV)	$ 25.00	$ 25.00		
Unit Gross Margin (UGM)	$ 29.00	$ 29.00		
× Forecast Annual Demand (FAD)	5,000	5,000		
Gross Margin Potential (GMP)	$ 145,000.00	$ 145,000.00		
× Unit Fill Rate (UFR)	92.00%	92.00%		
Gross Margin (GM)	$ 133,400.00	$ 133,400.00		
Leadtime Forecast Error % (LFEP)	140%	140%		
Leadtime (Days)	72	72		
Purchase Order Cost (POC)	**$ 402.00**	**$ 100.00**		
Safety Stock Inventory Value (SSIV)	$ 60,630	$ 60,630		
+ Lot Size Inventory Value (LSIV)	**$ 7,391**	**$ 3,686**	$ 3,705	50%
+ Pipeline Inventory Value (PIV)	$ 24,658	$ 24,658		
Average Inventory Value (AIV)	**$ 92,679**	**$ 88,974**	$ 3,705	4%
× Inventory Carrying Rate (ICR)	46%	46%		
Inventory Carrying Cost (ICC)	**$ 42,632**	**$ 40,928**	$ 1,704	4%
Inventory Turn Rate (ITR)	**1.24**	**1.29**	0.05	4%
GMROI	**144%**	**150%**	6%	4%
Inventory Value Added™	**$ 90,768**	**$ 92,472**	$ 1,704	2%
Lost Sales (LS)	$ 21,600	$ 21,600		
Shortage Factor (SF)	30%	30%		
Lost Sales Cost (LSC)	$ 6,480	$ 6,480		
Inventory Policy Cost (IPC)	**$ 49,112**	**$ 47,408**	$ 1,704	3%

added, and inventory policy cost are on a similar, negligible scale, ranging from 2 percent to 4 percent.

As a result, in this situation, work to reduce purchase order and setup cost should take a back seat to higher priority work on safety stock and pipeline inventory. That is not always the case. In many projects we engage, lot size inventory comprises the majority of total inventory value and excess inventory. In those cases lot size inventory should be the focal point for inventory optimization.

4.5 Inventory Deployment Optimization

Sometimes it's not the amount of inventory but its location in the supply chain that determines its service and financial effectiveness. The allocation and assignment of inventory to multiple locations is inventory deployment. It is one of the most complex inventory strategy decisions because it opens up interdependencies with customer response times, transportation costs, and redeployment costs and concerns. I always advise our clients that all things being equal, fewer stocking locations is better than more.

What is the likelihood of a mis-deployment if there is only one facility? Zero. Once the multi-facility deployment can of worms is opened, the range of deployment scenarios is nearly endless. Determining where to land in that spectrum of scenarios is deployment optimization. To do so, we recommend a rigorous process to narrow the options to a few high-potential candidate deployment scenarios for evaluation. The process includes collecting and analyzing a comprehensive database to support the decision making, brainstorming to identify candidate deployment scenarios and scenario evaluation criteria, and rigorous analytical modeling. We have been down those roads a few times. The best way to teach deployment optimization may be to share a few examples.

Everybody Wants a Warehouse

A few years ago we developed a supply chain strategy for the spares group in a large semiconductor company. The catalyst for the project was a request from their sales group to provide each customer with their own spares warehouse located inside each customer's facility. That's great customer service, but exceedingly expensive. It was an easy thing for sales to ask for since they were not paying for inventory or supply chain expenses.

We were engaged to help the company determine conditions under which customers "earned" their own warehouse. We developed a deployment simulation system to help them answer the question on an ongoing basis (Figure 4.22).

Figure 4.22 Deployment optimization for semiconductor parts

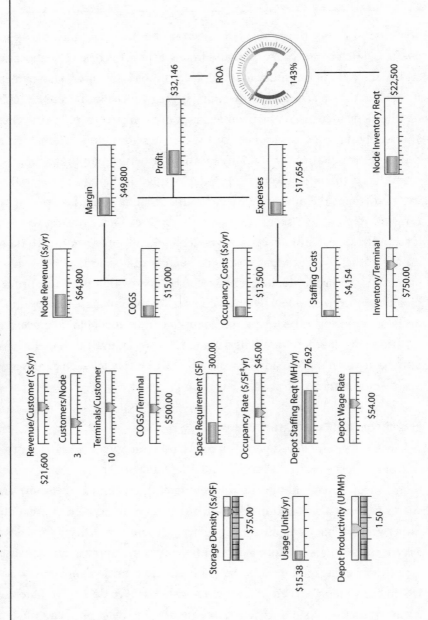

We began by working with their finance team to develop a return on asset threshold for customer warehouses. Based on estimated revenue, inventory consumption, and location logistics, we estimated the return on assets (ROA) for on-site stocking for each customer. Customers were assigned on-site inventory based on their predicted ROA. Customers who did not qualify for the on-site spares program were also given the option to increase business volumes in order to qualify.

Sales and marketing accepted the responsibility of the additional supply chain costs of supporting on-site inventories. The key was having finance, sales, and supply chain collaborating to work through the decision with reliable data and a real-time decision support tool.

Predeploy It!

One of our clients is a large food company delivering on a DSD basis to grocery chains around the southeast. Their historical deployment strategy had been to centralize and hold inventory, delaying deployment as late as required delivery windows would permit. The approach was based on the Lean principle of inventory postponement; holding back inventory in a central location until an order is received. It could be called delayed deployment or deploy-to-order.

Based on their outbound transportation cost I suspected the approach might be overly expensive. They were willing to have a look at some other options. The resulting analysis is presented in Figure 4.23. The figure is a screenshot from our Multi-Echelon Inventory Optimization System. The system considers multiple network configuration options for each SKU. Network configuration options are defined as the number of central warehouses, the number of regional warehouses, and the number of local warehouses. In the example a single central warehouse serves 12 sales centers, which each serve 17 small depots. Based on minimizing total supply chain cost including transportation, inventory carrying, and lost sales cost, an optimal inventory deployment emerges. The key is to understand the optimal allocation and assignment of inventory for each type of SKU. In

Figure 4.23   Multi-Echelon deployment optimization

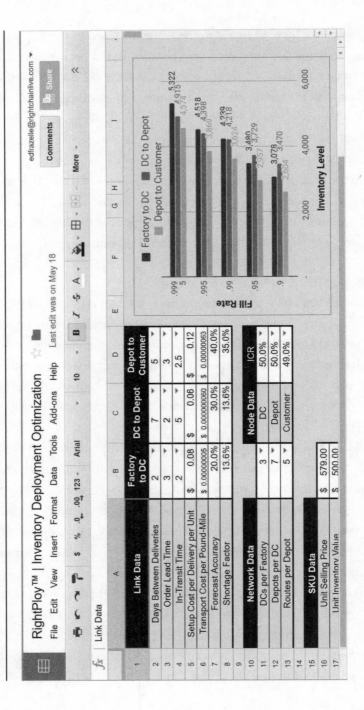

this particular case the recommended deployment is 20/30/50; 20 percent of the inventory held centrally, 30 percent held regionally, and 50 percent deployed in depot locations near large customers. The previous deployment had been 60/20/20. The revised deployment was worth $12,000,000 in total supply chain cost savings.

4.6 Inventory Visibility Optimization

Inventory levels to a large degree are about trust. Since we tend to not trust what we can't see, any blind spots or poor visibility in the supply chain will be places where excess inventory accumulates. The value of visibility is *replacing information about inventory for inventory.*

During a project with a home improvement company I sat with one of their buyers for an hour to get familiar with his work. Early in the hour he placed a large order for a replenishment of lumber. Toward the end of the hour he placed the same order for the same quantity with the same vendor. I asked why. He explained that if he did not receive electronic notification from the vendor that they had received the order, then he reordered. I asked him if he had cancelled the original order. He said no. I asked why he had not cancelled the original order. He said that he wanted to make double sure the vendor received the order. I asked him if he was afraid of having too much inventory. He said no, explaining that the person in his position prior to him had been fired for running out. The lack of visibility, in this case the lack of an electronic acknowledgment from the supplier, led to excess inventory.

Inventory accuracy also plays a major role in visibility. Suppose you are a buyer for a retailer and you get to keep your job if the stores in your region do not run out of stock. However, the warehouse for your region has an inventory accuracy of 60 percent, as was the case in a recent engagement. How much extra inventory will you procure? At least 40 percent, but potentially more. If the accuracy is that poor, then it would be difficult to trust any number reported by that DC.

The appetite for inventory visibility in the supply chain is nearly insatiable. With bar codes, QR codes, RFID tags, and GPS, nearly any level of inventory visibility is feasible. The difficult question is what level and type of visibility is valuable. Just like other investment decisions, there are marginal returns toward the tail end of the benefits curve. The proper approach is to develop progressively more comprehensive visibility scenarios, estimate the return and investment for each, and choose a visibility path forward. We call that RightSight, determining the most appropriate points, transactions, and types of inventory visibility in the supply chain.

Our RightSight scenario generation template is provided in Figure 4.24. We consider each document, each transaction, each node, and each link in the supply chain and recommend the optimal level and type of visibility. We measure the degree of visibility as the percent of SKUs and percent of supply chain transactions in compliance with the visibility program.

4.7 Inventory Carrying Rate Optimization

Inventory carrying rate is the cost of carrying a dollar of inventory for one year. It includes the opportunity cost of capital, the cost of storage and handling, loss and damage, obsolescence and markdowns, and insurance and taxes. The rate determines the financial viability of holding inventory. If it is inexpensive to carry inventory, then it becomes less expensive to provide higher fill rates and shorter response times. Inventory carrying rate is a critical factor in nearly all inventory calculations, yet very few organizations recognize it or compute it.

Since few organizations have an inventory carrying rate, very little understanding of its impact on inventory strategy has been developed. Even when companies have an inventory carrying rate, they assume it is fixed. They overlook the fact that it, like forecast accuracy, lead time, purchase order cost, setup cost, and so on, plays a major role in inventory optimization. Inventory carrying rate should be evaluated as potential for

Figure 4.24   RightSight visiblity solution template

		Documents							Inventory			
		PO	ASN	BOL	Forecast	BOM	Work Order	Mnt Sched	At Supplier	In Transit	In Warehouse	At Customer
Supplier	Response	Seconds	Minutes	Hours	Days	x Days	Days	Weeks	Seconds	Seconds	Seconds	Seconds
	Frequency	Daily	On Demand	Daily	Weekly	Weekly	Daily	Weekly	On Demand	On Demand	On Demand	On Demand
	Granularity	Order Line	Doc #	Doc #	Unit	Doc #	Order Line	Order Line	Order Line	Order Line	Order Line	Order Line
	Format	XML	XML	Email	Email	XML	Efax	Email	EDI	XML	EDI	EDI
Client	Response	x Seconds	Minutes	Hours	Days	x Days	Days	Weeks	Seconds	Seconds	Minutes	Hours
	Frequency	On Demand	On Demand	On Demand	On Demand	Weekly	On Demand	On Demand	On Demand	On Demand	On Demand	On Demand
	Granularity	Order Line	Order Line	Unit	Order Line	Order Line	Unit	Order Line	Order Line	Order Line	Order Line	Order Line
	Format	MMS	MMS	MMS	Efax	MMS	MMS	MMS	MMS	Fax	XML	MMS
Customer	Response	Minutes	Minutes	Hours	Days	x Days	Days	Weeks	Seconds	Seconds	Hours	Seconds
	Frequency	On Demand	On Demand	On Demand	Hourly	Hourly	On Demand	On Demand	On Demand	On Demand	On Demand	On Demand
	Granularity	Order Line	Order Line	Order Line	Order Line	Order Line	Order Line	Order Line	Order Line	Doc #	Order Line	Unit
	Format	MMS	MMS	XML	MMS	Efax	MMS	Fax	MMS	EDI	MMS	MMS
4PL	Response	Minutes	Minutes	Hours	Days	x Days	Days	Weeks	Seconds	x Hours	Seconds	Hours
	Frequency	On Demand	Hourly	On Demand	Daily	On Demand	On Demand	On Demand	On Demand	On Demand	On Demand	On Demand
	Granularity	Order Line	Doc #	Order Line	Unit	Order Line	Order Line	Order Line	Unit	Order Line	Unit	Doc #
	Format	MMS	Fax	MMS	MMS	MMS	Email	MMS	MMS	Fax	MMS	MMS

process improvement and investment. For example, warehouse process improvements and related investments in material handling equipment and warehouse management systems typically yield higher warehouse labor productivity, higher warehouse storage density, higher levels of inventory accuracy, and lower damage and loss rates. As a result, storage and handling costs can be significantly reduced, yielding a much lower inventory carrying rate. In addition, relocating to locales with lower interest, tax, and duty rates yields lower inventory carrying rates. One of our industrial supplies clients moved their distribution operations three blocks and paid for the move and a fully automated DC with the savings they achieved in inventory carrying costs. The savings accrued from a lower inventory carrying rate. The lower rate was the result of lower inventory taxes in the adjacent county and the free trade zone status available in the new facility.

RightRate Simulation

An inventory strategy considering relocation and DC automation was being considered in the example in Figures 4.25 and 4.26. There was the potential to reduce the inventory carrying rate from 46 percent to 20 percent per year. The expected inventory investment increases slightly, by 4 percent; however, the cost to carry the inventory drops dramatically, by 55 percent, yielding a 26 percent increase in inventory value added and a 43 percent decrease in inventory policy cost. In this case, those percentages represented savings in excess of $7,000,000 per year in inventory carrying and total supply chain costs; an increase of over $3,000,000 per year in inventory value added and EVA to the client. Those savings easily paid for the $2,500,000 investment required for warehouse process improvements and MHE/WMS investments.

Figure 4.25   RightRate simulation for a large toy company

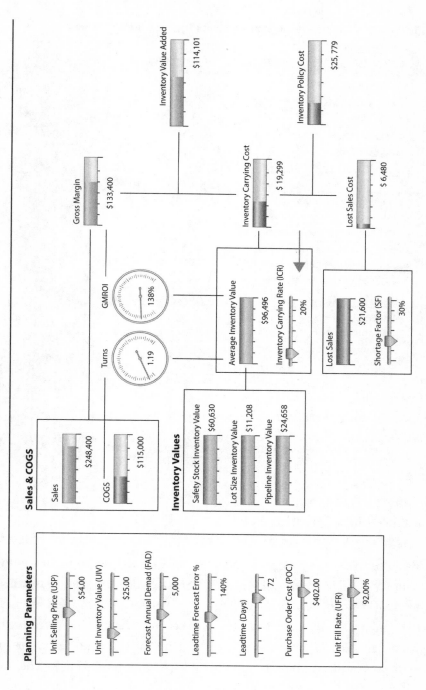

Figure 4.26   RightRate simulation results for a large toy company

Factor	Baseline	RightRate™	Delta	%
Unit Selling Price (USP)	$ 54.00	$ 54.00		
– Unit Inventory Value (UIV)	$ 25.00	$ 25.00		
Unit Gross Margin (UGM)	$ 29.00	$ 29.00		
× Forecast Annual Demand (FAD)	5,000	5,000		
Gross Margin Potential (GMP)	$ 145,000.00	$ 145,000.00		
× Unit Fill Rate (UFR)	92.00%	92.00%		
Gross Margin (GM)	$ 133,400.00	$ 133,400.00		
Leadtime Forecast Error % (LFEP)	140%	140%		
Leadtime (Days)	72	72		
Purchase Order Cost (POC)	$ 402.00	$ 402.00		
Safety Stock Inventory Value (SSIV)	$ 60,630	$ 60,630		
+ Lot Size Inventory Value (LSIV)	$ **7,391**	$ **11,208**	$ (3,817)	–52%
+ Pipeline Inventory Value (PIV)	$ 24,658	$ 24,658		
Average Inventory Value (AIV)	$ **92,679**	$ **96,496**	$ (3,817)	–4%
× Inventory Carrying Rate (ICR)	46%	20%		
Inventory Carrying Cost (ICC)	$ **42,632**	$ **19,299**	$ 23,333	55%
Inventory Turn Rate (ITR)	**1.24**	**1.19**	(0.05)	–4%
GMROI	**144%**	**138%**	–6%	–4%
Inventory Value Added™	$ **90,768**	$ **114,101**	$ 23,333	26%
Lost Sales (LS)	$ 21,600	$ 21,600		
Shortage Factor (SF)	30%	30%		
Lost Sales Cost (LSC)	$ 6,480	$ 6,480		
Inventory Policy Cost (IPC)	$ **49,112**	$ **25,779**	$ 23,333	48%

4.8 Inventory Optimization

Because they are synergistic in their effect, a well-developed inventory strategy should consider all seven RightStock principles—SKU assortment, forecast accuracy, lead time, lot sizing, deployment, visibility, and inventory carrying rate—together. That was our accepted recommendation for this particular client. The results are presented in Figures 4.27 and 4.28. Forecast error was reduced from 140 percent to 80 percent. Lead time was reduced from 72 days to 40 days. Purchase order cost was reduced from $402 to $100 per transaction. Inventory carrying rate was reduced from 46 percent per year to 20 percent per year. As a result, every type of inventory was reduced dramatically, yielding an overall reduction in total inventory investment of 58 percent. Inventory carrying cost for the simulated SKU was reduced from $42,632 per year to $7,707 per year; an 82 percent decrease. Inventory turns increased from 1.24 to 2.98; a 140 percent increase. GMROI increased from 144 percent to 346 percent. Inventory value added increased from $90,768 to $125,693; a 38 percent increase. Inventory policy cost declined from $49,112 to $14,187; a 71 percent decline.

Is a 58 percent reduction in inventory, an 82 percent reduction in inventory carrying cost, a 140 percent increase in inventory turns, an increase in GMROI from 144 percent to 346 percent, a 38 percent increase in inventory value added, and a 71 percent decrease in inventory policy cost with no decrease in an already optimized service level worth the time, effort, and investment? In this case that combination of numbers represented over $40,000,000 worth of inventory, $10,000,000 per year savings in inventory carrying cost, $6,500,000 additional inventory value added, and $10,000,000 in inventory policy cost reductions, easily paying for the $3,500,000 investment required to accomplish them.

Figure 4.27   RightStock simulation for a large toy company

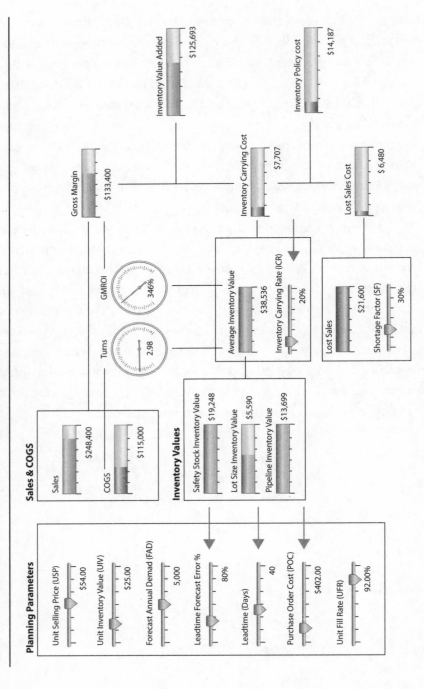

Figure 4.28   RightStock simulation results for a large toy company

Factor	Baseline	RightStock™	Improvement	%
Unit Selling Price (USP)	$ 54.00	$ 54.00		
− Unit Inventory Value (UIV)	$ 25.00	$ 25.00		
Unit Gross Margin (UGM)	$ 29.00	$ 29.00		
× Forecast Annual Demand (FAD)	5,000	5,000		
Gross Margin Potential (GMP)	$ 145,000.00	$ 145,000.00		
× Unit Fill Rate (UFR)	92.00%	92.00%		
Gross Margin (GM)	$ 133,400.00	$ 133,400.00		
Leadtime Forecast Error % (LFEP)	140%	80%	60%	43%
Leadtime (Days)	72	40	32	44%
Purchase Order Cost (POC)	$ 402.00	$ 100.00	$ 302	75%
Safety Stock Inventory Value (SSIV)	$ 60,630	$ 19,248	$ 41,382	68%
+ Lot Size Inventory Value (LSIV)	$ 7,391	$ 5,590	$ 1,801	24%
+ Pipeline Inventory Value (PIV)	$ 24,658	$ 13,699	$ 10,959	44%
Average Inventory Value (AIV)	$ 92,679	$ 38,537	$ 54,142	58%
× Inventory Carrying Rate (ICR)	46%	20%	26%	57%
Inventory Carrying Cost (ICC)	$ 42,632	$ 7,707	$ 34,925	82%
Inventory Turn Rate (ITR)	1.24	2.98	1.74	140%
GMROI	144%	346%	202%	140%
Inventory Value Added™	$ 90,768	$ 125,693	$ 34,925	38%
Lost Sales (LS)	$ 21,600	$ 21,601		
Shortage Factor (SF)	30%	30%		
Lost Sales Cost (LSC)	$ 6,480	$ 6,480		
Inventory Policy Cost (IPC)	$ 49,112	$ 14,187	$ 34,925	71%

CHAPTER 5

RightBuys
Sourcing Strategy

"She considers a field and buys it;
from her profits she plants a vineyard."
—SOLOMON

I have led more than 300 supply chain seminars and conference programs. I have had only one situation where students were literally willing to fight over an issue. It happened when I was teaching our RightBuys seminar. One of the students was the head of sourcing and procurement for a large auto company. In the prior month one of his company's assembly lines was shut down for a couple of days because of an interruption in the supply of car seats. As it would happen, another student in the class had custom ordered a car from that company that was supposed to be produced during those same days in the factory where the shutdown occurred. Evidently, the student wanted the new car to impress a friend or business associate. In anger and in retaliation over not receiving his car on the day it was promised, he decided to try to humiliate the auto company's head of sourcing by loudly elaborating on the supply chain deficiencies of the auto company. The procurement chief was quick to defend himself and his organization. When the disgruntled customer started to speak again I worked to politely calm the nerves. When he and the procurement chief continued to debate under the tone of my lecture I finally had to ask them to either step outside or dismiss themselves from the seminar. Can you imagine a high noon draw over a car seat?

Sourcing and procurement decisions set up the supply chain for ultimate success or failure. Unfortunately, the professionals who work in those areas are the least likely to be educated in supply chain management, and are the least equipped with tools to work through the difficult trade-offs in sourcing and procurement. I remember being so surprised and encouraged the day the head of sourcing and procurement at Honda called and asked that we lead them through our full set of supply chain courses. I knew they were headed to a good place in their supply chain if those folks could understand the 360 degree supply chain ramifications of the decisions they were making. Sure enough, not long after the training, Honda's supply chain performance began a dramatic turnaround. They surpassed Toyota and every other auto company in nearly every aspect of supply chain performance. The same principles shared with them are the ones shared here in a highly concentrated form.

Over the years I synthesized sourcing success or failure into the presence or absence of the following eight principles, which applied in sequence comprise our RightBuys methodology (Figure 5.1).

The first step in the RightBuys methodology is Supplier Certification, basically prequalifying suppliers as candidates to participate in a sourcing footprint. The second step is a set of analytics we developed for allocating business to international and domestic suppliers called Supplier Optimization. The third is a means of organizing sources called Supplier Rationalization. The fourth is a means of measuring the supply base called Supplier Evaluation. Next is a means of partitioning supply flows called Supplier Stratification. Number six is the partnering step of supplier relationships we call Supplier Integration. Number seven anchors integrated suppliers into what we call Supplier Collaboration. Eight is the timing of flows with suppliers we call Supplier Synchronization.

Figure 5.1   RightBuys methodology

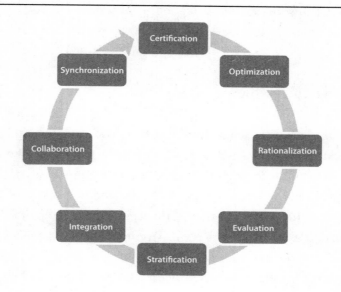

5.1 Supplier Certification

A vital step in supply strategy is the creation of a set of prequalifying supplier certification criteria—a set of performance measures, supply chain capabilities, and other business requirements that must be met or exceeded to qualify a supplier as a candidate to participate in a supply base. A typical set of supply chain certification criteria would include but not be limited to the following:

- Advanced shipment notice capability
- Bar coding and/or RFID tagging capability
- ISO certification
- Cartonization and palletization capability
- On-time delivery performance minimums
- Fill rate performance minimums

- Damage free performance minimums
- Real-time inbound information accuracy
- Reasonable capacity risk exposure (Figure 5.2)

5.2 Supplier Optimization

Limited domestic labor availability, high domestic labor costs, the domestic demand for a great variety of unique products, global communication systems availability, lower trade barriers, increasing sophistication and capability of international suppliers, and developing pockets of production expertise unique to specific world regions have all led to the need for all corporations to create global sourcing strategies. Global sourcing strategies have paid enormous dividends for U.S. corporations. Nike, with 100 percent global sourcing, is an iconic U.S. example. Unfortunately, many U.S. companies have swung the pendulum too far toward global sourcing, overlooking the benefits of domestic sourcing including shorter in-transit times, lower transportation costs, lower inventory levels, cultural compatibilities, and rapid and reliable communications. Sourcing optimization reveals an optimal mix of internal and external, global and domestic sources based on total acquisition cost, global business strategy, and high-level sourcing policies.

The first sourcing decision for each item is whether to make it or buy it. The decision should take into account long-term business strategy, core competencies, the capabilities of optional supply sources, total ownership cost, and quality implications associated with internal vs. external sourcing. Internal sources should be held accountable to the same supplier certification criteria as external sources.

A variety of factors should be used in selecting an external supplier. However, one of the most important is the total acquisition cost. Total acquisition cost analysis goes well beyond traditional unit purchase cost considerations to include the cost of inbound transportation, inventory

Figure 5.2   RightBuys supplier risk assessment

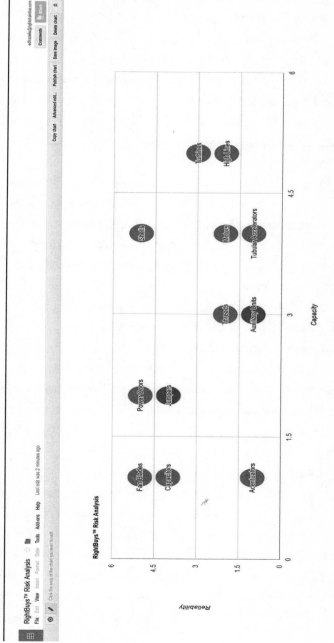

carrying, lost sales, warehousing, international logistics fees, and the cost of poor quality. Total acquisition cost should be computed and compared for each item for all sourcing alternatives. TAC analysis is especially important when considering global sourcing alternatives where a low unit purchase cost may be offered, but may be more than offset by high costs of transportation, lost sales, inventory carrying, and international logistics. In addition to the total acquisition cost, RightBuys analysis incorporates gross margin, inventory turns, gross margin return on inventory, and inventory value added.

An example RightBuys sourcing optimization is presented in Figure 5.3. The example is from a recent supply chain strategy project in which the client was considering moving a large portion of their supply base to China and eastern Europe. In fact, the far-sourcing train had a lot of momentum when we were asked to help them consider the full supply chain ramifications of the decision.

Initial Unit Cost (First Cost)

Our analysis considers the three main cost elements of sourcing decisions. The first is the *initial unit cost* (sometimes referred to as the first cost) offered from each supplier. Those costs ranged from $4,101.40 per unit from the eastern European candidate to $6,906.00 per unit from the incumbent domestic suppler.

Landing Costs

The second group of costs are *landing costs*. Landing costs include inbound freight, customs brokerage, freight forwarding, export compliance, sourcing organization fees, duties, banking fees, and the cost of poor quality. In this case the unit landing costs ranged from $146.12 with the incumbent domestic supplier to $998.00 per unit from the Chinese supplier. The unit landing costs added to the initial unit costs make up the *unit landed cost*. In this case the unit landed cost ranged from $4,628.00 per unit to $6,914.00 per unit.

Figure 5.3   RightBuys sourcing optimization for a global manufacturer

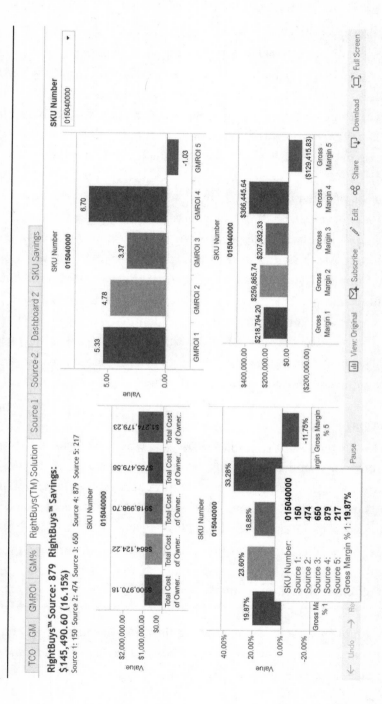

Inventory Carrying Costs

Some sourcing analyses consider landing costs, but few consider inventory carrying costs. Here, we include the three buckets of inventory described earlier—safety stock, lot size, and pipeline inventory. As expected, inventory carrying costs from the international suppliers are much higher. The inventory carrying costs for each option range from $11,005 from a candidate domestic supplier to $20,246 from the Romanian supplier.

Total Acquisition Cost

The sum of initial, landing and inventory carrying cost is the *total acquisition cost*. In this case the total cost of acquisition ranges from $1,408,646 to $2,085,405. The unit cost of acquisition ranges from $4,695.49 per unit from the Romanian supplier to $6,951.35 per unit from the domestic incumbent.

It is rare for one sourcing option to dominate the evaluation criteria, but that was the case here. The eastern European option had the lowest total acquisition cost, the highest margin, the highest return on sales, the highest inventory value added, and the shortest payback period.

Sourcing Footprint

Our RightBuys optimization was used on every SKU and was the major factor in developing a new global sourcing footprint. The strategy takes into account total acquisition cost, supply chain economic value, risk, and many other factors but leans heavily on the RightBuys recommendations. The resulting sourcing footprint is illustrated in Figure 5.4.

5.3 Supplier Rationalization

The RightBuys methodology distinguishes three sourcing schemes—(1) sole sourcing, (2) primary/secondary sourcing, and (3) transactional sourcing. Sole sourcing may be required for patented products and/or when there

Figure 5.4   RightBuys sourcing optimization footprint

| COMMODITY | GEOGRAPHY | | | | | | | |
| | China | | India | | EU | | LA | |
	Current	Optimal	Current	Optimal	Current	Optimal	Current	Optimal
Electronics	$7.40	$6.10	$0.70	$1.20	$7.40	$4.80	$2.90	$6.40
Machining	$13.10	$9.40	$10.30	$17.80	$21.30	$14.50	$1.80	$6.90
Castings	$8.10	$1.90	$2.10	$5.90	$1.80	$0.70	$6.60	$6.80
Composites	$4.80	$3.20	$3.30	$7.20	$8.80	$4.30	$4.20	$8.10
	$33.40	$20.60	$16.40	$32.10	$39.30	$24.30	$15.50	$28.20

is literally only a single source for a product. Sole sourcing is feasible when the sole source has the capacity, commitment, and proven track record to earn the trust required in sole sourcing. Sole sourcing may even be preferred when the economies of scale are sufficient to outweigh any risks of service interruption.

In primary/secondary sourcing, a primary source is used as long as they have availability to meet our requirements and have continued to meet or exceed supplier performance targets. If there is some slippage in a primary supplier's performance, demand can be shifted to the secondary supplier in proportion to the degree of slippage.

Transactional sourcing allows three or more prequalified suppliers to bid on less strategic requirements as the needs arise.

The objective in supply base rationalization is to optimize the number of suppliers while satisfying all the quality and cost objectives of the sourcing policy. That said, in general, supply chains operate more effectively with fewer suppliers rather than more as long as capacity risk is covered.

There are three main reasons for consolidating the supply base. First, increasing the volumes contracted with a smaller supplier base yields unit purchase price reductions. Second, raising quality standards automatically disqualifies many suppliers. Third, long- and short-term supply chain initiatives aimed at enhancing customer service and reducing total supply chain cost are much easier to implement with a few highly integrated and highly capable suppliers than with a large mix of loosely integrated, inconsistently capable suppliers.

5.4 Supplier Evaluation

One of our clients likes to say, "Either manage the suppliers or they will manage you." One of the most important facets of supplier management is supplier performance measurement and an associated accountability plan. Though commonsensical, many companies operate their supply chains without any formal performance measures or accountabilities for their suppliers. The presence or absence of those measures and accountabilities sends a very strong signal to the supply base.

The RightBuys methodology includes four categories of supplier performance measures—finance, quality, cycle time, and compliance.

Finance
As described earlier, our primary financial evaluation of a supplier is the total cost of acquisition and the related financial metrics including gross margin return on inventory and inventory value added. Those metrics were defined earlier.

Quality
We recommend two high-level supplier quality metrics—supplier fill rate and perfect purchase order percentage.

Supplier fill rate is a critical quality metric because every percentage point differential between the supplier fill rate and the customer fill rate is a percentage difference that must be made up in extra inventory carrying cost. For example, if a supplier provides a 94 percent fill rate, and I want to provide a 98 percent customer fill rate to the customers, how do I make up the 4 percent gap? Extra inventory.

The second indicator is the perfect purchase order percentage. All the facets of the perfect order we described earlier are applied to a purchase order. On a broad scale, for every percent difference between the perfect order percentage that we want to offer our customers and the perfect purchase order percentage offered by suppliers, we have to make up in extra inventory, excess inspection, excess transportation costs, etc. In our experience, the gap between a company's perfect customer order percentage offering to its customers and the perfect purchase order percentage received from its suppliers can explain a large portion of the excess supply chain costs incurred by the company.

Cycle Time

The two cycle time indicators we monitor are purchase order cycle time and its variability. Purchase order cycle time includes the elapsed time to process a purchase order including order entry time, order processing time, manufacturing time (if required), and in-transit time. We also monitor the variability because we often have to plan for the worst case. In some cases we select suppliers who offer the best worst case as opposed to the best average case or minimum case purchase order cycle time.

Compliance

All of the supplier certification criteria that were established early on must be continually monitored. Some of our clients currently use vision systems at receiving to automate certification compliance and to enact non-conformance charges.

Supplier Accountability

An important component of supplier certification criteria is the design of rewards and penalties for extraordinary performance or non-conformance to established criteria. Typical rewards are high-profile vendor recognition, long-term contracts, and sole sourcing. Typical penalties include fines for specific violations of the certification criteria, sourcing reductions, and/

or rejected receipts. One of our retail clients inspects each receipt, takes a digital picture of each non-conformance, invoices the supplier for each violation based on its published penalty charge, and includes the digital picture with the non-conformance invoice. Another organization classifies their vendors into "white hat" and "black hat" categories based on their historic delivery quality. "Black hat" vendors are charged $50 per hour for every hour spent in receiving inspection. The most severe non-conformance penalty program I am aware of is a client who charges each vendor twice the retail value of all the contents of an inbound truckload if there is *any* non-conformance in the entire truckload.

An important tool in supplier accountability is the ongoing measuring and reporting of each supplier's performance in the accountability criteria. Our RightBuys Scoreboard measures and reports each supplier's financial, quality, and cycle time performance (Figure 5.5).

5.5 Supplier Stratification

Based on performance to established targets and inbound logistics volumes, suppliers should be filtered into three or four strata. A template for stratifying suppliers and items for the purposes of inbound supply chain planning is provided in Figure 5.6.

A items coming from the A suppliers are probably full truckloads. B and C items coming from B and C suppliers may offer opportunities for inbound transportation consolidation. C items coming from C vendors might require a higher percentage receiving inspection than A items coming from A vendors.

Figure 5.7 is a supplier stratification we developed for a company introducing hypermarkets into their retail portfolio. Suppliers are classified by size and performance into A, B, C, and D categories. Seven commodities and A, B, C, and D classes of items based on unit sales and item popularity are also specified. For each cross-section of suppliers and items an optimal

Figure 5.5   RightBuys Scoreboard

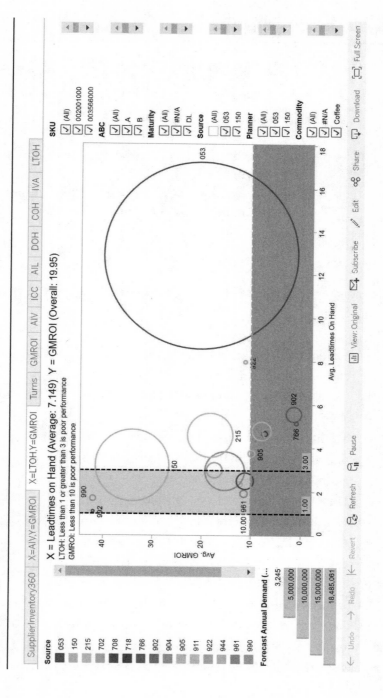

Figure 5.6   RightBuys supplier stratification

		Supplier Classifications		
		A Suppliers	B Suppliers	C Suppliers
Item Classifications	A Items	A Items from A Suppliers	A Items from B Suppliers	A Items from C Suppliers
	B Items	B Items from A Suppliers	B Items from B Suppliers	B Items from C Suppliers
	C Items	C Items from A Suppliers	C Items from B Suppliers	C Items from C Suppliers

inbound supply chain strategy is recommended. The optional strategies include:

- Vendor managed inventories (VMI) for stable, popular items coming from reliable suppliers
- Cross-docking for time-sensitive products inbound from reliable suppliers
- Traditional warehousing and delivery for slower moving products and commodities inbound from suppliers who may require additional oversight
- Direct store delivery for perishables
- Consignment inventory for promotional items
- Outsourcing to wholesalers for the slowest moving items in all categories

Color codes connote the recommended inbound supply chain strategy. For example, the A, B, and C perishables coming from A, B, and C suppliers move via direct store delivery. They have a very short shelf life and don't have time to sit in a warehouse. A and B dry grocery items inbound

Figure 5.7   RightBuys inbound supply chain strategy

SUPPLIERS	Clothing				Dry Grocery				General Merchandise				Healthy & Beauty				Housewares				Perishables				Promotions
	A	B	C	D	A	B	C	D	A	B	C	D	A	B	C	D	A	B	C	D	A	B	C	D	A
A	XD	DC	DC	X	XD	XD	DC	X	XD	DC	DC	X	XD	DC	DC	X	XD	DC	DC	X	DSD	DSD	DSD	X	Consignment
B	DC	DC	DC	X	XD	XD	DC	X	DC	DC	DC	X	DC	DC	DC	X	DC	DC	DC	X	DSD	DSD	DSD	X	Consignment
C	DC	DC	DC	X	DC	DC	DC	X	DC	DC	DC	X	DC	DC	DC	X	DC	DC	DC	X	DSD	DSD	DSD	X	Consignment
D	X	X	X	X	X	X	X	X	X	X	X	X	X	X	X	X	X	X	X	X	X	X	X	X	Consignment

COMMODITIES

VMI
BMI

XD   Cross Dock
DC   DC Flow
X   Eliminate
VMI   Vendor Managed Inventory
BMI   Buyer Managed Inventory
DSD   Direct Store Delivery

from A and B vendors are cross-docked and placed under vendor management. The inbound flow and suppliers are reliable enough to justify cross-docking. C dry grocery items inbound from the A, B, and C suppliers flow through the distribution center. For promotional items, our client had enough leverage with these vendors to retail them on a consignment basis.

5.6 Supplier Integration

The supplier base is really an extension of the enterprise. As such, supplier relationships (face-to-face, telecommunications, Internet) need be developed as aggressively and strategically as customer relationships. The reliability, predictability, and value added in links with suppliers is the foundation for the ability to serve customers reliably, predictably, and with increasing value. Wal-Mart's supplier relationships (though criticized as heavy-handed in many circles) are the foundation of their business success. Dell Computer and Harley-Davidson's on-site supplier community serve as the foundation for their supply chain successes.

Those relationships have been developed through a formal supplier relationship management (SRM) program. SRM programs include annual conferences where supply chain trends in all organizations are shared, upcoming business initiatives that will impact the supplier community are presented, and agreements are reached for future supply chain standards and capabilities.

Supplier integration and excellence in supplier relationship management (SRM) is difficult to measure, but it is easily recognized by the presence or absence of the following practices:

- Vendor managed inventory (VMI)
- Forecast sharing

- Supply chain collaboration, optimization, scheduling, and simulation
- Pre-receiving
- Standard, economic handling increments

Vendor Managed Inventory (VMI)

Some supplier relationships have evolved to the point of permitting the supplier (or vendor) to manage customer inventory levels. VMI programs require the supplier to maintain inventory visibility, place replenishment orders (with themselves) on behalf of the customer, and achieve target customer service levels. As a result, VMI programs require a high degree of trust between the parties and extensive supply chain capabilities on both sides.

Three of the most successful VMI programs are the BOSE JIT II program, where suppliers monitor component inventory levels from offices inside the BOSE speaker factory; Harley-Davidson's supplier city; and Dell Computer's on-site supplier program. In each case the initial concerns were the "fox in the chicken coop" syndrome. However, in each case the foxes learned that the best way to keep their good standing in the chicken coop was not to eat the chickens, but to coddle and protect them with excellent customer service and reasonable pricing.

Demand Information Sharing

Demand information could be point-of-consumption data, future demand period forecasts, existing orders, and/or future growth plans. In the absence of this information, suppliers are left to guess the amount and timing of future demand. Since most reputable suppliers err on the side of providing enough inventory for the worst case, excess inventory is built up at every point in the supply chain where guessing occurs. Demand information sharing minimizes the guesswork, the associated inventory, and the associated excess supply chain costs and eliminates the guesswork in supply chain and inventory planning.

Pre-receiving

A more practical manifestation of supplier integration is pre-receiving or pre-clearing receipts from suppliers based on receiving certification and historic performance in a variety of delivery quality measures. Bar code license plates and/or RIFD tags on all inbound unit loads, advance shipment notifications, low to near-zero in-transit damage, and high purchase order to receiving quantity match percentages are typical requirements for pre-receiving.

Standard, Economic Handling Increments

Another practical manifestation of supplier integration is the use of standard, economic handling units inbound from the supplier. Ideally, product should flow in full case (with broken case customer demand), layer, full pallet (with full case customer demand), and/or full truckload quantities in standard case, pallet, and truckload configurations to minimize transportation and warehousing costs.

Paperless Information Exchange

Paperless, electronic, real-time information exchange is a key enabler of supplier integration. Forecasts, automatic replenishments, manufacturing resource planning (MRP) requirements transmitted as purchase orders, electronic funds transfer, and advance shipment notifications should all flow through electronic links with suppliers and carriers. The Internet, intranets, EDI, and even fax (a poor man's EDI) can, have, and should be used to reduce the coefficient of friction of information exchange with suppliers.

Perpetual PO Status Visibility

The status of all purchase orders (in process, in verification, in manufacturing, in picking, in packing, awaiting parts, loading, in transit, etc.) should be updated and visible in real time at all times. The updates are required manufacturing scheduling, transportation planning, warehouse management, and customer order status inquiries.

5.7 Supplier Collaboration

For every factory there is an optimal production schedule that minimizes the total production and inventory carrying cost given labor and material availability, manufacturing and storage capacity, and demand requirements. In like manner, for every supply chain there is an optimal supply chain schedule that minimizes the total cost to consumption including inventory carrying, transportation, warehousing, and lost sales given the supply chain's production, transportation, and warehousing capacity and inventory requirements at every node in the supply chain. In some supply chains a fourth party (Figure 5.8) is used to produce the optimal schedule. Each major player (supplier, customer, carrier) in the supply chain shares their true demand and capacity with the fourth party who computes an optimal supply chain schedule including retail receiving hours, warehouse shipping and receiving schedules, transportation schedules, and production schedules.

Figure 5.8   Supply chain collaboration optimization

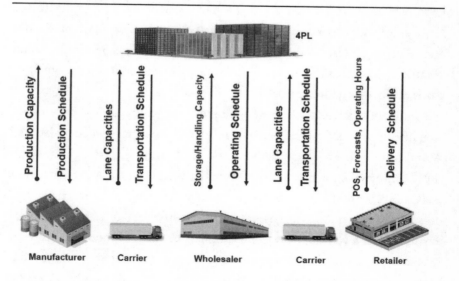

5.8 Supplier Synchronization

In a traditional supply chain, manufacturers try to drive down their manufacturing unit cost by making long production runs. The tactic creates large inventories. To make quarter end revenue projections and to free up space for new inventory, manufacturers use discounting to push that quarter's inventory out their door to wholesalers. Wholesale buyers are energized by the push because it means they can buy at a discount, as long as they buy a lot. Most wholesalers have very large warehouses designed to accommodate discount lot buying. When sales don't materialize for that inventory, and the end of the quarter comes with its anxiety for sales and earnings, wholesalers turn to the retailers, looking to use discounts to push their excess inventory out their doors into the retail channel. Retail buyers are energized because they are measured on how low a price they can pay, which they can as long as they buy a lot. At the end of the next quarter the cycle repeats as retailers turn to consumers to make their sales and earnings estimates. It is not a coincidence that the most common inventory turn rate in American business is four.

Over time some organizations have woken up and orchestrated their supply chains to combat the quarterly cycle. For example, in our RightChain design for one of America's largest wholesale/retail entities (Figure 5.9), we stratified flows based the degree of supply chain synchronization that could be achieved.

Full truckload A items from A suppliers move directly from a production line into outbound trailers for direct store delivery. A mix of palletized A and B items from A suppliers move directly from palletizing lines into outbound trucks for more direct store deliveries. Those A/B items from A/B suppliers that can't justify direct store delivery move in and out of cross docking centers in just a few hours. Synchronized ordering and delivery with A/B-level suppliers yields a tight schedule of inbound deliveries, inbound/outbound dock assignments, and outbound departure times that provide their retail stores with a steady stream of next-day, daily deliveries.

Figure 5.9   Supplier synchronization design

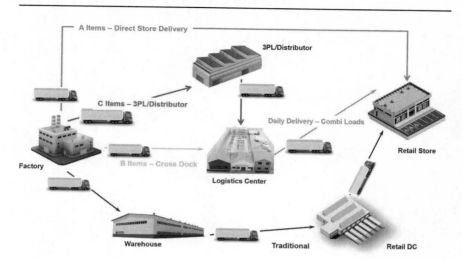

The schedule is derived daily based upon the previous day's store orders, inventory, and delivery requirements computations.

One other technique that enhances this practice is what's called a combi-load. A combi-load accommodates frozen space, refrigerated space, and ambient temperature space on the same truck. That fleet configuration supports a program of daily store deliveries. Daily deliveries free up backroom space for selling and help reduce total supply chain inventories.

C items could not be ignored because they were the very items that differentiated our client's stores from their competitors. Instead of clogging the main flow paths of the A and B items with the C items, we found a third-party wholesaler who specialized in logistics for slow-moving items in the food industry. We treated that third party as if they were just another A/B item supplier and gave them their daily delivery shipping requirements to our logistics center. Their C-item flows merged into the A/B items cross-dock flows and became a normal part of the daily cross-docking for daily store delivery.

CHAPTER 6

RightTrips
Transportation Strategy

"Whoever travels life in integrity and straight lines travels securely,
but whoever travels crooked paths will be found out."
—SOLOMON

A few years ago we were working with a large frozen food company. A group of us were in the executive board room waiting for the CEO to show up. I was seated next to the CFO. While we were waiting, he decided to take me through their financial statements. He was especially proud of their expense statement for the prior 12 months. He insisted on showing me that all but one of their expense items had been reduced as compared to the prior year. He indignantly pointed out that the single line item that had increased in comparison to the prior year was transportation. He then asked me what I thought they should do about their transportation expenses.

Instead of replying right away, I asked him what had happened to profit during the period that transportation expenses had increased. He said that profit was up. I asked him what had happened to market share during the period in which transportation expenses had increased. He said that market share was up. I asked him what had happened to customer satisfaction during the period when transportation expenses had increased. He said that customer satisfaction had increased. He got upset and impatiently asked, "But Dr. Frazelle, what should we do about transportation expenses? They are increasing." I said, "It looks to me like you should spend even more on transportation, because it seems to be working." That was the last time he spoke to me. Six months later it was the last time he spoke to anyone in the company because he was let go. I expect he was let go because he was bound and determined to reduce every single expense in the company, even at the cost of lower profits, lower revenue, and poor capital utilization.

For many reasons, transportation should be viewed as a strategic component of supply chain and business strategy, and an area crying for additional resources and focus.

- Transportation is the physical means of connecting with customers and a vital contributor to the customer experience.
- Transportation is typically the single most expensive supply chain activity.
- Strategic spending on transportation may help reduce inventory carrying cost and improve customer service.
- In many organizations, transportation is the activity where the least amount of science is applied, and carriers are often the least sophisticated and innovative of all the players in a supply chain.
- Transportation is the means by which a business must navigate the increasingly competitive and complex logistics landscape. The basic ability to deliver goods to customers used to be taken for granted. Not anymore. In the face of growing and grave security concerns, unreliable access to transportation capacity, dire operator shortages, frequent strikes and critical transportation choke points, and a crumbling transportation infrastructure—there is no such thing as "Ship it and forget it."

- Transportation is the means by which a business plugs into the growing myriad of delivery modal alternatives—drones; autonomous vehicles, ships, trains, and planes; mega-ships and mega-planes; and traditional trucks, ships, trains, and planes; fuel alternatives—electricity, hydrogen, solar, and fossil; and response time alternatives ranging from a few hours to a few weeks is confounding at best.

While there are many questions that need answers in transportation, a transportation strategy answers the following:

- How should the supply chain **network** and its flows be configured?
- What **shipping plan** addressing modes of transportation and shipment frequency optimizes supply chain performance?
- What **fleet** size, configuration, and operating model optimizes supply chain performance?

6.1 Network Strategy

Customers and suppliers are continually relocating. Product and packaging sizes and weights and configurations are continually changing. Mergers and acquisitions create a constantly changing competitive landscape. Real estate, capital, and labor availability and rates are dynamic. Governments and government regulations come and go at the swipe of a pen. Mode, carrier, and port availability are unpredictable. Network congestion is at an all-time high. Security risks and requirements are proliferating. Free trade agreements are in total flux. Consumer demographics and transience are in flux.

It is in that context that supply chain network optimization determines the number of logistics layers, the number of distribution points in each layer, and the location of each distribution point. Accordingly, supply chain network design has a major impact on response times, inventory levels, fill rates, and supply chain costs including transportation costs, warehousing costs, inventory carrying costs, and lost sales costs.

The optimal network design minimizes the total supply chain cost while satisfying customer response time requirements and complying with any network constraints.

Objective Function
Minimize total supply chain costs.

Constraints
1. Meet all customer response time requirements.
2. Meet all lane flow requirements.
3. Do not violate any lane throughput capacities.
4. Do not violate any facility storage capacities.
5. Do not violate any facility throughput capacities.

Network Trade-Offs
Before we delve into our network design methodology, there are some key trade-offs at work in logistics network design that will guide the evaluation and design of alternative networks.

Network Configuration and Inventory Carrying Cost
Supply chain inventory levels logically increase as the number of stocking locations in the network increases. The increase is a result of the greater number of deployment decisions, the associated forecast errors, and the resulting additional safety stock. Consequently, a supply chain network is often optimized by identifying the fewest number of logistics facilities that will meet customer response time requirements (Figure 6.1).

Figure 6.1   Supply chain network and inventory trade-off analysis

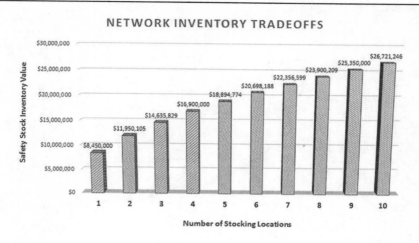

Network Configuration and Travel Times

Any network optimization analysis also needs to consider the impact of the network design on customer service times (Figure 6.2). Assuming the facilities are placed logically, as the number of facilities increases, the average distance to customers decreases. Correspondingly, the response time to the customer base decreases.

Network Design and Transportation Cost

Assuming the same transportation modes are employed, as the distance to customers decreases, so should the outbound transportation cost. That phenomenon is reflected in Figure 6.3 in a network analysis recently completed for a large retailer. Note that as the number of facilities increases, inventory carrying cost increases. However, total transportation cost decreases. The sum of those two, the total logistics cost, is minimized with four facilities.

Network Cost and Service

When we add inventory carrying and transportation costs and include customer response times in the same consideration, we get the optimization

Figure 6.2   Network design impact on the distance and time to the customer base

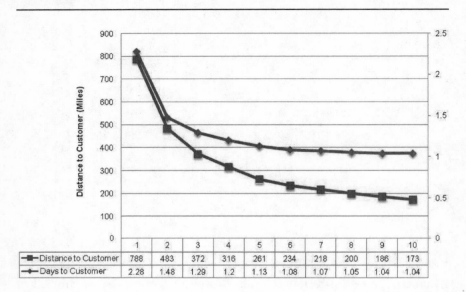

	1	2	3	4	5	6	7	8	9	10
Distance to Customer	788	483	372	316	261	234	218	200	186	173
Days to Customer	2.28	1.48	1.29	1.2	1.13	1.08	1.07	1.05	1.04	1.04

presented in Figure 6.4. In this case, the supply chain service policy required us to reach the customer base in no less than 48 hours. The least-cost design that allowed us to meet that requirement required six facilities.

RightNodes Methodology

Since each corporation's vendor and customer base are unique, so too is its optimal supply chain network. We developed the RightNodes methodology to help our clients develop and evaluate network scenarios that meet their unique objectives and provide the ongoing capability to consider new scenarios as business objectives and network constraints change over time (Figure 6.5).

1. **Assess and evaluate the current network performance.** Each alternative network configuration must be compared with the financial,

Figure 6.3   RightNodes optimization for a large retailer

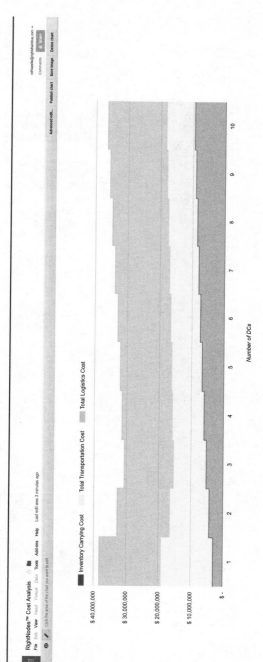

Figure 6.4   RightNodes optimization for a large spares organization

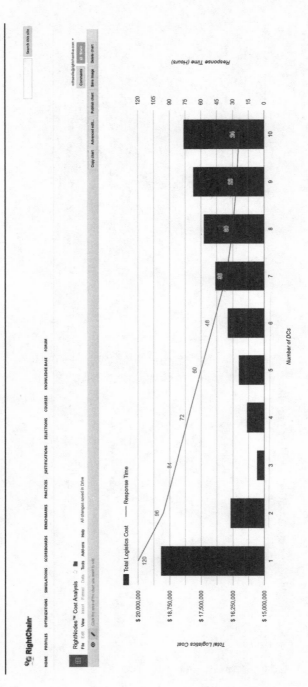

Figure 6.5   RightNodes network optimization methodology

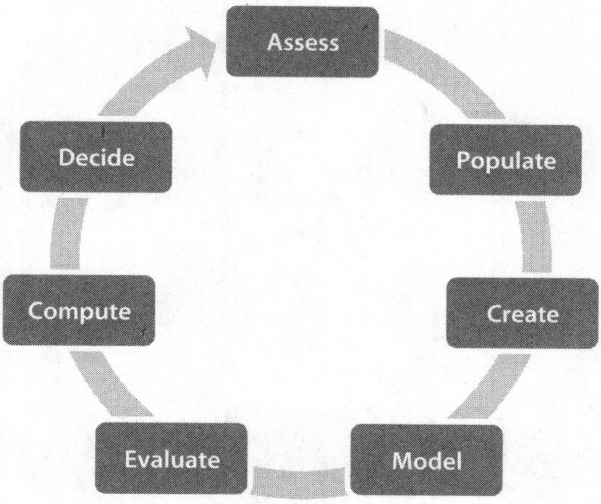

service, and risk performance of the current network. To that end, a first step in network reconfiguration is an assessment of the performance of the current network. We use the RightChain Scoreboard presented in Chapter 2 as the baseline network performance assessment (Figure 6.6).

2. **Design and populate the network optimization database.** One of the most cumbersome and time-consuming steps in network optimization is collecting, purifying, rationalizing, and profiling the database of origins, destination, volumes, weights, cubes, facilities, costs, and constraints that typify a network optimization database. At a minimum the database should specify geocoded locations and modal travel speeds along each lane connecting pickup, delivery, and distribution locations; fixed and variable warehousing, inventory carrying, and transportation costs; response time requirements for each delivery point (and time windows if specified); product availability at each source and product demand at each delivery point; any immovable locations; location throughput and storage constraints;

Figure 6.6   RightChain Scoreboard

											Year	2010
											Month	July
											Channel	Grocery
											Category	Waters
											State	TN

Category	Sub-Cat	Selling	Planning	Manufacturing	Sourcing	Transportation	Warehousing	Delivery	Merchandising	SUPPLY CHAIN
Service / Customers	Quality	94.0% PSO	56.0% Fcst Accuracy	99.0% PMOP	81.0% PPVOP	92.0% PDP	72.0% PWVOP	98.0% PDP	93.0% PMCO	72.0% POP
	Cycle Time	1.9 SCT	4.7 IPCT	7 MCT	14.3 POCT	8.2 TCT	2.4 VTS, WCT	5.4 DCT	12.8 MCT	17.3 SCCT
	On Time	93% % on-time	92%	92% % adherance	92% % OT Pos	92% % loads on-time	92% % order on-time	92% % loads on-time	92% % merch on-time	92% SCCT
GPTW / Employees	Safety	4,250.0 MH/I	7,653.0 MH/I	3,822.0 MH/I	8,788.0 MH/I	9,145.0 MH/I	9,987.0 MH/I	9,650.0 MH/I	8,998.0 MH/I	9,001.0 MH/I
	Satisfaction	81.0% % yes	91.0% % yes	93.0% % yes	94.0% % yes	91.0% % yes	81.0% % yes	79.0% % yes	98.0% % yes	85.0% % yes
	Development	9.2 out of 10	8.1 out of 10	8.1 out of 10	8.5 out of 10	8.7 out of 10	7.3 out of 10	9.2 out of 10	8.8 out of 10	8.7 out of 10
Finance / Shareholders	Cost	1.23 $/case	1.22 $/case	2.99 $/case	0.99 $/case	1.88 $/case	2.11 $/case	1.82 $/case	4.21 $/case	12.24 $/case
	Capital	12,000,000 $s	48,000,000 $s	207,000,000 $s	2,000,000 $s	50,000,000 $s	60,000,000 $s	70,000,000 $s	80,000,000 $s	529,000,000 $s
	ROIC	6.00% SROA	12.00% GMROA	33.00% GMROA	21.00% GMROA	9.00% GMROA	45.00% GMROA	33.00% DROA	8.00% MROA	19.00% SCROIC
Productivity	Labor	67 orders/MH	43 $x/FTE	78 cpmh	34 cpmh	124 cpmh	112 cpmh	100 cpmh	21 cpmh	12 cases/FTE
	Space	0.998 GM/cube	0.876 GM/cube	0.776 GM/SF	0.601 GM/cube	0.398 GM/cube	213 cases/SF	0.511 GM/cube	0.991 GM/cube	18.99 cases/SF
Utilization	Labor	28.0% % buy util	34.0% % labor util	81.0% % labor util	99.0% % labor util	34.0% % labor util	44.0% % labor util	39.0% % labor util	69.0% % labor util	83.0% % labor util
	Capital	91.0% % buy util	92.0% % buy util	91.0% % prod util	65.0% % buy util	73.0% % cap util	82.0% % cap util	62.0% % buy util	89.0% % buy util	81.0% % cap util
	Space	93.0% % space util	80.0% % space util	78.0% % space util	79.0% % space util	77.0% % space util	80.0% % space util	89.0% % space util	89.0% % space util	80.0% % space util
TOTAL		18.91 TSCC/PSO	13.45 TIC/PIO	11.10 TMC/PMO	9.97 TSC/PSO	8.88 TIC/PTO	9.12 TWC/PWHO	11.10 TDC/PDO	12.55 TMCC/PMO	26.93 TSCC/PNetOrder
	Practices	2.1 out of 5	2.8 out of 5	2.8 out of 5	2.8 out of 5	2.8 out of 5	2.8 out of 5	2.8 out of 5	2.2 out of 5	2.4 out of 5
	Complexity	2,000 orders	500 SKUs	3,000 SKU-lines	2,000 SKU-suppliers	3,000 SKU-stops	5,000 locations	1,000 SKU-stops	10,000 accounts	26,500 complexity
	Risk	4.1 Out of 5	2.8 Out of 5	3.1 Out of 5	2.1 Out of 5	4.8 Out of 5	3.5 Out of 5	3.2 Out of 5	2.5 Out of 5	3.1 Out of 5

and lane volumes in weight, cube, frequency, and monetary value and units. This step may take from a few to several weeks to complete depending on the number and variety of pickup/delivery points, commodities, transportation modes, and alternative flow paths.

Mapping is a powerful data visualization platform for network data because it can quickly suggest network alternatives for consideration and quickly eliminate some that may have been in the consideration set. We developed the mapping in Figure 6.7 for one of the world's largest aerospace companies. They were considering supply chain hubs in a variety of locations around the world. Once the map was published, our design team quickly focused on a northeast hub for the new assembly center (Figure 6.8).

Our recent mapping of customer activity for a European biotechnology company quickly identified three logical sites for consideration to reach all of their European customers by truck within 24 hours (Figure 6.9).

Our recent mapping of a global healthcare network identified redundancies in the European Union, Americas, and Asia-Pacific and led to a rapid consolidation into an EU logistics center near Amsterdam, an Americas center in Miami, and an Asia-Pacific center in Singapore (Figure 6.10).

3. **Create network design alternatives.** A supply chain modeling tool can only evaluate the scenarios it is given to consider. Hence, the creation of the alternatives for consideration is one of, if not the most important step in the RightNodes methodology.

The charge is to challenge current supply chain paradigms and brainstorm as many feasibly effective scenarios as possible to consider in the evaluation. That requires considering new supply chain flow patterns for each commodity including direct shipping, cross-docking, consignment inventory, inbound and outbound consolidation, and merge-in-transit schemes.

Figure 6.7   RightNodes mapping for a global aerospace supply chain

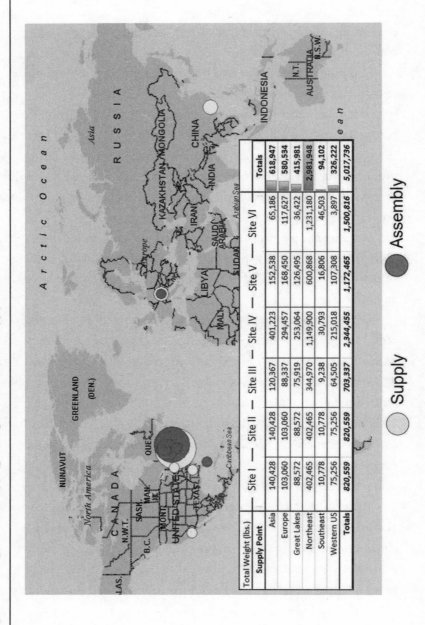

Total Weight (lbs.) Supply Point	Site I	Site II	Site III	Site IV	Site V	Site VI	Totals
Asia	140,428	140,428	120,367	401,223	152,538	65,186	618,947
Europe	103,060	103,060	88,337	294,457	168,450	117,627	580,534
Great Lakes	88,572	88,572	75,919	253,064	126,495	36,422	415,981
Northeast	402,465	402,465	344,970	1,149,900	600,868	1,231,180	2,981,948
Southeast	10,778	10,778	9,238	30,793	16,806	46,503	94,102
Western US	75,256	75,256	64,505	215,018	107,308	3,897	326,222
Totals	820,559	820,559	703,337	2,344,455	1,172,465	1,500,816	5,017,736

Supply   Assembly

Figure 6.8   RightNodes mapping for a global assembly center

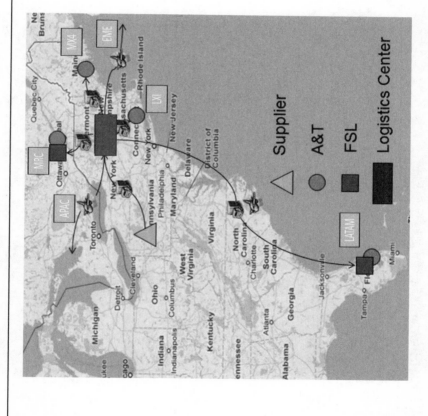

Figure 6.9   RightNodes optimization for a European biotech company

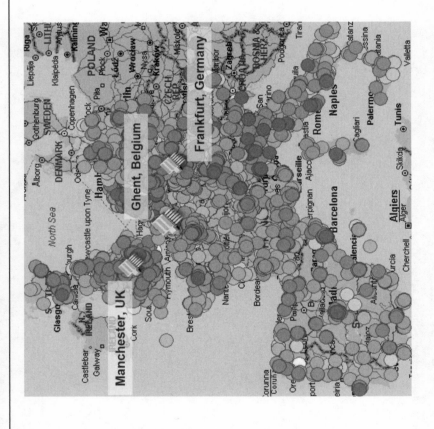

Figure 6.10   RightNodes optimization for a global healthcare company

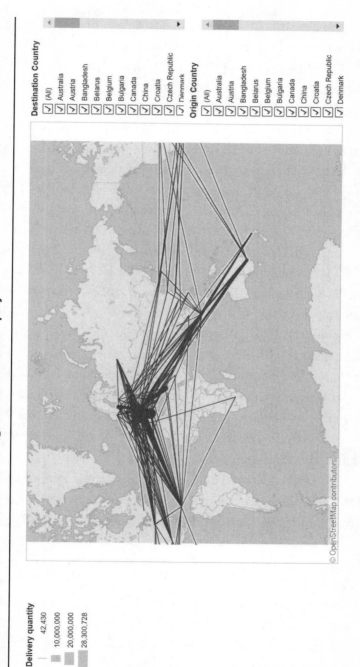

Delivery quantity

42,430
10,000,000
20,000,000
28,300,728

Destination Country

☑ (All)
☑ Australia
☑ Austria
☑ Bangladesh
☑ Belarus
☑ Belgium
☑ Bulgaria
☑ Canada
☑ China
☑ Croatia
☑ Czech Republic
☑ Denmark

Origin Country

☑ (All)
☑ Australia
☑ Austria
☑ Bangladesh
☑ Belarus
☑ Belgium
☑ Bulgaria
☑ Canada
☑ China
☑ Croatia
☑ Czech Republic
☑ Denmark

We use flow path optimization to help our clients consider those myriad flows. Flow path optimization begins with an enumeration of all the potential flow paths in a network. An example enumeration completed for a large healthcare company is provided in Figure 6.11.

This step may also require pre-modeling analysis. An example is the RightFlows analysis we recently conducted to help a client determine SKU-level optimal supply chain flow paths. The alternative flow paths for each item are illustrated and evaluated in Figure 6.12.

We also consult the supply chain real estate community when we are evaluating candidate network locations. We take this step for two important reasons. First, we want to avoid considering locations that are unprofitable market-wise. Second, as strange as it may sound, there is a very limited range of options for locating major logistics facilities. Knowing those locations in advance can save many weeks on a supply chain network project timeline.

One real estate option we often consider is what we call an urban strike point (USP). An urban strike point is located in close proximity to multiple points of heavy supply and demand, is removed from the congestion of the heavy supply and demand, is in close proximity to multiple interstate access points, is near a high quality and reasonably priced workforce, offers reasonable occupancy costs, and has minimal risks of supply chain disruption.

When those criteria are applied, the potential locations for major logistics facilities narrow quickly. In a recent project with a major retailer, their flow path optimization highlighted the need for a major West Coast distribution center (DC) near their West Coast ports of entry and a major East Coast DC (Figure 6.13). The urban strike point analysis for their West Coast DC quickly highlighted the Moreno Valley area with close proximity to their inbound Port of Long Beach; their customers in California and across the western United States; good weather; access to Interstates 5, 10, 15, and 415; new DC construction opportunities; and an excellent workforce (Figure 6.14).

Figure 6.11   RightFlows flow path enumeration

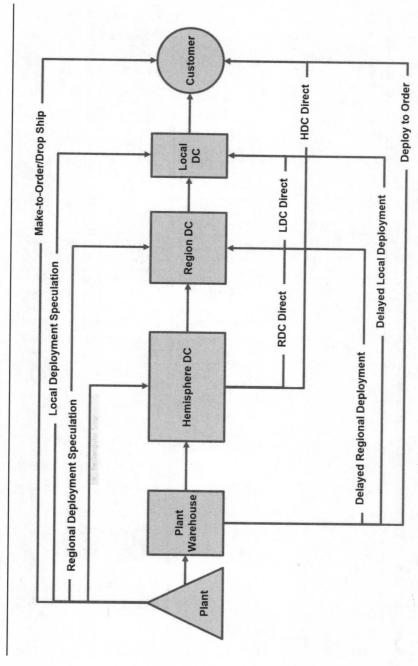

Figure 6.12 RightFlows optimization for a food manufacturing firm

Flow Path	Touches	Pipeline Days	Fill Rate	Inventory Carrying Cost per Unit	Transportation Cost per Unit	Warehousing Cost per Unit	Total Logistics Cost per Unit	Manufacturing Cost per Unit	Total Cost per Unit	Selling Price per Unit	Unit Margin	Average Inventory Value	GMROI
Non-Stop	2	3	99.5%	$2.30	$4.10	$ -	$ 6.40	$11.50	$17.90	$ 31.00	$13.10	$ 5.00	262%
One-Stop	4	5	99.0%	$2.80	$4.50	$0.70	$ 8.00	$10.20	$18.20	$ 34.50	$16.30	$ 5.50	296%
DC Direct	4	6	98.0%	$3.00	$4.70	$1.20	$ 8.90	$ 9.80	$18.70	$ 37.00	$18.30	$ 6.00	305%
DSD	6	10	92.5%	$5.00	$6.10	$2.80	$13.90	$ 9.40	$23.30	$ 38.50	$15.20	$ 7.00	217%
Surge	8	40	93.7%	$7.00	$8.20	$4.10	$19.30	$ 7.10	$26.40	$ 31.00	$ 4.60	$ 8.00	58%
Distributor	6	30	94.1%	$8.00	$7.50	$1.70	$17.20	$10.75	$27.95	$ 30.00	$ 2.05	$ 8.50	24%
Warehouse	6	15	97.0%	$4.00	$7.10	$2.50	$13.60	$11.10	$24.70	$ 31.25	$ 6.55	$ 8.75	75%
Cust Direct	4	16	98.2%	$4.50	$6.90	$2.60	$14.00	$11.30	$25.30	$ 31.75	$ 6.45	$ 7.50	86%

Figure 6.13   RightFlows optimization for a major retailer

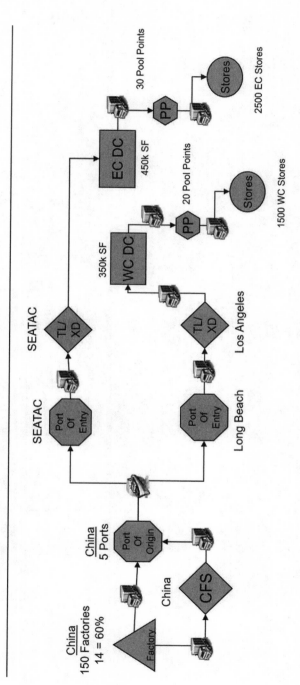

Figure 6.14   Urban strike point analysis for a major retailer

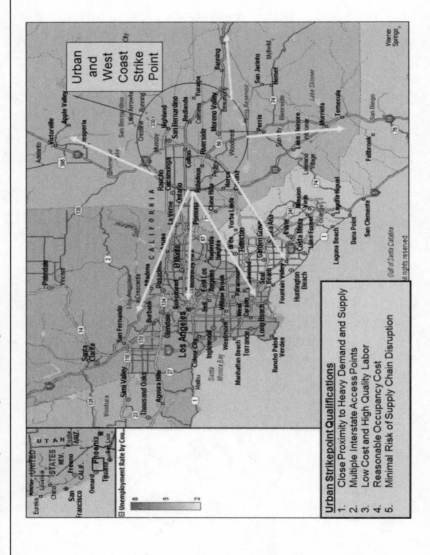

4. **Develop network optimization model.** The next step is to formalize the network optimization model, expressing the network operating scenarios mathematically in the form of mathematical programs. The mathematical program should include an objective function (typically to minimize the total supply chain costs associated with the design) and a set of constraints (typically focused on the response time and demand requirements of the customer locations). At this point, our RightChain modeling tools are pre-configured to consider the full range of possible network models and scenarios.

5. **Evaluate alternative network designs.** The next step is to evaluate each scenario on the basis of cost, service, and risk. The evaluation summaries allow executives to quickly decide from among alternative network designs since the cost and service trade-offs are quantified and presented graphically. A few of our recent network evaluations are presented below.

RightNodes Biotech

One of the joys of teaching is the friendships that develop with the students. One of my favorite (yes, teachers have favorites) students of all time is the vice president of logistics for a large biotechnology company. Dave is one of the best logisticians I have ever worked with. His management of inter- and intra-facility logistics is exceptional.

Dave called me one day distraught. I asked him what was wrong. He said, "Our CEO just came into our new East Coast DC and closed it." I asked him why. He said, "One of our employees had a bad attitude toward him, and the CEO shut the place down on the spot. We're moving all our inventory to the West Coast." I said, "But all your customers are on the East Coast." He said, "That's right. Our logistics costs are going to go through the roof, and our service levels are going to plummet."

About 18 months later Dave called again. I asked him what was going on. He said, "Our CEO is very angry that our logistics costs are going through the roof and our customer service levels have plum-meted. He wants to optimize our supply chain immediately, and I'd like your help."

The preliminary network mapping led to a total of five network scenarios (Figure 6.15). Two of those scenarios called for a single distri-bution point, in one case a parcel carrier's air hub and in another case a 3PL (third-party logistics) location on the Chicago O'Hare campus. The other three scenarios were bicoastal.

The cost and service trade-offs are presented in the figure. In this case one scenario presented the lowest cost, best service, and least risk to supply chain disruption—reopening the facility they had previously closed and continuing to operate in California. Fortunately, the origi-nal facility had not yet been sold or occupied. In addition, anticipating the scenario, Dave had maintained communication with the former employees. The solution relocated our client in the middle of the two largest biotech markets with a low-cost, highly responsive, low-risk supply chain.

RightNodes E-commerce

Lou is another one of my favorite students. When he began his stint as chief supply chain officer, he inherited an overexpanded network bloated in response to unprecedented e-commerce growth. As demand growth slowed, their supply chain cost-to-sales ratio exploded. Lou asked for our help in optimizing their network.

The network optimization is presented in Figures 6.16 and 6.17. Note that there were six scenarios under consideration, effectively clos-ing an additional DC in each scenario. The decision came down to a network of three (Atlanta, Harrisburg, and Reno) vs. two (Atlanta, Reno) DCs. The total logistics cost between the two options was nearly identical, but the three-DC network reached an additional 5 percent of the U.S. population within two days. That additional service was deemed worth the additional management complexity of an extra

Figure 6.15 RightNodes network optimization for a large biotech company

| | Centralized - Single DC | | East Coast/West Coast Distribution | | |
| | Airborne Hub | Best Central | Current | Frederick | Best East |
	Wilmington	Chicago/ND	GI/CA	FR/CA	BE/CA
Total Transportation Cost	$10,468,913	$10,938,410	$10,632,484	$9,236,174	$9,208,574
Total Warehousing Cost	$10,126,253	$9,451,169	$8,668,028	$8,848,997	$9,011,017
Inventory Carrying Cost	$10,038,450	$10,038,450	$9,936,520	$10,038,450	$10,038,450
TOTAL LOGISTICS COST	$30,633,616	$30,428,029	$29,237,032	$28,167,191	$28,258,041
Order Cutoff Time	12:00 AM	7:00 PM	7:00 PM	8:30 PM	7:00 PM
Supply Chian Failure Risk	High - SPF	Moderate	Low	Lowest	Moderate
# of Network Airports	1	2	2	6	4
Shipment Consolidation	Yes	Yes	No	Yes	Yes
Weather Related Service Interruptions	Moderate	Worst	Moderate	Best	Moderate
Marketplace Proximity	Poor	Worst	Good	Best	Best
Same-Day Capability	No	No	No	Yes	Yes
New Facilities Required	Yes	Yes	Yes	No	Yes
Learning Curve	Difficult	Most Difficult	Easiest	Easy	Moderate
Notes	5% AB Rate Discount	North Dakota	Proximity to CS	Less to Canada	Proximity to NY

Figure 6.16   RightNodes optimization map for e-commerce fulfillment

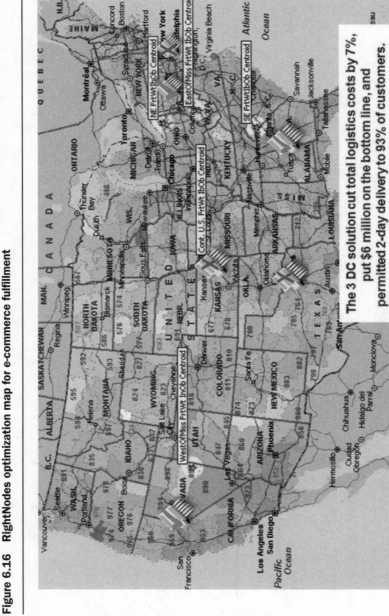

The 3 DC solution cut total logistics costs by 7%, put $6 million on the bottom line, and permitted 2-day delivery to 93% of customers.

Figure 6.17   RightNodes optimization for e-commerce

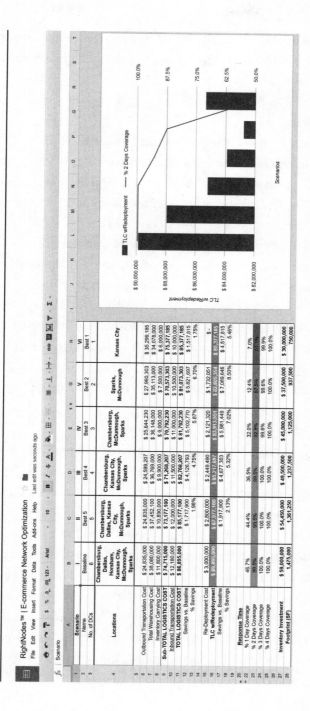

distribution center. The extra distribution center on the East Coast also helped to mitigate the risk of fuel price increases and supply chain disruptions.

Network Holes

Logistics zones, also known as service territories, determine the assignment of customers to their primary distribution or service point. Ideally, each customer will be served from its closest, minimum travel time, and/or minimum cost distribution point. However, due to DC capacity constraints, that may not always be possible.

One of our clients is the largest retailer in Mexico. The company is adding nearly 1,000 stores per year to its current base of 10,000 stores. The rapid growth keeps the capacity, capacity planning, and new construction under constant strain. We were asked to develop a long-term logistics zone optimization. A screenshot from the optimization is provided in Figure 6.18. By continually optimizing the logistics zones, the cumulative savings will be more than $23,000,000, while ensuring that each of their stores is served with increasing delivery frequency and shorter response times.

6. **Compute reconfiguration cost-benefit.** No matter how cost effective a new network design may be, the savings as compared to the baseline may not be sufficient to offset the cost of reconfiguring the existing network. Those reconfiguration costs include the cost of relocating personnel, severance, relocating inventory, opening and closing costs, and potential disruption to customer service.

7. **Make go/no-go decision.** At this point we've done our homework and presented management with the best analysis we can provide. We can make a recommendation, but the decision ultimately rests with the highest level executives in the corporation. I've seen many network modeling analyses ignored in the final decisions made by a CEO or COO. They go with their experience, intuition, gut feel, or

Figure 6.18   RightZones optimization for a large retailer

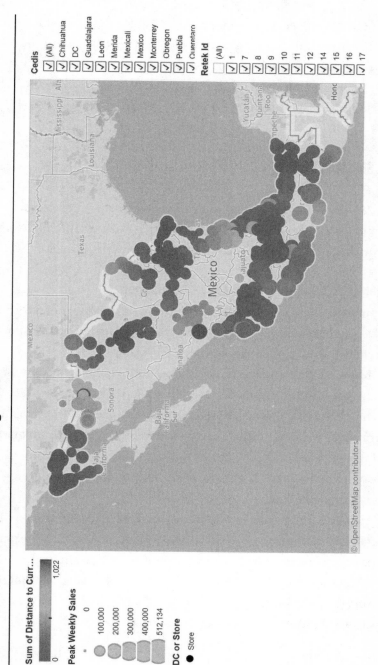

political influence of one aspect of the organization over another. That is executive prerogative. That's OK. The objective of the modeling effort is to present management with the best representation of supply chain cost and service trade-offs associated with network design decisions.

6.2 Shipping Strategy

We define a shipment simply as a collection of orders that travel together. Shipping strategy determines the shipping frequency and mode for those shipments.

RightStops | Shipping Frequency Optimization

Shipping frequency optimization determines the number of days between deliveries that minimizes total supply chain cost including transportation, warehousing, inventory carrying, and lost sales.

More frequent deliveries yield lower supply chain inventory levels and higher customer fill rates. Overall in-transit, lot size, and safety stock inventory levels and costs are reduced because there is less inventory in-in transit at any one time, the recipient is receiving smaller lot quantities, and there are more opportunities to react to shifts in demand or supply. Customer satisfaction is enhanced since customers are receiving goods more reliably more often.

However, more frequent deliveries increase transportation and warehousing cost (Figure 6.19). Transportation costs increase because the number of trips increases, the overall travel distance increases, and any transportation economies of scale are lost. Warehousing costs increase as delivery frequency increases because smaller unit load quantities are more expensive to pick than larger unit load quantities.

Figure 6.19 Shipping frequency supply chain trade-offs

Shipping Frequency	Inventory Carrying Costs			Transportation Costs		
	In-Transit	Lot Size	Safety Stock	Freight Costs	Administration Costs	Customer Satisfaction
More Often	↓	↓	↓	↑	↑	↑
Less Often	↑	↑	↑	↓	↓	↓

Retail Shipping Frequency Optimization

An example shipping frequency optimization for a large retailer is presented in Figure 6.20. As you read from left to right, the number of days between deliveries increases. Moving from left to right we consider the impact of daily deliveries (one day between deliveries), every-other-day deliveries (two days between deliveries), and continue until we get to weekly deliveries.

Note the rapid decline in transportation cost as the days between deliveries increase (delivery frequency decreases), in this case moving from a high of $1,664 to a low of $238. Note also the rapid increase in inventory carrying cost as the days between deliveries increase (delivery frequency decreases), in this case moving from a low of $960 to a high of $6,720. Finally, note that out-of-stocks move from a low of 0.1 percent to a high of 10 percent as the days between deliveries increase (delivery frequency decreases).

The optimal delivery frequency for this particular store is every other day. That delivery cadence for that store yields the lowest total supply chain cost and an acceptable fill rate. The answers for each store, however, are unique based upon each store's volume and distance from the distribution center. A summary delivery frequency analysis for all stores is presented in Figure 6.21. Note that the optimal shipping frequency is greater for those stores with higher sales rates and in closer proximity to the distribution center.

Figure 6.20   RightShip optimization example

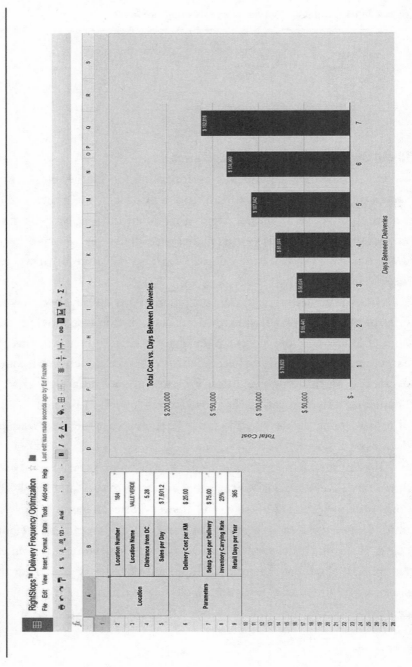

Figure 6.21   RightStops delivery frequency optimization map

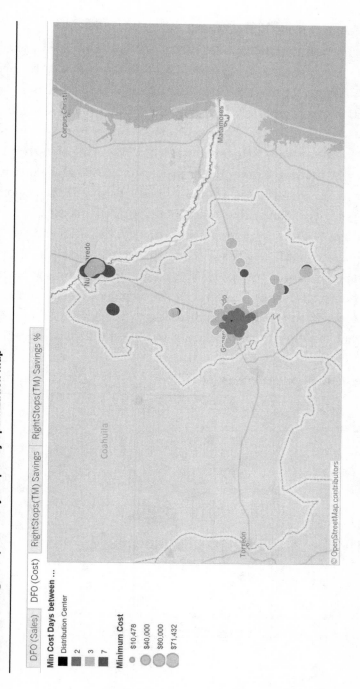

RightModes | Mode Optimization

Choosing transportation modes also plays a significant role in determining service response time. The faster the transportation mode, the shorter the response time, the lower the in-transit inventory, and the higher the transportation cost. Conversely, the slower the transportation mode, the longer the lead time, the greater the pipeline inventory and associated safety stock inventory, and the higher the inventory carrying costs. However, the slower the mode, the lower the transportation costs. Mode optimization, RightModes, identifies the transport mode that meets the response time requirements and offers the lowest total supply chain cost.

There is more to mode optimization than meets the eye. At first thought, how hard can it be to decide whether to put something on a truck, train, plane, or ship? What difference does it make, anyway? As it turns out, quite a bit (Figure 6.22). Trucks, trains, planes, and ships move at different speeds, run on different schedules, hold varying types of cargo, offer different levels and types of security, operate at different frequencies, and

Figure 6.22   RightModes trade-offs

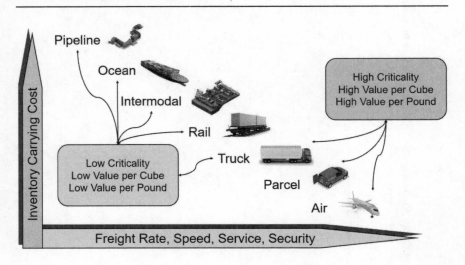

have widely varying price points. Accordingly, the choice of transportation mode has a significant impact on total supply chain cost and customer service. Hence, the choice of transportation mode also has a major impact on some of the all-encompassing supply chain financial metrics such as gross margin return on inventory (GMROI) and inventory value added.

Global Health and Beauty Aids Mode Mix Optimization

One of our clients is a global health and beauty aids manufacturer and distributor located on the West Coast of the United States. They ship to countries in Asia via air and ocean from the ports of Los Angeles, and they are constantly wrestling with the service and cost trade-offs of air vs. ocean shipping. We were retained to develop a mode mix optimization.

Figure 6.23 presents the results of a mode mix optimization for one of their SKUs. Note that the two air options offer significantly lower inventory policy costs (the sum of inventory carrying and lost sales cost), but significantly higher total transportation cost (the sum of total freight cost and transportation setup cost). The sum of all those costs is lowest for Ocean Carrier No. 4, but Air Carrier No. 2 is very close in cost. Air Carrier No. 2 wins the GMROI and inventory value added (gross margin less inventory carrying cost) battles.

So, what's the answer? That's where finance and transportation meet! The answer depends on the financial objective of the company. If it is strictly cost, then Ocean Carrier No. 4. If it is a value-based metric, then Air Carrier No. 2. Like so many answers in supply chain strategy decision making, it depends!

RightShip | Shipment Plan Optimization

A shipment plan simultaneously optimizes the mode *and* frequency of shipping (Figure 6.24). More frequent deliveries result in lower inventory, lower safety stocks, and higher fill rates. Less frequent deliveries result in higher inventories, higher safety stocks, and typically lower fill rates. Faster transportation modes (air vs. ocean or truck vs. rail) yield shorter

Figure 6.23   RightShip optimization for a health and beauty company

RightModes™ | Mode Optimization ☆ ▪
File Edit View Insert Format Data Tools Add-ons Help   Last edit was on October 6

Product Parameters

Product Parameters	Unit Inventory Value	Unit Selling Price	Inventory Carrying Rate	Forecast Annual Demand	Fill Rate	Leadtime Forecast Error	Weight (pounds)
	$ 4,000.00	$ 7,000.00	35%	2,400	95.00%	45.00%	12

Mode/Carrier Parameters	Truck 1	Truck 2	Truck 3	Air 1	Air 2	Rail	Ocean
Transit Times Door-To-Door	2	2.5	3	1.5	1	4	7
Frequency of Shipment Arrival	7	5	7	28	14	21	21
Freight Cost Door-to-Door ($/pound)	$ 12.00	$ 10.00	$ 8.00	$ 17.00	$ 20.00	$ 7.00	$ 3.00
Transportation Setup Cost ($/shipment)	$ 1,200.00	$ 1,500.00	$ 3,000.00	$ 3,600.00	$ 2,400.00	$ 3,800.00	$ 1,900.00
On-Time Arrival Percentage	95.00%	93.00%	94.00%	90.00%	92.00%	94.50%	87.50%
Tardiness (days)	0.50	0.30	4.00	6.30	7.30	8.30	9.30
Inventory Carrying Cost	$ 67,895	$ 67,514	$ 87,596	$ 161,260	$ 87,537	$ 171,751	$ 231,418
Lost Sales Cost	$ 360,000	$ 360,000	$ 360,000	$ 360,000	$ 360,000	$ 360,000	$ 360,000
Total Freight Cost	$ 345,600	$ 288,000	$ 230,400	$ 489,600	$ 576,000	$ 201,600	$ 86,400
Transportation Setup Cost	$ 62,571	$ 109,500	$ 156,429	$ 46,929	$ 62,571	$ 66,048	$ 33,024
Total Logistics Cost	*$ 836,066*	*$ 825,014*	*$ 834,425*	*$ 1,057,789*	*$ 1,086,108*	*$ 799,398*	*$ 710,841*
TLC per Unit	$ 348.36	$ 343.76	$ 347.68	$ 440.75	$ 452.55	$ 333.08	$ 296.18
GMROI™	3712%	3733%	2877%	1563%	2879%	1467%	1089%
LGMROI™	3281%	3305%	2543%	1333%	2445%	1304%	981%
Inventory Value Added™	$ 7,132,105	$ 7,132,486	$ 7,112,404	$ 7,038,740	$ 7,112,463	$ 7,028,249	$ 6,968,582
Supply Chain Value Added™	$ 6,003,934	$ 6,014,986	$ 6,005,575	$ 5,782,211	$ 5,753,892	$ 6,040,602	$ 6,129,159
In-Transit Inventory	13.15	16.44	19.73	9.86	6.58	26.30	46.03
Safety Stock Inventory	12.33	15.35	19.83	13.27	9.92	27.34	50.23
Lot Size Inventory	23.01	16.44	23.01	92.05	46.03	69.04	69.04
Total Inventory							

Figure 6.24   Shipment planning optimization trade-offs

MODE	FREQUENCY	Time	In-Transit Inventory	Lot Size Inventory	Total Inventory	Freight Cost
Fast	High	Shortest	Least	Least	Least	Highest
	Low			Most	In Between	In Between
Slot	High	Longest	Most	Least	In Between	In Between
	Low			Most	Most	Lowest

Figure 6.25   RightShip optimization for a large healthcare company

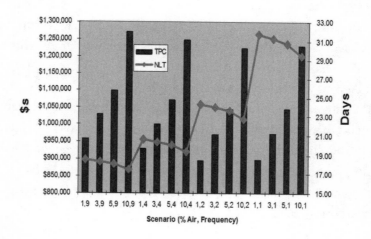

response times and less in-transit inventory, but higher freight rates. Conversely, slower transportation modes yield longer response times and more in-transit inventory, but lower freight rates.

RightShip Health and Beauty

An example RightShip optimization is illustrated in Figure 6.25. The deliverable is from a global health and beauty aids client. Shipment plans are (x/y) pairs where x is the proportion of shipping via air (as opposed to ocean) and y is the number of shipments per month. As expected, the plan with the highest proportion of air shipping with the greatest frequency has the highest associated logistics cost, but the lowest inventory cost. Conversely, the plan with the highest portion via ocean and the greatest time between shipments has the lowest logistics cost, but the highest inventory carrying cost, lowest fill rate, and slowest response time. Our optimization considers the full range of pairs to determine the optimal shipping plan.

We considered 1 percent, 3 percent, 5 percent, and 10 percent of shipping by air and 9, 4, 2, and 1 shipments per month to each country in the Asia-Pacific region. The analysis compares the total supply chain cost of each scenario with the door-to-door delivery cycle times experienced by countries in the Asia-Pacific. Since the customers in the Asia-Pacific region were not willing for their lead times to exceed 24 days, we recommended the scenario yielding the lowest total supply chain cost among those with net lead times less than 24 days. In this case that shipment solution was to ship 1 percent via air four times per month.

The current air shipping percentage was close to 10 percent with shipments made eight or nine times per month. The high air shipping percentage and shipment frequency was due primarily to inadequate advanced planning capability and insufficient communication links between the United States and Asia. The optimization netted more than $12,000,000 for their bottom line.

RightShip Telecom

A few years ago a large global telecommunications company approached us for assistance with their supply chain strategy. One of the featured components of the strategy was the total revamping of their global supply chain flows and modes.

The three major questions concerned their consolidation points, the shipping frequency, and the modes of transportation. Since any of those decisions individually is radically complex, the combined decision is nearly insolvable. Our RightShip algorithm iterates between the three to develop a near-optimal solution. The resulting RightShip decision tree for this telecom operation is illustrated in Figure 6.26.

Figure 6.26   RightShip algorithm for a global telecom supply chain

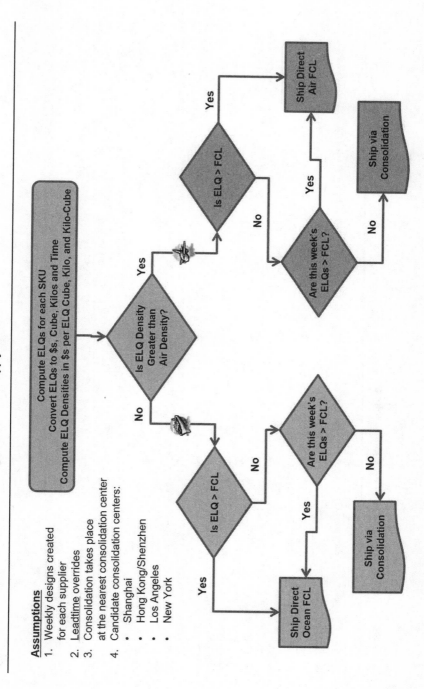

Assumptions
1. Weekly designs created
   for each supplier
2. Leadtime overrides
3. Consolidation takes place
   at the nearest consolidation center
4. Candidate consolidation centers:
   • Shanghai
   • Hong Kong/Shenzhen
   • Los Angeles
   • New York

Compute ELQs for each SKU
Convert ELQs to $s, Cube, Kilos and Time
Compute ELQ Densities in $s per ELQ Cube, Kilo, and Kilo-Cube

Is ELQ Density
Greater than
Air Density?

Is ELQ > FCL

Is ELQ > FCL

Ship Direct
Air FCL

Ship Direct
Ocean FCL

Are this week's
ELQs > FCL?

Are this week's
ELQs > FCL?

Ship via
Consolidation

Ship via
Consolidation

Yes

No

Yes

No

Yes

No

Yes

No

Yes

No

Figure 6.27   RightShip optimization for a global telecom

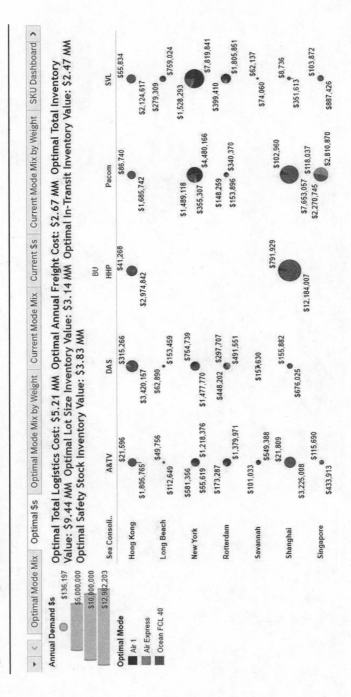

The resulting shipping solution is portrayed in Figure 6.27. The result was a 32.8 percent reduction in total supply chain costs.

6.3 Fleet Strategy

The objective in fleet sizing is to employ through ownership, lease, and/or rental the fewest number of vehicles and containers possible to meet the hourly, daily, weekly, monthly, and annual shipping requirements. The decision is much like the decision of how much inventory to make available to customers. Increasing availability yields fewer lost sales, improved customer service, and higher inventory carrying costs. In fleet sizing, increased availability yields fewer lost sales, shorter customer cycle times, and improved customer service, but higher fleet costs. The graph in Figure 6.28 illustrates the trade-offs in play and suggests the optimal solution is the minimum fleet size that satisfies a prespecified level of customer service during peak and average periods.

Figure 6.28   Fleet sizing trade-offs

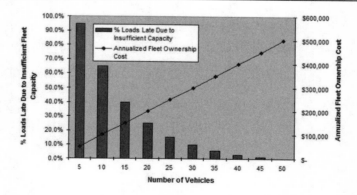

RightFleet Optimization

We recently completed a fleet strategy for a large furniture company. The assignment was to determine the optimal fleet size and operating model to deliver from their nationwide network of plants to furniture stores across the United States and to recommend the optimal operating model considering private and dedicated contract alternatives (Figure 6.29).

Our RightFleet algorithm was used to determine the fleet size requirements to minimize fleet costs and meet all service requirements. An example RightFleet optimization for their Midwest territory is provided in Figure 6.30.

The next step in the analysis was to determine for each plant the optimal mix of private, dedicated, and rental fleet tractors and trailers. With bid pricing provided by three large dedicated contract carriage providers, we were able to optimize the mix of private, dedicated, and rental fleet. The RightFleet design saved our client in excess of $32 million annually, representing a 35 percent reduction in their total supply chain cost per delivered piece (Figure 6.31).

Figure 6.29   RightChain optimized supply chain footprint

Figure 6.30 RightFleet optimization example

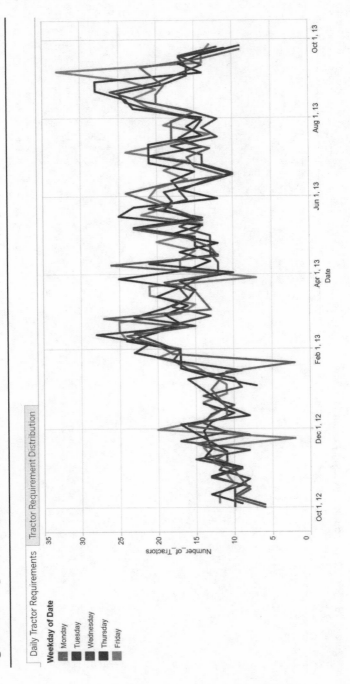

Figure 6.31   RightFleet savings example

BU I Location	BU II Location	RightNodes™ Location	Total Logistics Cost - Current	Total Logistics Cost - Model	LCPP Current	LCPP Future	Current Tractors	RightFleet™ Tractors	Pieces Current	Pieces Future	Fleet Pieces Current	Fleet Pieces Future	% Carrier Current	% Carrier Future	Fleet Miles per Piece - Current	Fleet Miles per Piece - Future	Fleet Miles Current	Fleet Miles Future
San Francisco, Oakland	Oakland	Oakland	$ 7,382,227	$ 6,885,325	$ 12.28	$ 11.46	10	9	601,017	601,017		359,665		2.6%		2.86		1,055,109
		Brooklyn		$ 2,135,607		$ 5.78				369,425								
Milwaukee		Milwaukee	$ 2,824,689	$ 5,359,469	$ 8.31	$ 7.48	13	13	339,715	716,685	270,111	704,319	20.5%	1.7%	5.21	3.73	1,406,266	2,630,438
Boston	Springfield	Springfield	$ 9,055,398	$ 2,397,257	$ 8.01	$ 5.44	31	17	1,130,512	568,423	776,535	568,423	31.3%	0.0%	3.65	1.88	2,833,178	1,069,770
Lancaster	Baltimore	Hazelton	$ 8,733,404	$ 4,589,450	$ 7.72	$ 5.44	25	21	1,131,738	993,652	677,724	993,652	40.1%	0.0%	2.53	2.15	1,715,578	2,137,822
Anderson	Charlotte	Charlotte	$ 5,527,965	$ 4,383,594	$ 8.83	$ 6.50	25	30	626,320	674,226	521,654	670,935	16.7%	0.5%	3.77	3.02	1,968,269	2,024,701
Atlanta	Augusta	Augusta	$ 8,906,279	$ 3,987,789	$ 9.51	$ 7.71	35	26	936,684	516,967	625,293	516,967	33.2%	0.0%	5.60	4.17	3,502,549	2,154,499
Boynton		Orlando	$ 3,854,232	$ 3,158,794	$ 6.85	$ 5.48	16	14	562,285	576,645	303,430	576,645	46.0%	0.0%	4.63	2.47	1,406,266	1,424,200
Chicago		Chicago	$ 3,531,593	$ 4,308,669	$ 9.11	$ 7.94	15	12	387,848	542,584	315,125	486,831	18.8%	10.3%	6.51	5.62	2,050,000	2,735,931
Baton Rouge		Baton Rouge	$ 2,395,006	$ 5,346,671	$ 7.20	$ 7.44	11	10	332,596	718,279	251,445	711,397	24.4%	1.0%	4.49	3.81	1,128,648	2,707,791
Birmingham		Mobile	$ 4,819,395	$ 3,631,923	$ 11.50	$ 8.41	17	15	419,182	431,763	238,426	406,382	43.1%	5.9%	7.96	4.74	1,897,965	1,927,454
Mason		Lexington	$ 3,418,831	$ 4,136,553	$ 6.82	$ 5.90	16	14	501,175	701,413	352,447	697,050	29.7%	0.6%	3.86	1.39	1,361,661	967,334
Tulsa		Tulsa	$ 2,017,748	$ 1,479,558	$ 10.77	$ 6.01	9	10	187,344	246,053	156,779	238,603	16.3%	3.0%	5.23	2.64	819,264	630,825
Louisville	Fort Wayne	Indianapolis	$ 9,365,264	$ 3,770,777	$ 8.04	$ 5.21	42	28	1,165,175	723,862	884,675	717,976	24.1%	0.8%	3.97	2.34	3,515,782	1,680,282
	Dallas	Dallas	$ 6,105,637	$ 1,387,523	$ 11.84	$ 5.22	24	8	515,657	265,979	428,712	247,854	16.9%	6.8%	5.67	2.16	2,431,189	534,607
Houston		Houston	$ 1,334,193	$ 2,365,570	$ 4.91	$ 4.81	7	16	271,908	491,649	235,351	471,862	13.4%	4.0%	2.06	1.86	485,728	876,192
Denver	Salt Lake	Salt Lake	$ 4,198,825	$ 2,538,369	$ 8.99	$ 5.72	18	17	466,858	454,286	406,762	422,637	12.9%	7.0%	3.80	3.52	1,544,341	1,486,901
Tucson	Phoenix	Phoenix	$ 3,649,172	$ 1,069,907	$ 7.27	$ 4.04	11	8	502,144	265,150	312,843	265,150	37.7%	0.0%	1.83	1.00	571,225	265,150
Palm Springs	Ontario	Victorville	$ 7,535,618	$ 6,367,441	$ 7.08	$ 4.94	25	21	1,064,603	1,290,181	981,455	1,262,042	7.8%	2.2%	1.22	1.91	1,298,185	1,089,901
		Honolulu	$ 648,088	$ 650,395	$ 17.64	$ 14.43	4	5	36,747	45,069	21,902	36,750	40.4%	18.5%	0.98	0.58	21,468	21,468
Portland	Seattle	Vancouver	$ 3,670,261	$ 2,362,566	$ 9.11	$ 6.07	14	15	402,713	388,913	308,495	360,971	23.4%	7.2%	3.40	2.50	1,047,510	902,317
		TOTALS	$ 98,973,824	$ 72,313,205	$ 8.55	$ 6.24	368	320	11,582,221	11,582,221	8,069,164	10,716,111	30.3%	7.5%	3.84	2.64	31,005,071	28,322,692

CHAPTER 7

RightHouse
Warehousing Strategy

*"A house is built by wisdom, and by understanding
it is entirely put in good order."*
—SOLOMON

I wrote the first edition of *World-Class Warehousing* in 1995. Back then people asked me why I was writing a book on warehousing when the JIT movement was aimed at eliminating warehousing. Today it's the Lean movement. The question is a legitimate one and the one I ask our seminar attendees every time I kick off a seminar or presentation on warehousing. "Why should we devote our time and energy to studying an activity that every supply chain professional and the Lean literature is trying to eliminate?" A better way to phrase the question might be to ask, "In what ways does warehousing add value in business and in supply chains?" If we can't come up with some good answers, then writing and reading this book really is a waste of time. As I'm sure you have already surmised, warehousing does in fact add value by playing vital roles in business and supply chain strategy.

7.1 The Role of Warehousing in Supply Chains

I developed the RightChain supply chain logistics model (Figure 7.1) in the mid-1990s. The model walks through our five components of supply chain strategy: customer service, inventory management, supply, transportation, and warehousing. Through those eyes the value of warehousing is clearly visible.

Figure 7.1   RightChain supply chain logistics model

Warehousing and Customer Service

One very important area where warehousing adds value in business and supply chains is customer service, including facilitating high-inventory availability, shorter response times, value-added services, returns, customization, and consolidation, among others.

Fill rate is the portion of a customer's demand satisfiable from on-hand inventory. In most cases a significant investment in safety stock is required to provide high customer fill rates. That safety stock must be housed somewhere, and that somewhere is typically a warehouse.

Warehouses in close proximity to the customer base and with short internal cycle times help reduce response times to customers. We have one client that provides same-day delivery of critical service parts. They accomplish that with a nationwide network of small warehouses with short order cycle times. One of our financial services clients supports their financial analysts with small warehouses located in the center of major financial districts, serving financial service offices via subway, courier, walking, and bicycles. One of our convenience store clients is increasing product freshness by increasing delivery frequencies to their 14,000 stores supported by a major increase in the number and capacity of their warehouses and distribution centers.

Following from the mass customization movement, the likelihood that an order will require customization in some form is increasing exponentially. The ability to execute the requisite value-added services such as custom labeling, special packaging, monogramming, kitting, coloring, pricing, and so on is and will continue to be a competitive supply chain differentiator. Warehouses are uniquely equipped with the workforce and equipment to execute those value-added services. In addition, by holding the noncustomized inventory and postponing the customization, overall supply chain inventory levels may be reduced. As the physical facility closest to the customer location, warehouses are also natural places to customize, kit, assemble, and/or countrify product in accordance with the principle of postponement—minimizing overall inventory investments throughout a logistics network by delaying the customization of product to the latest moment. For example, one of our health and beauty aids clients produces shampoo into blank bottles for storage. Once an order is confirmed from a specific country, the labeling required for that specific country is applied in line with the picking and shipping process. One of our consumer products clients houses large quantities of finished goods that are packaged into customer-unique kits and displays of those goods.

One customer service that is foundational to our culture's expectations of logistics systems and is often taken for granted is consolidation. For example, if you order a shirt and a pair of pants from a mail-order company, rarely would you want the shirt showing up one day in one package and the pants showing up another day in another package. For those items to show up at the same time in the same package, they most likely need to be housed under the same roof, i.e., in a warehouse.

Returns is another customer service facilitated through good warehousing practice. The more convenient and inexpensive the returns process for customers, the higher the sales rate and the higher the customer satisfaction ratings. Warehouses and distribution centers are typically already located in close proximity to the customer base and have the workforce and material handling equipment uniquely suited to handling returns.

Though not directly considered a customer service, in many parts of the world physical market presence is an important cultural competitive differentiator. Warehouses and distribution centers are an important and well-recognized means of establishing physical market presence.

Warehousing and Inventory Management

Since warehouses house inventory (or wares), warehousing adds business and supply chain value in all the same ways including support for production economies of scale, optimizing factory utilization via seasonal inventory builds, and mitigating supply chain and business risk by holding contingency and disaster inventory.

Despite all efforts to reduce setup and changeover cost and time, there will always remain expensive and time-consuming setups. In those situations it would be economically foolish to produce short runs. When long production runs are economical, the resulting lot size inventory must be housed—most effectively in a warehouse. For example, one of our large food and beverage clients was running lot sizes 50 percent below optimal, incurring excessive changeover and production costs as a result. Once corrected, an additional 150,000 square feet of warehousing space was required, yielding a significant return on investment in warehousing (Figure 7.2).

Many corporations have significant peaks and valleys in their demand. One of our clients, Hallmark Cards, is an extreme example. The large majority of the demand for greeting cards falls in the Christmas and Valentine's seasons. If their production capacity was designed for those peaks,

Figure 7.2   Coca-Cola's distribution center near Raleigh, North Carolina, with expanded warehousing square footage to accommodate larger lot sizes and an optimal activity density

their production capacity would be cost-prohibitively underutilized for 75 percent of the year. To balance the production and optimize their supply chain costs, Hallmark produces greeting cards at a fairly balanced pace during the year, resulting in a large storage requirement for a majority of the year. That "seasonal inventory" is stored in large seasonal warehousing pictured in Figure 7.3.

The Schwan's food company is another one of our clients. One of their flagship products is frozen pie. They are the world's largest manufacturer of frozen pies, the majority of which are consumed between Thanksgiving and Christmas. As was the case with Hallmark, to optimize their supply chain costs they must balance production throughout the year and utilize third-party frozen warehousing to hold seasonal build inventory January through September.

Contingency and disaster inventory ensures against unexpected situations outside the realm of those covered by traditional safety stock

Figure 7.3   Hallmark Cards warehousing complex, Liberty, Missouri (Sized to accommodate inventory buildups in support of extreme seasonal peaks.)

inventory. Those situations include natural disasters, labor strikes, and other abnormal supply chain disruptions. For example, in our work with telecommunications and utilities clients we often plan for contingency and disaster inventory to maintain service in the increasingly likely event of hurricanes, floods, and snowstorms.

Warehousing and Sourcing

One of our clients is one of the world's largest chocolate candy companies. Of course, the main ingredients are chocolate and sugar. In addition to production, those raw material costs also make up the majority of the total landed product cost. To help determine the optimal timing of the purchase of sugar and cocoa, the company operates some of the world's most advanced weather forecasting systems and some of the most advanced predictors of the future price of sugar and cocoa. When they believe the price is right, they may literally buy boatloads of sugar and cocoa. That sugar and cocoa must be housed somewhere, and that somewhere is a warehouse.

After raw materials, the next most expensive cost component of their total landed cost is production. To help keep those costs low they operate with extremely long production runs. Since margins are high, inventory carrying rates are low, the risk of obsolescence is low (I have never personally refused a candy bar due to technical or packaging obsolescence), and shelf lives are long, total landed supply chain costs are optimized with long production runs. Those long production runs create large batches of inventory that must be housed somewhere. That somewhere is a warehouse. Special opportunities to procure at a discount and/or at the end of product life for critical materials or components are two of the means by which warehousing adds value in sourcing.

Another means by which companies seek to reduce material cost is low-cost foreign sourcing. The likelihood that an order entering a warehouse originated in a foreign country and the likelihood that an order departing a warehouse is destined for a foreign country have never been greater. Warehouses can add significant value in the supply chain by facilitating the efficient inbound and outbound processing of international orders. One example is our client, Payless Shoes, one of the world's largest shoe retailers and global importers. The large majority of their shoes are imported from China and arrive in the United States via the Port of Long Beach (Figures 7.4 and 7.5). Goods arriving there are transloaded into 53-foot containers and trucked to their West Coast DC (Figure 7.6) in Redlands, California, or their East Coast DC near Cincinnati, Ohio. Similar West Coast DC missions are carried out by the massive concentration of distribution centers in or near Redlands known as the Inland Empire. A similar empire of DCs has grown up around the Port of Savannah, Georgia, where Home Depot, Ikea, and Pep Boys, among many others, inject imported product into their East Coast logistics networks (Figure 7.7).

By postponing title possession, on-site vendor managed inventories are another means by which warehousing can add value in business and

Figure 7.4 **The Inland Empire is approximately one hour's drive from the ports of Long Beach and Los Angeles; located at the crossroads of major Interstates I10, I15, and I215; and home to a high-quality workforce. It is also home to perhaps the world's largest concentration of warehouses.**

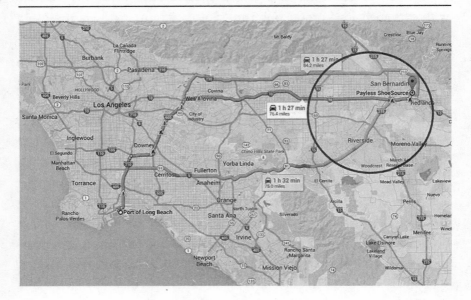

supply chain logistics. The photo in Figure 7.8 is from one of our mining client's maintenance parts VMI warehouse locations. The warehouse is located near the large maintenance shops in one of the world's largest copper mines.

Warehousing and Transportation

As supply chains reduce inventory by shipping more frequently in smaller quantities, warehouses can help provide transportation economies of scale by working as consolidation points for accumulating and assembling small shipments into larger ones; less-than-truckload shipments into full truckloads, less-than-container loads into full container loads, transloading 40-foot containers to 53-foot containers, etc. (Figure 7.9).

A frequently overlooked transportation expense is customs duties. Bonded warehouses allow consignees to delay duty payment until their goods are withdrawn from the bonded warehouse. Bonded warehouses located in free trade zones also permit in-transit goods to pass through without duties being charged at all.

Warehousing and Warehousing

Despite all of the initiatives in e-commerce, supply chain integration, efficient consumer response, quick response, Lean Six Sigma, and just-in-time delivery, the supply chain connecting manufacturing with end consumers will never be so well coordinated that warehousing will be completely eliminated. In fact, the length of supply chains due to global sourcing, the potential for disruption due to increasing numbers, and severity of climatic and security incidents are increasing the need for warehousing and the value warehousing adds in business and supply chain. As all these initiatives take hold, the role and mission of warehouse operations are changing and will continue to change dramatically.

Warehousing Through the Years

Warehousing has evolved from a simple activity devoted primarily to material storage in the 1950s and 1960s (Figure 7.10). With the adoption of just-in-time principles in the 1970s and 1980s came smaller order sizes more often, less inventory, and a greater need for order assembly activities occupying the space made available by inventory reductions. Warehouses were transformed into distribution centers, beginning the reimaging of warehousing from a career-killing profession to a career neutral profession. With the adoption of customer-driven designs, third-party logistics, postponement, mass customization, supply chain integration, and global logistics in the 1990s, a variety of cross-docking and value-added service activities were added in the warehouse. As a result, logistics centers were created out of distribution centers combining customized labeling and packaging, kitting, international shipment preparation, customer-dedicated

Figure 7.5   Aerial view of a concentration of warehouses and distribution centers in the Inland Empire

Figure 7.6   Aerial view of Payless Shoes West Coast distribution center in Redlands, California

Figure 7.7   East Coast Inland Empire in Savannah, Georgia

Figure 7.8   Rio Tinto's vendor management inventory warehouse in support of maintenance operations for their Kennecott copper mine located outside Salt Lake City, Utah

Figure 7.9   Transloading is the transfer of cargo from 20-foot or 40-foot ocean containers into domestic 48-foot or 53-foot trailers. Depicted is Pep Boy's East Coast transload facility located near the Port of Savannah.

Figure 7.10   Warehousing through the years

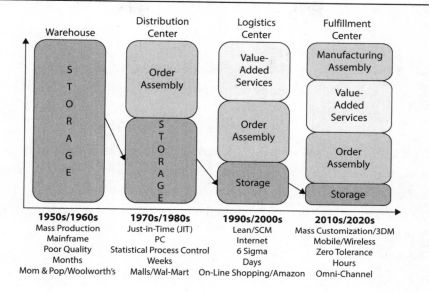

Warehouse	Distribution Center	Logistics Center	Fulfillment Center
S T O R A G E	Order Assembly / **S T O R A G E**	Value-Added Services / Order Assembly / Storage	Manufacturing Assembly / Value-Added Services / Order Assembly / Storage
1950s/1960s	**1970s/1980s**	**1990s/2000s**	**2010s/2020s**
Mass Production	Just-in-Time (JIT)	Lean/SCM	Mass Customization/3DM
Mainframe	PC	Internet	Mobile/Wireless
Poor Quality	Statistical Process Control	6 Sigma	Zero Tolerance
Months	Weeks	Days	Hours
Mom & Pop/Woolworth's	Malls/Wal-Mart	On-Line Shopping/Amazon	Omni-Channel

processes, and cross-docking with the traditional activities of storage and order assembly. The distinction between manufacturing, transportation, and warehousing activities is blurred in a logistics center. The margin for error is near zero.

All of these changes add up to put warehouse managers under a lot of pressure. Under the influence of e-commerce, supply chain collaboration, globalization, quick response, and just-in-time, warehouses today are being asked to:

- Execute more, smaller transactions
- Handle and store more items
- Provide more product and service customization
- Offer more value-added services
- Process more returns
- Receive and ship more international orders

At the same time warehouses today have:

- Less time to process an order
- Less margin for error
- Less young, skilled, native-speaking, literate personnel
- Less WMS capability (a byproduct of Y2K investments in ERP systems)

I call this rock-and-a-hard-place scenario the plight of the warehouse manager. Never has the warehouse been asked to do so much and at the same time been so strapped for resources. It makes it even more important to understand the fundamentals and best practices of warehousing. That begins with a basic classification of the roles of warehousing in a logistics network.

Roles for Warehouses

As we have explained, the warehouse is not going away but continues to play many valuable roles. Those roles have names (Figure 7.11).

Raw material warehouses hold inventory near or in factories where the timely support of production and assembly schedules is the key to success (Figure 7.12).

Work in process warehouses hold inventory in or near factories and primarily serve as variation buffers between production schedules and demand.

Finished goods warehouses (or plant warehouses) typically hold large quantities of finished goods awaiting deployment to distribution centers.

Overflow warehouses, typically located near plant warehouses, often hold seasonal inventory and are frequently operated by a third party. Nearly two-thirds of all plant warehouses have overflow warehouses.

Figure 7.11   Roles for warehouses in the supply chain

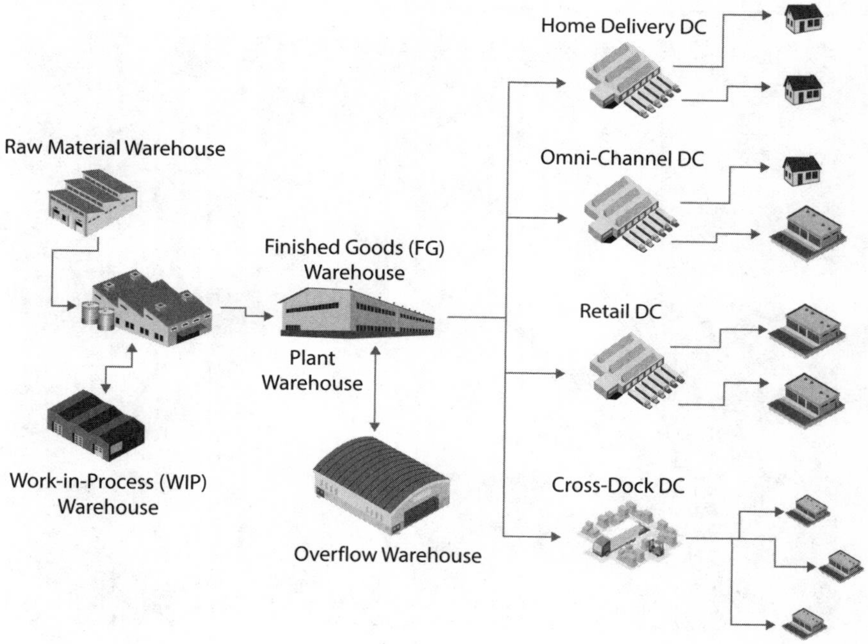

Distribution center warehouses are located much closer to the customer base than are plant warehouses. DCs typically receive product from many plant warehouses and serve customers with same or next-day delivery. The delivery point for the DC determines its name. Home delivery DCs deliver to homes. Retail DCs deliver to retail stores. Omni-channel DCs deliver to a mix of homes and retail stores. Cross-dock DCs do not hold product but simply mix and sort.

Bonded warehouses typically sit inside free trade zones and facilitate delayed duty payments.

Public warehouses are operated by third-party warehousers and are open to the public for what are typically short-term storage agreements.

Figure 7.12   Plant finished goods and raw materials warehouses supporting H.P. Hood's Winchester dairy plant

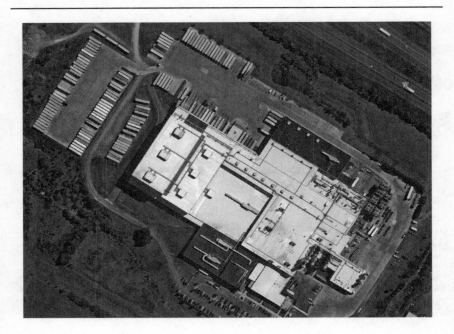

Contract warehouses are operated by third-party warehousers and typically dedicated to single users for extended periods.

Retail back rooms, tool cribs, storerooms, and parts lockers are also forms of warehouses that don't carry the "warehousing" name.

7.2 Inbound Warehousing Strategy

As we discussed in Chapter 1, the performance of any system diminishes with increasing complexity. Supply chain logistics systems are no different, where the number of handling transactions is one of the greatest contributors to system complexity. Hence, minimizing work content, mistakes,

Figure 7.13   RightFlows optimization for a large semiconductor company

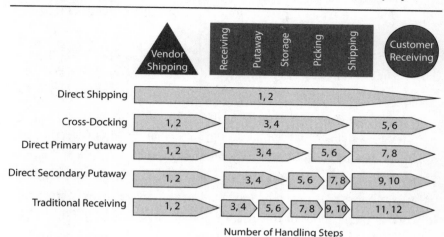

time, and accidents is accomplished in supply chain logistics by reducing handling steps. Figure 7.13 illustrates the reduction in handling steps that can be achieved by applying advanced receiving and putaway practices.

In order from least handling steps to most the inbound strategies are as follows:

- **Direct shipping** bypasses the warehouse completely, requiring only two touches: one to load the outbound truck at the origin and one to receive the inbound truck at the destination.
- **Cross-docking** requires six moves with product moving directly from the inbound dock to the outbound dock.
- **Direct primary putaway** requires eight touches and checks to see if there are any empty primary locations and directs putaways to those locations, thus bypassing receiving inspection, putaway, storage, and replenishment.

- **Direct secondary putaway** bypasses receiving staging and inspection and moves product directly from unloading into reserve locations.
- **Traditional receiving** requires receiving staging, receiving inspection, reserve putaway, and replenishment to a primary picking location.

There are many more opportunities to mishandle, misplace, miscoordinate, and/or miscommunicate in 12 handling steps than there are in 10, 8, 6, or 2. The costs of those extra steps are reflected in the receiving flow optimization we recently completed for a large food company (Figure 7.14). It includes the number of touches, inventory days on-hand, damage percentage, fill rate, and cost per case related to direct shipping, cross-docking, direct primary putaway, direct secondary putaway, and traditional receiving. The cost per case ranges from a low of $0.83 per case with direct shipping to $3.56 per case with traditional receiving.

Direct Shipping

For some materials, the best receiving is no receiving! In direct (or drop) shipping vendors bypass our warehouse completely and ship directly to the customer. Since the items never arrive at the DC, they do not have to be unloaded, staged, put away, replenished to a forward pick location, picked, packed, checked, staged, or loaded. Hence, all the labor, time, and equipment normally consumed and all the mistakes and accidents that often occur in the warehouse are eliminated.

Opportunities for direct shipping include large, bulky items; made-to-order items; and combinations of items for which the regular shipping volume occupies at least a full truckload. For example, one of our large mail-order clients ships canoes, large tents, and furniture direct to customers from their point of origin instead of from their central DC. An increasing number of our food, beverage, and consumer products manufacturing clients are producing and assembling store

Figure 7.14   RightFlows receiving flow optimization for a large food company

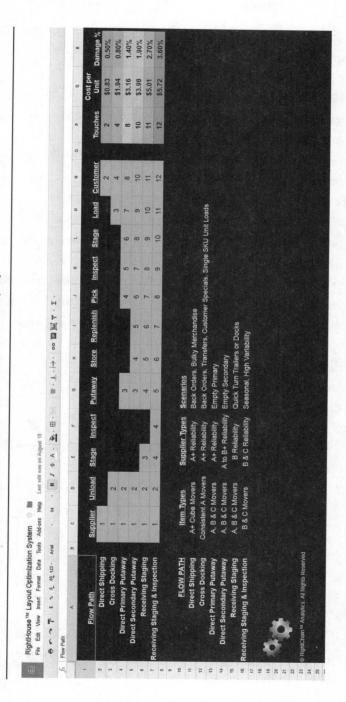

orders at their factories for direct delivery to their retail customers' store locations.

Direct Shipping and Cross-Docking in the Food Industry

As described earlier as an example of supplier synchronization, a classic example of direct shipping and cross-docking is from a $2 billion grocer headquartered in Grand Rapids, Michigan (Figure 7.15). "A" movers (based on cube movement) are shipped in truckload quantities from food manufacturers to grocery retail stores. B movers are precisely scheduled into a central DC for daily cross-docking to build consolidated (frozen, refrigerated, and ambient temperature) loads for retail stores. C movers are stored in a contiguous DC specially designed for dense storage and batch picking of slow-moving items. A daily batch is of C items is picked and inducted into the cross-docking operation. (Of course, to take advantage of this operating philosophy, warehouse activity profiling is critical and must be executed continuously.)

Cross-Docking

When material cannot be shipped direct, the next best option may be cross-docking (Figure 7.16). In cross-docking:

- inbound loads are scheduled for delivery into the warehouse from vendors,
- inbound materials are sorted immediately into their outbound orders,
- outbound orders are transported immediately to their outbound dock,
- without receiving staging or inspection, and
- without product storage.

In so doing the traditional warehousing activities involving receiving inspection, receiving staging, putaway, storage, pick location replenishment, order picking, and order assembly are eliminated.

Figure 7.15   RightFlows optimization in the food industry

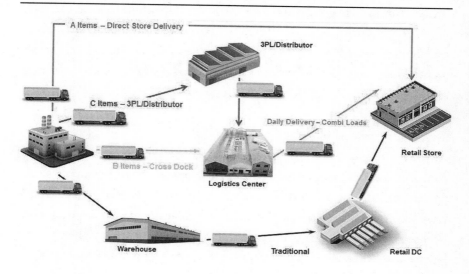

Figure 7.16   Cross-docking simulation for a large consumer products company

In addition to normal order flows, backorders, special orders, and transfer orders are good candidates for cross-docking because the sense of urgency to process those orders is high, the inbound merchandise is prepackaged and labeled for delivery to the ultimate customer, and the merchandise on those orders does not have to be merged with other merchandise to complete customer requirements.

Cross-Docking the Amway Way

Amway is a major manufacturer and direct-to-consumer distributor of consumer and personal products including soaps, cleaning supplies, and cosmetics. At its central distribution center in Ada, Michigan, receipts from manufacturing are scheduled and all incoming pallets have bar code license plates (Figure 7.17). As a lift truck operator unloads a trailer, a pallet license plate (bar code) is scanned to inform the warehouse management system that the pallet is on-site. The warehouse management system then directs the operator to move the inbound pallet to its assigned warehouse location. The first priority for the pallet is cross-docking. In fact, if the item is required in an outstanding order that is currently being loaded (and if there is no violation of code-date expiration windows for pallets in inventory of the same item), the operator is directed to move (cross-dock) the pallet to that dock for shipping. The next priority is direct-putaway to a primary pick location if there is an opening for the pallet in the primary pick location. The last priority is to move the pallet to its reserve warehouse location. Even in that case, there is no staging of the product since locations are either preassigned or assigned in real time.

Cross-Docking at Sony Logistics

At Sony Logistics' distribution center just outside of Tokyo, a cart-on-track conveyor system is used to move full pallet loads between dock doors (Figure 7.18). Each dock door may be used for inbound or outbound loads, thus dramatically increasing the utilization of any given dock door. Also note that the entire cross-dock operation is executed without labor.

Figure 7.17   Receiving flows concept plan for Amway Logistics

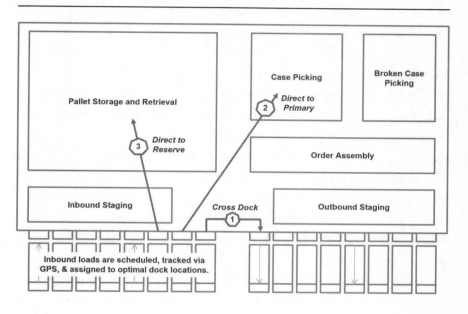

Figure 7.18   Sony Logistics cross-docking

Direct Putaway

When material cannot be cross-docked, material handling steps can be minimized by bypassing receiving staging and putting material away directly to primary picking locations—essentially replenishing primary locations from the receiving dock. Direct primary putaway is recommended if there is an opening for an inbound pallet or case in the primary pick location and shelf life requirements will not be violated. In direct putaway systems, staging and inspection activities are eliminated. Hence, the time, space, and labor associated with those operations is eliminated.

Toward that end, one of our large healthcare clients does not allow staging space in their warehouse layouts. They "force" warehouse operators to put goods away immediately upon receipt as opposed to the delays and multiple handlings that are characteristic of traditional receiving and putaway activities.

Vehicles that serve the dual purpose of truck unloading and product putaway facilitate direct putaway. For example, counterbalanced lift trucks can be equipped with scales, cubing devices, and online RF terminals to streamline the unloading and putaway function.

If there is no primary putaway requirement, the next best move would be to transport inbound goods immediately to their secondary reserve location. Even in that case, there is no staging of the product since locations are either preassigned or assigned in real time.

The world's most advanced logistics operations are characterized by automated, direct putaway to storage locations. The material handling technologies that facilitate direct putaway include roller-bed trailers and extendable conveyors (Figure 7.19).

An excellent example of automated putaway is at Scroll's omni-channel distribution center just outside of Nagoya, Japan (Figure 7.20). There inbound cartons are automatically unloaded onto inbound telescoping conveyors. Those conveyors feed conveyor lanes that lead directly to the input stations of an automated storage and retrieval system. Cases are sorted into their assigned lanes with an in-line sorting system.

Figure 7.19   Automated direct putaway at KAO's Iwatsuki City DC

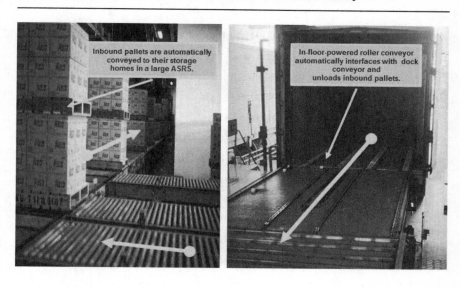

Figure 7.20   Automated putaway to ASRS at Scroll360

7.3 Warehouse Storage Strategy

A storage strategy determines for each item its (1) optimal storage mode, (2) optimal allocation of space, and (3) optimal storage location in its appropriate storage mode. As a result, slotting has a significant impact on all of the warehouse key performance indicators—productivity, shipping accuracy, inventory accuracy, dock-to-stock time, warehouse order cycle time, storage density, and the level of automation. Yet when we begin our RightStore projects we typically find that less than 15 percent of the items are slotted correctly. Most warehouses are spending 10 percent to 30 percent more per year than they should because the warehouse is mis-slotted.

Our RightStore methodology is based on 20-plus years of research in storage optimization. After looking back on all those projects and all those different types of items—cans, bottles, rolls of carpet backing, sweaters, brake parts, spools of yarn, computer hardware, vials of nuclear medicine, automotive service parts, paper products, frozen food, and chainsaws—I identified the common denominators of the projects, and developed this storage optimization methodology and supporting analytics to assist in storage strategy projects (Figure 7.21).

Populate the Storage Database

Fortunately, the number of data elements required for storage optimization is not overwhelming. For each item we need the following: item number, item description, material type, number of requests, total quantity requested, storage environment (frozen, refrigerated, flammable, hazardous, etc.), shelf life, dimensions (L, W, H), item unit cube, weight, units per carton, cartons per pallet, and base unit of measure.

This information should be readily available from the product or item master file. Just the process of evaluating the accuracy and availability of this data is helpful as a data integrity audit.

Figure 7.21   RightStore decision tree

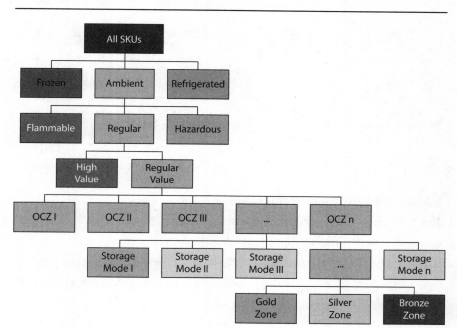

For each customer order we need the customer identification, the unique items requested on the order and the quantities of each, and order date and time. This information should be available from the sales and/or order history file. The sample size required depends heavily on the seasonality of the industry. If there are large annual surges of demand, such as in the mail-order and retailing industries, then a 12-month sample is necessary to cover seasonal fluctuations. If the demand is fairly stable over the course of a year, as in automotive service parts, then a three- to six-month sample will be adequate.

Compute Storage Statistics

Once the raw data is captured, the computation of storage statistics is fairly straightforward (Figure 7.22).

Figure 7.22 RightSlot statistics and formulas (RightChain Analytics)

Statistic	Symbol	Unit(s) of Measure
Item	i	
Popularity	P(i)	Requests for Period for Item i
Turnover	T(i)	Units or Pieces Shipped per Period for Item i
Unit Cube	UC(i)	Cubic Feet or Inches for a Piece of Item i
Cube Movement	CM(i) = T(i) x UC(i)	Cubic Feet or Inches Shipped per Period for Item i
Pick Density	PD(i) = P(i)/CM(i)	Requests per Cubic Foot or Inches Shipped for Item i
Demand Increment	DI(i) = T(i)/P(i)	Units or Pieces per Request of Item i
Cube Increment	CI(i) = CM(i)/P(i)	Cubic Feet or Inches per Request of Item i

Assign Items to Environmental Families

The next step is to assign items to storage environment families based on
requirements for storage temperature (frozen, refrigerated, and ambient),
flammability, toxicity, and security. These storage environment families
will specify the need for special building requirements, special racking
requirements, and special material handling zones.

Assign Items to Order Completion Zones

Within each storage environment, assign items to order completion zones
based on the order completion and demand correlation analysis completed
in warehouse activity profiling. Order completion zones will create warehouses within the warehouse for highly efficient order picking.

Assign Items to Storage Mode Families

Based on productivity, storage density, picking error rates, and system
investment requirements, a storage mode economic analysis should determine the least-cost storage mode for each item. The items assigned to a
particular storage mode become the members of that storage mode's family.
Our RightStore optimizations compute the annualized cost of assigning
each item to each storage mode. The least-cost mode and optimal space allocation are recommended for each item. Example output (Figures 7.23 to 7.25)
illustrates the assignment of item activity families to storage mode families.

Figure 7.23   RightStore storage mode optimization before and after

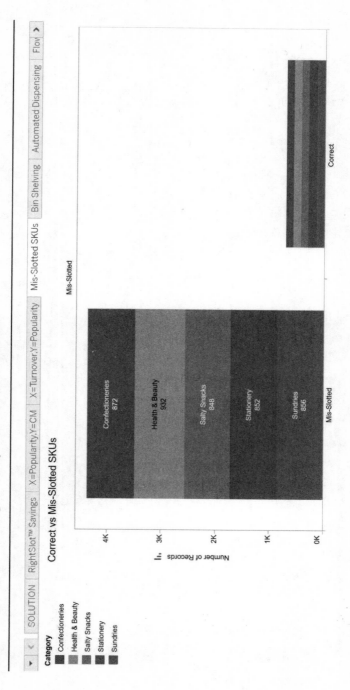

Figure 7.24   RightStore preference regions

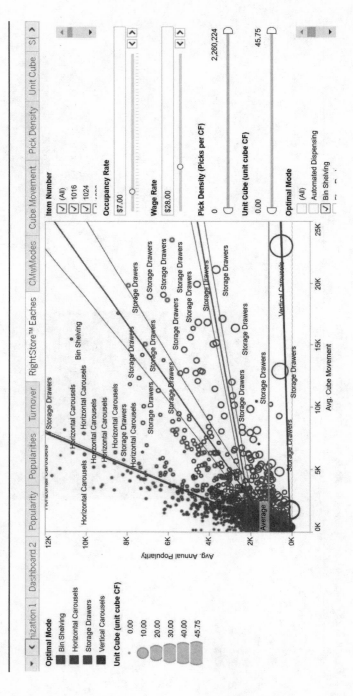

Figure 7.25   RightStore annual savings example

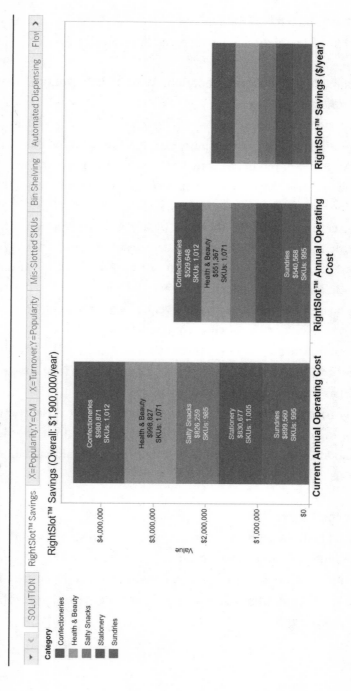

Rank Items Based on Pick Density

Rank items from highest to lowest based upon picking density (Figure 7.26).

Map Individual Warehouse Locations Within Each Storage Mode into Picking Activity Zones

The first step in slot location mapping is to plot the pick path through each storage mode. Once the pick path through the pick line has been determined, the definition of the activity zones is fairly straightforward.

The two most popular pick paths are the serpentine pick path and the mainline path with side trips (Figure 7.27).

In serpentine picking, the order picker will by definition travel down each aisle and by each location. Hence, to designate an A activity zone near one end of the pick line will not reduce travel time. In fact, it may create congestion problems. Instead, the A activity zone should be defined as the locations that are at or near waist level for broken case picking, and at or near floor level for case picking from pallet rack.

In mainline picking with side trips, the objective is to minimize the number and length of the side trips. Hence, the A activity zone should be defined as the locations along the mainline.

In order picking from a pod of two or three carousels, picking from alternating carousels should eliminate any idle time for the order picker waiting on the carousel, and the A activity zone should be defined as the locations at or near waist level.

Follow the Map to Slot

Simply stated, the principle of golden zoning is to store the most popular items in the most accessible locations. In this example (Figure 7.28) at Bertelsmann's book distribution center a worn place in the carpeted picking floor is a good indicator that pickers are most often working near the center of the picking zone.

Figure 7.26   RightSlot Rankings screenshot

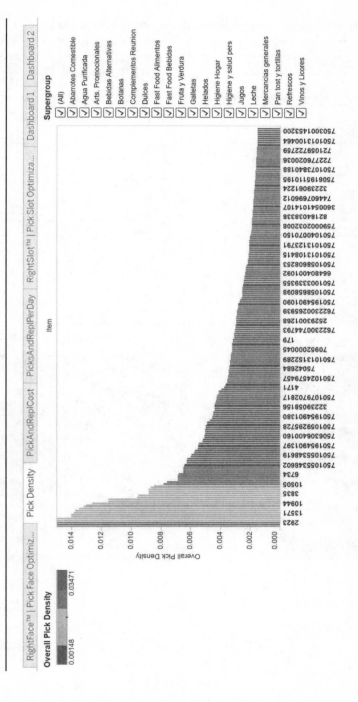

Figure 7.27   Serpentine picking and mainline picking with side trips

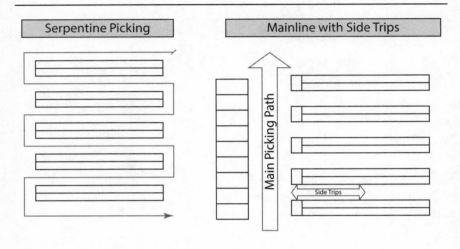

Figure 7.28   Golden zoning in a Bertelsmann distribution center

7.4 Outbound Warehousing Strategy

We developed the RightPick taxonomy and decision tree to help our clients create and evaluate alternative outbound flow strategies. The taxonomy simultaneously addresses the three most important questions in outbound warehousing strategy:

1. Should orders be **batched** for picking and shipping, and if so, how?
2. Should the outbound processing area be organized into **zones**?
3. How should outbound transactions be **sequenced** for processing?

In our RightPick taxonomy of picking schemes (Figure 7.29), the first decision is whether to pick from primary/forward or secondary/reserve storage locations.

Figure 7.29   RightPick taxonomy of picking schemes

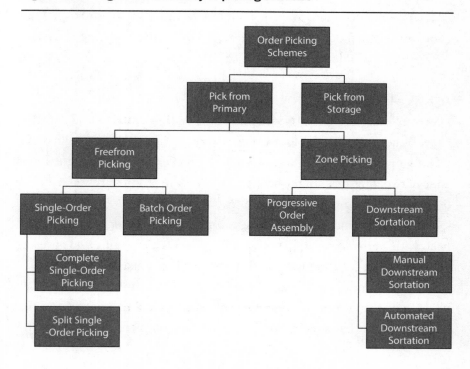

Pick from Primary

Once we have decided to pick from primary pick locations, the next decision is whether or not to designate order picking zones. A picking zone is defined as a portion of an aisle, multiple aisles, or machines (carousels, ASRS machines) assigned to an operator for picking. The key distinguishing feature is that each operator is assigned to a single zone. In order picking this also means that the operators do not have order completion accountability since the lines on an order will be filled from different zones and hence by different order pickers. (A storage zone is distinguished from a picking zone. Storage zones are defined to facilitate efficient and safe storage. For example, storage zones may be established for bulky items, floor storage items, small items, bar stock items, refrigerated items, frozen items, flammable items, explosive items, and so on. These zones are specified in slotting.)

The opposite of zoning for order picking is free-form picking. In free-form picking, order pickers are responsible for picking every line on each order assigned to them, and they are free to move to any order picking zone in the warehouse. The pros and cons of creating picking zones are highlighted in Table 7.1.

Xerox Service Parts

I recently toured a Xerox service parts distribution center outside of Chicago, Illinois. During the tour I spent nearly an hour observing the order picking operation. In that operation, order pickers are each assigned to a zone of two long aisles of bin shelving. Orders are progressively assembled by conveying an order tote from zone to zone.

I especially enjoyed meeting the top-performing order picker. She had been with Xerox for over 20 years and had worked the same two aisles in the warehouse for the previous three years. The housekeeping, productivity, and accuracy in her zone were the highest in the warehouse. Her pride in her job was also evident by the near-perfect arrangement of the merchandise in her zone. I could not help but comment to her about the

Table 7.1   To Zone or Not to Zone?

Zoning Pros	Notes and Comments
Operator travel time is reduced since operators are assigned to small, dedicated work areas.	I always prefer to play zone defense in basketball since I do not have to chase anyone around the court and since I do not have responsibility for an opposing player's scoring outbursts!
Operators become familiar with the products and locations in their zone.	Product familiarity should yield improved picking productivity and picking accuracy. (See Xerox Service Parts below.)
Congestion is minimized since not more than one operator is in an aisle at a time.	Minimizing congestion is the most important justification for zone picking. In some operations the volume is so great that free-form picking creates gridlock.
There is operator-zone accountability.	The order picking performance (productivity, accuracy, housekeeping) can be recorded and posted by zone. The trade-off is the loss in accountability for orders. (See True Value Hardware below.)
Minimizes excessive socializing.	Since operators are assigned alone to dedicated work zones, there is little or no opportunity during a pick wave for excessive socializing. Some socializing is healthy, but zone picking helps to control and monitor it.

excellent performance record she had and on the neatness of her work area. During the conversation I noticed that the merchandise in the bin closest to the front of her zone and next to the takeaway conveyor was not nearly as neatly arranged as the other bins. It was so unusual compared to other bins in her zone that I asked her about the arrangement of that particular bin. She told me the bin contained merchandise that customers were going to order that day. How did she know that? She did not have ESP or claim to function as the world's greatest forecasting system. The items in that bin were A-movers that had not been properly re-slotted. The order picker grew tired of traveling to the end of her zone for those popular items. She simply moved some of the inventory for those items close to the front of the zone. This simple process improvement would have been impossible without the product and location familiarity that comes with zone picking.

True Value Hardware

At True Value Hardware, each of its small-item order picking areas is configured in single-aisle zones. A takeaway belt conveyor runs down the center of each zone, allowing an operator to make one pass through the zone during a pick wave. During a picking wave, each operator works with a roll of picking labels. The labels present items in location sequence to the order picker, who picks an item, places a bar code label on the item, places the labeled item on the belt conveyor, and moves to the next location. The takeaway belt conveyor feeds a downstream sortation system that sorts the items coming from each zone into retail store orders. At the end of each zone, the performance statistics including picking productivity, picking accuracy (via internal audit), and housekeeping for the zone are posted. Talk about public accountability!

The benefits of zone picking—reduced travel time, minimal congestion, product-location familiarity, and operator-zone accountability—may or may not pay for the associated costs and inherent control complexities presented by zone picking. Table 7.2 describes some of those costs and control difficulties.

Free-Form Picking

As described earlier, in free-form picking order pickers are free to operate outside the confines of picking zones. In free-form picking, the toughest decision is whether the order picker should work on a single order (single order picking) or multiple orders (batch picking) during a picking tour.

Single Order Picking

In single order picking, each order picker completes one order at a time. For picker-to-stock systems, single order picking is like going through a grocery store and accumulating the items on your grocery list into your cart. Each shopper is concerned with only his or her list.

The major advantage of single order picking is that order integrity is never jeopardized. The major disadvantage is that the order picker is likely

Table 7.2 Zone Picking Costs and Control Complexities

Zone Picking Costs and Control Challenges	Notes and Comments
Order assembly.	The major difficulty and cost factor in zone picking is the need to assemble the order across order picking zones. The two methods for order assembly, progressive assembly by passing the contents of the order from zone to zone and wave picking with downstream sortation, can be excessively expensive. They can also reduce the operating flexibility of the warehouse, and significantly increase the level of sophistication of warehouse control systems.
Workload imbalances can create bottlenecks, gridlock, and low worker morale.	It is nearly impossible to perfectly balance the workload between zones on a daily basis. To do so requires advanced slotting techniques, or, as is the case with highly sophisticated zone picking schemes, dynamic floating zones are used. In those operations the size of the zone varies as a function of the associated workload. In either case, the controls are an order of magnitude more complex than those used in free-form picking.

to traverse a large portion of the warehouse to pick a single order. Consequently, the travel time per line item picked is high if the order does not contain several line items. (For large orders, a single order may yield an efficient picking tour.) In addition, in some systems, response time requirements do not allow orders to accumulate to create efficient batches for order picking. For an emergency order, the customer service motivation should override the efficiency motivation, and we should pick the single emergency order.

Batch Picking

Batch picking (Figure 7.30) can be thought of as going to a grocery store with your shopping list and those of some of your neighbors. In one traversal of the grocery store, you will have completed several orders. As a result, the travel time per line item picked will be reduced by approximately the number of orders per batch. For example, if an order picker picks one order with two items while traveling 100 feet, the distance traveled per pick

Figure 7.30   Picking two orders, one per pallet, with a double pallet jack is a classic example of free-form batch picking. (Oxxo, Monterrey, Mexico)

is 50 feet. If the picker picked two orders with four total items, the distance traveled per pick is reduced to 25 feet.

Single-line orders are a natural group of orders to pick together. Single-line orders can be batched by small zones in the warehouse to further reduce travel time.

The major disadvantages of batch picking are the time required to sort line items into customer orders and the potential for picking errors.

Zone Picking

The major decision in zone picking is how to establish order integrity for those orders with lines picked in multiple zones. The two options are progressive order assembly and downstream sortation.

Progressive Order Assembly

In progressive assembly (or pick-and-pass) systems (Figure 7.31), the contents of an order are passed from one zone to the next until the order is completely assembled. The contents of the order may move in a tote pan or carton on a conveyor from zone to zone, may be manually moved on a cart from zone to zone, or may move on pallets on a towline conveyor, automated guided vehicle, lift truck, or pallet jack from zone to zone. Intelligent progressive order assembly systems will only move an order's container to a zone if there is an SKU for the order in that particular zone. This practice is called zone skipping.

Figure 7.31   Progressive order assembly

Downstream Sortation

In zone picking with downstream sortation, there is no designation of an order during the picking process. Order pickers work in parallel, making full passes of their pick zone during a wave. Product is typically bar code labeled as it is picked and placed into a large cart or onto a conveyor belt that passes alongside the pick line. The contents of the cart and/or the items on the takeaway conveyor are then inducted into a sortation system that sorts the merchandise into customer orders. The cost of downstream sortation systems can run into the millions of dollars. Hence, the incremental productivity benefits of zone picking with downstream sortation compared to progressive order assembly must be sufficient to justify the incremental investment.

Manual Downstream Sortation

Lanier Worldwide is a multibillion distributor of copiers, fax machines, and dictation equipment. A major portion of its revenue comes from service parts and supplies that support its installation base. For parts and supplies picking, we helped Lanier devise a zone picking scheme with manual downstream sortation. Parts and supplies are stored in traditional bin shelving. Operators are assigned to zones of two aisles of shelving (see Figure 7.32). Orders are released to the picking floor in 20-minute waves, just long enough to allow efficient picking tours and just short enough to maintain the attention and sense of urgency of the order pickers. Each order picker takes a specially designed picking cart through his or her zone. Each picking cart is subdivided into eight compartments. Before each picking tour, an empty tote labeled with that zone and operator's identification is placed in each of the eight containers. At the beginning of each wave, an order picker is given a pick list that walks the operator through his or her zone in location sequence. On each line on the pick list is the location, the item identification, the quantity to pick, and the number of the compartment (1–8) on the cart to place the item into. At the end of a tour, each order picker brings his or her cart to a large storage rack that is subdivided into

Figure 7.32   Lanier manual wave picking concept

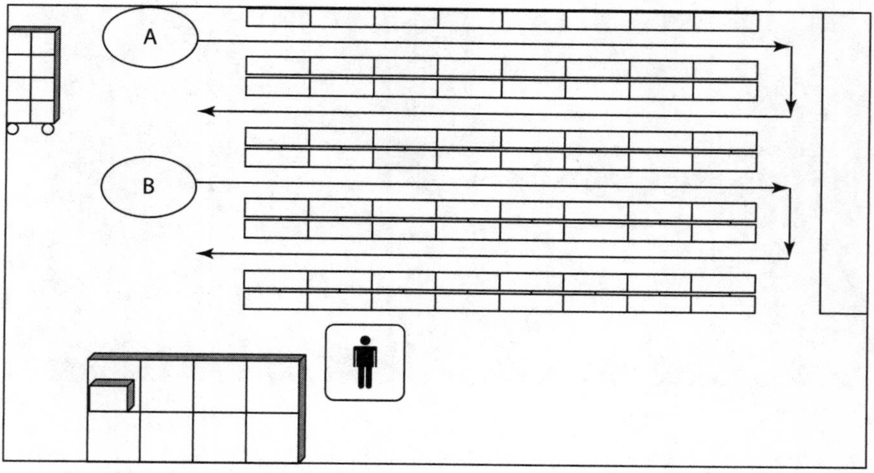

(you guessed it) eight compartments. Each operator puts his or her #1 tote in the #1 compartment, #2 tote in the #2 compartment, and so on. Standing on the other side of the storage compartment is an operator whose job is to sort the merchandise in each compartment into orders, check the order for accuracy, and pack the contents of the order for shipping. This operation yields manual picking productivity in excess of 120 lines per person-hour and exceptionally high picking accuracy.

Automated Downstream Sortation

Scroll's mail order distribution center outside of Nagoya, Japan, is an excellent example of zone picking with automated downstream sortation (Figures 7.33 and 7.34).

1. A returnable carton is used as a physical kanban indicating a replenishment is required from a supplier, the inbound shipping container, and the picking carton.

Figure 7.33   Zone Picking with automated downstream sortation

Figure 7.34   Zone Picking with automated downstream sortation, *continued*

2. Inbound cartons flow directly from inbound trailers into a mini-load ASRS.

3. Picking aisles are on mezzanines on the opposite side of the storage/retrieval aisle. Picking occurs on two shifts. During the third shift the ASRS machine reconfigures the entire pick line for the next day's picking activity.

4. Each piece has a bar code label, and pickers apply a bar code label to each polybagged garment as it is picked into a picking cart.

5. A simple batch picking cart holds two corrugated totes.

6. Order pickers work in dedicated picking zones—one aisle is one zone.

7. Once full, each completed corrugated tote is conveyed to a sorter induction station. The contents of each tote are spilled into an induction station.

8. Induction operators orient each piece so that it is read by an overhead bar code scanner by which each piece is assigned to a section on a cross-belt sorter.

9. The cross-belt sorter conveys each piece to its assigned packing lane and diverts it down the lane.

10. Packers move among the three or four lanes assigned to them and sort several pieces into their orders, pack them, and place them on an outbound shipping conveyor running below the bottom of the sorting lane.

11. A mobile packing station makes it easy to move between sortation lanes.

Pick from Storage

A traditional U-shape warehouse layout (Figure 7.35) incorporates receiving docks, receiving staging, receiving inspection, putaway to reserve storage, reserve pallet storage and pallet picking, case pick line replenishment from pallet storage, case picking, broken case pick line replenishment from case

Figure 7.35   Traditional U-shape warehouse configuration

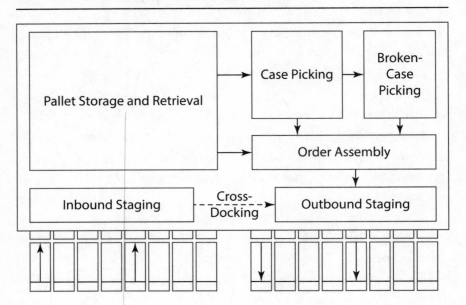

storage, broken case picking, packing, accumulation, shipping staging, and shipping docks.

Why do we need so many different storage and picking areas? Why do we need separate forward areas for case and broken case picking? The reason is that broken and full-case picking productivity from a large reserve pallet storage area is unacceptably low. The forward areas are small and compact, are uniquely configured for the picking task, and may have specialized equipment. As a result, the picking productivity in these areas is 10 to 20 times what the productivity would be in a large reserve storage area where the entire inventory for a single item would be housed. The picking productivity gain is almost always so great (as compared to picking from reserve storage locations) that the cost penalties paid for replenishing the forward areas and the space penalty paid for establishing these stand-alone areas are rarely considered.

Now, suppose we could achieve forward picking rates from a reserve storage area. In so doing, we can have our cake and eat it too—excellent picking productivity, no forward area replenishment, and no extra space set aside for forward areas. Is it possible? It is in Ford's service parts distribution centers.

Ford Service Parts

At Ford's service parts distribution centers (see Figure 7.36), receipts arrive by rail in wire baskets, each identified with a bar code license plate. The wire baskets are moved by a lift truck operator to an automated receiving station. At the receiving station the receiving operator scans the bar code to let the warehouse management system know that the item and cage are on-site. The system then directs the operator to distribute the contents of the cage into one or more tote pans, each with a bar code license plate. Each tote is in turn assigned to and conveyed to one of 54 horizontal carousels

Figure 7.36   Pick-from-storage order picking concept

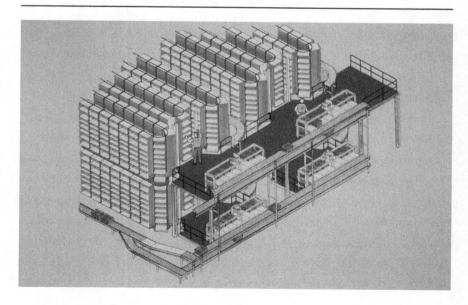

for putaway by the carousel operator. The carousel operators each work a pod of three carousels.

A real-time warehouse management system interleaves the putaway and picking tasks. All picking is light-directed, and the operator is also light-directed to distribute each pick into order totes housed in flow rack adjacent to the carousels. Eighty percent of all part numbers and a corresponding portion of the activity in the DC is handled this way.

Is this picking from storage? Yes, because the 54 carousels act as the reserve storage area. The entire inventory for an item is housed in the carousel system, but not necessarily in the same carousel location. There is no replenishment within the system, and there is no space set aside for backup stock.

This operating concept gives Ford a significant competitive advantage in service parts logistics. The concept requires a highly sophisticated logistics information systems (random storage, intelligent slotting, activity balancing, dynamic wave planning), a high degree of mechanization (to move the reserve storage locations to the order picker), and a disciplined workforce. This operating philosophy is not meant for every situation, but when the operating volumes are large enough and the necessary resources are available, the pick-from-storage concept can yield tremendous productivity gains.

Shiseido

Since a majority of a typical order picker's time is spent traveling to/from and/or searching for pick locations, one of the most effective means for improving picking productivity and accuracy is to bring the storage locations to the picker; preferably reserve storage locations. A large cosmetics distributor recently installed systems that bring reserve storage locations to stationary order picking stations for batch picking of partial case quantities and direct induction into a cross-belt sortation system (Figure 7.37). In so doing, order picking travel time has been virtually eliminated. In addition, the same system can transfer storage locations to/from receiving, prepackaging, and inspection operations, virtually eliminating travel

Figure 7.37   Pick-from-storage concept for health and beauty aids

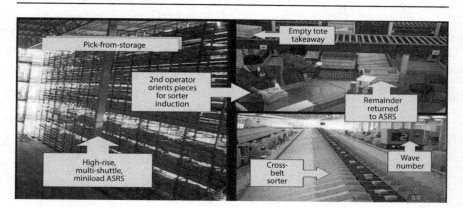

throughout the warehouse. Though expensive, the systems may be justified by increased productivity and accuracy.

To decide from among these picking schemes, we recommend that a concept be developed, evaluated, and sometimes simulated for each. Beginning with single order picking and moving through more expensive and sophisticated picking schemes, each scheme should be financially justified against all the others. From that justification process, a policy should be selected and implemented.

CHAPTER 8

RightSource
Supply Chain Outsourcing Strategy

"Blessings on all who play fair and square."
—SOLOMON

Several years ago we were asked by one of the world's largest retailers to review a third-party logistics contract that was in the works leading to the complete outsourcing of their national network of distribution centers. At the time it would have been one of the world's largest retail supply chain outsourcing initiatives. The document was the most convoluted and confusing supply chain outsourcing contract I have read in my 25-plus years in the field. I literally red inked every other sentence.

The day came to review the contract with their supply chain team. Their chief supply chain officer sat at one end of their boardroom table, and I sat at the other end. The team members were seated between us along the sides of the table. As the meeting began, the attention quickly focused on the contract document I had placed in front of me. I began the meeting by quickly flipping through the 45 pages of red ink for all to see. I shared with the team what I just shared with you—that it was the most convoluted and confusing supply chain outsourcing contract I had ever come across. Needless to say, there was a lot of silent apprehension in the room. I then said,

"Before I get into reviewing the contract edits, what is the motivation of the outsourcing? I can't find it in the contract, and my suspicion is that the lack of clear motivation is making it very difficult to put words to the terms of the agreement." It went dead silent in the meeting room, for a time well past the point of awkward. Finally the chief supply chain officer started laughing. Then everyone except me burst into laughter. I asked them what was so funny. The chief supply chain officer finally fessed up. He said, "We have no idea why we are outsourcing our logistics. Our CEO told us we weren't very good at logistics and to go find a third party who could do a better job."

I was incredulous. Having run our supply chain benchmarking research for many years, I knew they were one of the retail industry's leaders in logistics performance and innovation. I shared with the team that not only were they not "lousy" at logistics, but they were one of the industry leaders, and if they outsourced their logistics they were actually outsourcing their core competency since their logistics innovation and performance were critical to their financial and competitive performance. They wanted to know, if that was the case, what they should be doing with their logistics. I encouraged them to leverage and invest in their competitive advantage. The advice was received with relief and encouragement. The CFO was in the meeting, and he convened an executive committee meeting that same afternoon for me to share my findings and recommendations. Their executive committee was relieved as well, sharing with me that it was their former CEO who had mandated the outsourcing and that he had recently been removed. His successor had asked for the external review of the contract.

One of the main concerns of the project team was what to do with the contract they were nearly committed to. I encouraged them to openly broach the subject with the third-party provider, to share their conclusions but to offer to compensate the third party for the work they had completed in developing the solution proposal. Fortunately the third party was amenable to the approach and an amicable settlement was reached.

Our client then asked for a supply chain strategy and investment proposal that would leverage and extend their competitive advantage in logistics performance. That led to a global network optimization, innovative DC operating concepts, and supply chain information systems that remain at the forefront of the retail industry.

All of that to say that a clear understanding of the motivations for outsourcing is perhaps the key to answering the questions of if, when, and how to outsource logistics.

We will start our outsourcing discussion with healthy motivations for outsourcing and follow that with the related topic of justification and selection strategies.

8.1 Motivations to Outsource

I typically open our course on logistics outsourcing by asking the participants to call out the motivations for logistics outsourcing. To make a long discussion short, the most common healthy motivations for outsourcing supply chain activities are (1) to focus on core competencies, (2) to explore new markets, (3) to gain short-term access to supply chain resources, (4) to improve competitiveness, (5) to gain access to new technology, (6) to restructure logistics management, (7) to gain access to preferred rates, (8) to reallocate strategic capital, and (9) to manage increasing supply chain complexity.

Focus on Core Competencies
Focusing on core competencies is by far the most common reason mentioned for outsourcing any activity, let alone a supply chain activity. It can be a very healthy motivation as long as the enterprise understands what are and what should be their core competencies.

According to Webster, *core* means "the basic, essential, enduring, inmost, and important part of something." *Competency* means "having requisite or adequate abilities or qualities." Putting the two together suggests that a *core competency* is "the essential capability or culture."

Invitrogen

Invitrogen is one of the world's most advanced life sciences companies. They retained us to help assess the suitability of outsourcing a wide variety of supply chain activities so that they could concentrate their investments and talent on the essential competency of their business—breakthrough research in the human genome. Figure 8.1 presents the results of their Right-Source diagnostic. Our diagnostic evaluates the suitability of outsourcing for each supply chain activity. In their case, the diagnostic revealed a very healthy suitability for outsourcing many of the aspects of physical logistics. Those activities became the subject of a formal and successful request for proposal to the logistics outsourcing industry.

Lam Research

Lam Research engages in the design, manufacture, marketing, and service of semiconductor processing equipment. Several years ago they retained us to assess the suitability and feasibility of outsourcing their distribution operations. Like Invitrogen, they rightly believed that their core competency was not and should not be supply chain logistics, but was and should be the engineering of semiconductor processing equipment.

The results of their RightSource diagnostic are illustrated in Figures 8.2 and 8.3 below. Note that the traditional activities of receiving, unloading, putaway, picking, packing, and shipping were "green-lighted" for outsourcing. Inbound inspection, outbound audit, outbound inspection, and returns processing required so much detailed product knowledge that they were not suitable for outsourcing. So, with a mix of DC activities that are and are not suitable for outsourcing, what's the answer?

In this case we developed a joint operating model with a third-party logistics firm working side by side with Lam Research employees (Figure 8.4). The culture match between the selected third party and Lam Research allowed and continues to allow the operation to function smoothly, at a lower cost, and with high quality.

Figure 8.1   RightSource diagnostic results for a large biotech company

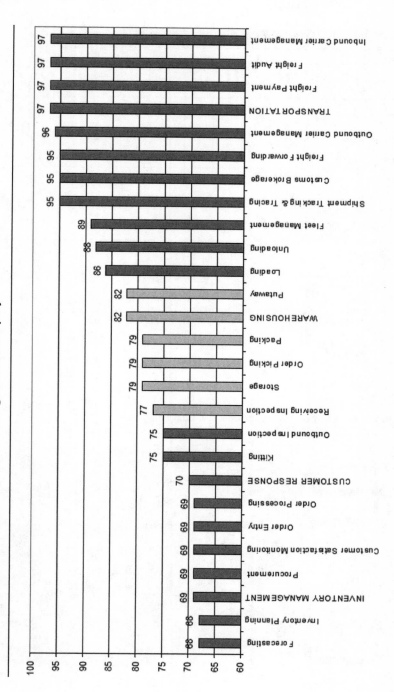

Inbound Carrier Management	97
Freight Audit	97
Freight Payment	97
TRANSPORTATION	97
Outbound Carrier Management	96
Freight Forwarding	95
Customs Brokerage	95
Shipment Tracking & Tracing	95
Fleet Management	89
Unloading	88
Loading	86
Putaway	82
WAREHOUSING	82
Packing	79
Order Picking	79
Storage	79
Receiving Inspection	77
Outbound Inspection	75
Kitting	75
CUSTOMER RESPONSE	70
Order Processing	69
Order Entry	69
Customer Satisfaction Monitoring	69
Procurement	69
INVENTORY MANAGEMENT	69
Inventory Planning	68
Forecasting	68

Figure 8.2   RightSource diagnostic for Lam Research

Process	Complexity	Customer Receptivity	Competitor Differentiator	Service Level Vulnerability	Customer Interaction Level	Product Knowledge Requirement	Process Knowledge Requirement	Exception Incidence	Learning Curve	Current Performance Index	3PL Ability to Assume Quickly and/or Improve	Index	Outsource Suitability and Success
Pre-Receiving	2	2	3	2	2	1	2	2	2	2	2	3.7	EASILY
Receiving Unload	2	1	1	2	2	2	2	2	2	3	5	4.1	EASILY
Inbound Inspection	4	4	1	4	2	5	4	2	4	3	2	2.4	UNLIKELY
Putaway	2	1	1	2	2	2	2	2	2	2	4	4.1	EASILY
Picking	1	3	1	3	2	2	2	2	1	2	5	4.1	EASILY
Outbound Audit	3	5	2	4	2	4	3	2	3	4	3	2.6	DIFFICULT
Outbound Inspection	4	5	3	4	2	5	4	2	4	5	2	1.9	UNLIKELY
Packing	1	2	1	2	2	2	2	2	2	3	5	4.1	EASILY
Manifesting	2	3	1	3	2	2	2	2	2	3	5	3.8	EASILY
Shipping	2	2	1	2	2	2	2	2	2	3	5	3.8	EASILY
Returns Processing	4	3	3	2	4	5	4	4	4	4	5	1.9	UNLIKELY

Figure 8.3   RightSource diagnostic results for Lam Research

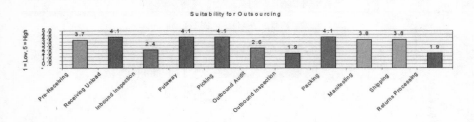

Figure 8.4   Joint operating model in a Lam DC

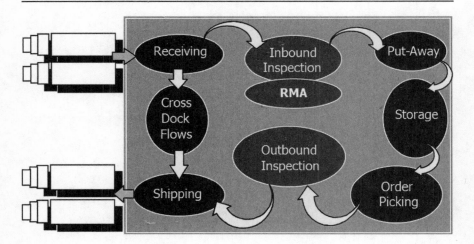

Explore New Markets

In some supply chain scenarios, a company may be exploring their prospects in new geographies where they may not have the requisite supply chain expertise or infrastructure. In order to get started in that geography they may utilize an outsource logistics provider up until the point they develop enough volume to justify an internalized infrastructure and/or up until the point when they develop sufficient supply chain expertise in the geography.

An industrial components company recently asked us to assist them with a global network strategy. The company is headquartered in Cleveland, Ohio, and serves North America, Europe, and Asia from there. Their Asian business had grown quite rapidly, and they suspected that an Asian distribution hub might be necessary and beneficial to improve customer service and reduce supply chain costs. It would certainly be faster and less expensive to serve Asia from Asia, wouldn't it? Not necessarily!

As we normally do, we developed a few candidate network scenarios (Figure 8.5). Since over half of their Asian business was in Japan, one candidate scenario was a Japan hub. It turned out that due to poor air cargo schedules out of Japan and excellent schedules provided by their carrier in Cleveland, it would take longer to serve their Asian clients from Japan than from Cleveland. In addition, because of the high cost of Japanese space and labor and the extra handling step required to add a hub, supply chain costs would have been higher.

Since Singapore was their second largest Asian market and since Singapore is an excellent logistics hub, a Singapore hub was the other option we considered. The Singapore option turned out to offer slightly better service but was still more expensive, $500,000 additional per year. Is a half-a-day better service worth $500,000? That is a question the executives must answer. In this case I suggested they pilot a small DC with a third-party logistics company (3PL) and monitor the result. The pilot is still running.

Figure 8.5   Asia-Pacific network optimization

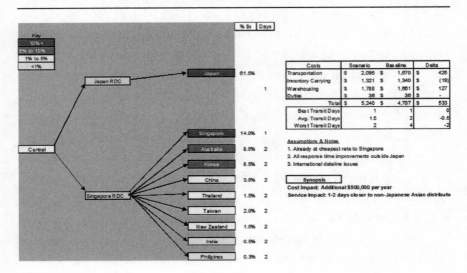

Short-Term Access to Supply Chain Resources

Most organizations experience dramatic peaks and valleys in their operations. Depending on the duration and size of the peak requirement, it
may make sense to employ temporary, outsourced resources (space, labor,
equipment) to cover the peak requirement.

As I mentioned earlier, one of our clients is a large frozen food manufacturer and one of the largest producers of frozen pies. The large majority
of those pies are purchased by consumers between Thanksgiving and
Christmas; a short 30-day window. The demand rate then is so much
greater than the demand rate during the remaining 335 days of the year
that to match manufacturing capacity to demand during those days would
render manufacturing virtually idle for 11 months of the year. Instead, the
company produces pies at a fairly even rate during the year and stores the
"build" inventory for the season in large, third-party frozen food warehouses. An example build plan is illustrated in Figure 8.6.

Figure 8.6   Inventory peak analysis for a large food company

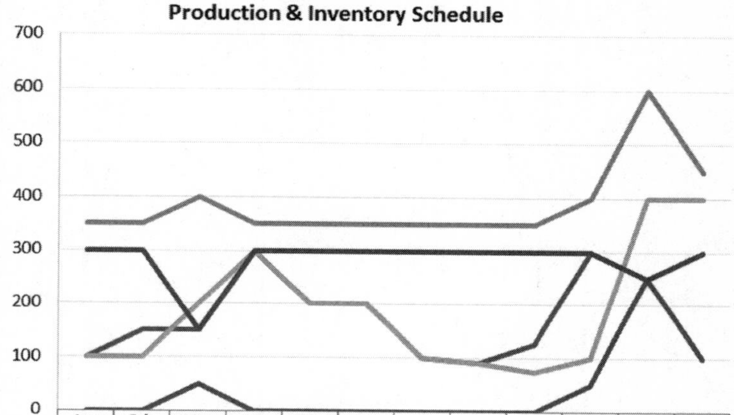

Production & Inventory Schedule

	Jan	Feb	Mar	Apr	May	Jun	Jul	Aug	Sep	Oct	Nov	Dec
Units Produced	100	150	150	300	200	200	100	90	125	300	250	300
Starting Inventory	-	-	50	-	-	-	-	-	-	50	250	100
Units Demanded	100	100	200	300	200	200	100	90	75	100	400	400
Production Capacity	300	300	150	300	300	300	300	300	300	300	250	300
Total Inventory	350	350	400	350	350	350	350	350	350	400	600	450

Improve Competitiveness

The appearance of a new competitor may require rapid access to new capabilities that can only be gained via outsourcing. Several years ago one of the world's largest telecommunications providers approached us as deregulation in one of their geographies was exposing significant weaknesses and making them vulnerable to newly permitted competition. Their supply chain practices gap is illustrated in Figure 8.7. Due to the lack of competition, they had become complacent in all areas of supply chain management. We estimated that it would have required them nearly two years and $24 million to bring their supply chain practices and technology up to a competitive level. They didn't have the $24 million or the two years; their new competition was showing up in 12 months. The only reasonable approach for them was to outsource their supply chain to an entity with the required

Figure 8.7   RightChain gap analysis for a large telecom

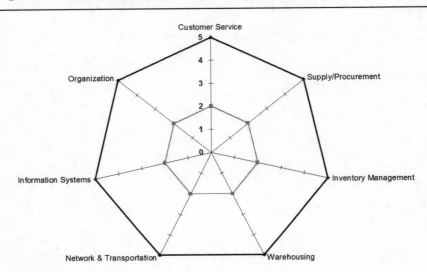

capabilities. The subsequent supply chain reconfiguration and outsourcing was the largest supply chain transformation in the telecommunications industry to date, and it is still running smoothly.

Access to New Technology

One of the most common motivations for outsourcing is gaining access to technologies that might not ordinarily be affordable or justifiable if accessed via a one-time up-front investment. Two examples follow.

In the first, a division of BP was considering investing in a new system for automating freight audit and payment to offset an expensive manual freight bill payment process. Instead of investing in the new system, I suggested they consider outsourcing the process to a freight pay and audit firm that had already made extensive investments in that same technology. The cost of paying a freight bill decreased from $1.14 to $0.76 with no investment and no implementation time required.

Figure 8.8   RightSource diagnostics for a service parts organization

	Baseline	SAP WMS	BOB I	BOB II	3PL I	3PL II
Total Annual Supply Chain Cost	$43,200,000	$40,000,000	$33,800,000	$29,200,000	$36,100,000	$35,600,000
Total Annual IT Cost	$3,900,000	$2,400,000	$2,800,000	$3,100,000	$1,700,000	$1,800,000
Total Annual Solution Cost	$47,100,000	$42,400,000	$36,600,000	$32,300,000	$37,800,000	$37,400,000
Annual Savings vs Baseline		$4,700,000	$10,500,000	$14,800,000	$9,300,000	$9,700,000
% Savings		9.98%	22.29%	31.42%	19.75%	20.59%
Solution Implementation Cost		$17,300,000	$8,300,000	$7,200,000	$5,100,000	$4,800,000
Solution Payback Period		3.68	0.79	0.49	0.55	0.49
Solution Risk	4.5	4.5	3	3	3.5	2.5
Customer Service Impact	2.5	3	4	4.5	3.5	3.5
DIFOT Impact	2	2.5	4	4	3.5	3
Supply Chain Visibility Impact	1.5	3	4.5	4.5	4	3.5
Productivity Impact	1	2.5	4	5	3.5	3

In another situation a large service parts organization was considering investing in their ERP's warehouse management system (WMS) or in a best of breed WMS. In addition, I encouraged them to consider outsourcing to a firm that already operated both that company's ERP WMS and two other best of breed warehouse management systems. The summary analysis is presented in Figure 8.8. In this case the organization decided to outsource the activity to reduce the implementation cost and time required to gain access to new WMS capability.

Restructure Logistics Management

A few years ago a large retailer approached us concerning their logistics management capability. They had reached the conclusion that they did not have the requisite skill set to manage a large logistics workforce of drivers and warehouse operators, nor the systems employed in overseeing their work, nor the facilities and vehicles required to support their work. They asked us to help them estimate what would be required for them to develop the requisite management capability. I also suggested that they consider outsourcing the entire activity and learn how to manage a large logistics outsource provider. They asked us to develop a business case for both approaches.

In the end, we found a 3PL that was able to help them reduce their overall logistics costs by 15 percent, provide a seamless transition into a new suite of logistics technology, and take on their entire logistics asset base. We were retained for the first two years of the contract to mentor our client in logistics provider management. Our client's culture was much more oriented toward managing supplier partners than a large population of employees and assets, and the agreement turned out to be very fruitful for all the parties.

One of the odd features of the agreement was the single line monthly invoice given to our client to cover all phases of logistics services during each month. Our client's accounting capability was so limited that a single line invoice was essentially all that they could process. All of their previous attempts at supply chain accounting had failed, and the single line invoice was one of the most attractive features of the new business arrangement. It was the first time in the retailer's history that they knew how much logistics was costing them.

Access Preferred Rates

Another common motivation for outsourcing is cost reduction through access to lower rates—freight rates, wage rates, occupancy rates, and/or procurement rates based upon the outsource provider's economies of scale in negotiating those rates.

One of the most expensive supply chain costs in Honda service parts is transportation to and from their dealers. Most auto dealers are located very near one another. If auto companies can combine transportation, then they can significantly reduce their transportation costs.

A RightSource diagnostic for Honda (Figure 8.9) suggested that transportation was very suitable for outsourcing. The subsequent bid yielded an 8 percent overall reduction in transportation costs with improved service levels. The reduction was available because their service parts were riding on lower rates that were available from carriers who had already established a network and auto dealer service delivery program.

Figure 8.9   RightSource diagnostic for Honda service parts

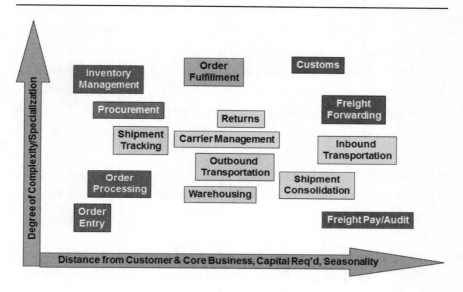

A couple of years after the transportation outsourcing I ran into their chief supply chain officer at an industry conference. I asked him how the outsourcing was going. He said, "I fired the provider and hired a different one." I knew the original provider had done a good job during the start-up and first year, so I asked why he fired them. He said, "They were saving us too much money." I asked him to explain. He explained that when we wrote the original contract it was clear to all involved that savings were important, but not to the point of missing any pickups and deliveries in their supply chain schedule. A missed pickup or delivery wreaked havoc on their entire supply chain. Under the direction of the original account manager, who had helped negotiate the contract and who was a veteran of the auto industry, everything ran smoothly and Honda enjoyed very significant savings. About 18 months into the contract, however, the logistics provider switched account managers to someone who had not been a part of the original negotiations and who had a background in an industry more sensitive to margin than delivery schedule reliability. After a few months under the new account manager, several pickups and deliveries had been missed. When the CSCO approached the manager about the missed deliveries, the account manager reported the additional savings he had helped Honda achieve. That conversation did not last long, and neither did the provider's relationship with Honda. A new provider was brought in who respected the terms of the contract and the critical nature of Honda's supply chain schedule.

Reallocate Strategic Capital

Another common and healthy motivation for outsourcing is the reallocation of capital to more strategic or better-performing assets.

BP Fabrics and Fibers

BP Fabrics and Fibers is a downstream business unit of the BP corporation. They make polypropylene-based fiber and fabrics for use in carpet backing. Each time a new business unit president was appointed, he rightfully asked why they had not outsourced their transportation fleet and drivers. In their case, the fleet was so well managed, so safe, so efficient, and so customer oriented that they were unable to make a business case for outsourcing their fleet to free up capital for new loom investments. In fact, what they learned was that their fleet was one of their most profitable assets and a candidate for additional funding (Figure 8.10).

Serta-Simmons Bedding

Mergers and acquisitions are a frequent catalyst for outsourcing decisions. When Serta and Simmons merged, they brought together two disparate models of fleet logistics. Serta had a long and successful history of operating an internal fleet connecting their factories with furniture stores across the United States. On the other hand, Simmons had a long and successful history of partnerships with dedicated contract logistics companies connecting their factories with their retail customers across the country. The

Figure 8.10   RightSource diagnostic for BP Fabrics and Fibers

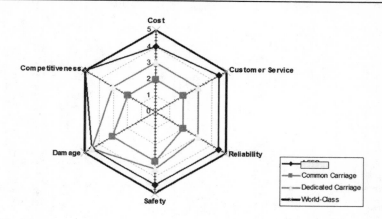

merged entity was also in the midst of heavily investing in furniture assembly automation in their large plants and wanted to free up as much capital as possible for those ventures.

We were asked to help them decide between the two logistics models. We recommended the evaluation of five alternative outsourcing models ranging from full insourcing (do-it-yourself) to full outsourcing. The models are explained in Figure 8.11.

In the end, both logistics managers had done such a good job with their particular models that a hybrid logistics solution was recommended based upon whose plant remained open after the factory rationalization between the two firms.

Manage Increasing Supply Chain Complexities

Another increasingly common motivation for outsourcing supply chain activities is the proliferation of supply chain complexities (Figure 8.12). One of our recent aerospace clients took the leap from a local sourcing footprint and local customer footprint to a global sourcing footprint and a global customer footprint. They asked for our assistance when their total supply chain costs grew exponentially and overwhelmed the unit cost savings they

Figure 8.11   RightSource optimization for Serta-Simmons

	Function	4PL	JOM I	JOM II	JOM III	DIY
Fleet Management	Replacement Management					
	Buy & Sell					
	Repair & Maintenance					
	Tracking & Visibility					
	Deployment					
	Fleet Financing					
	Status Management				Outsource	
Driver Management	Hiring					
	Wages & Benefits					
	Recruiting					
Fleet Administration	Licensing			Outsource		
	Insurance					
	Taxes		Outsource			
Carrier Management	Sourcing					
	Bidding	Outsource				Insource
	Scheduling					
	Contract Management					
	Relationship Management					
	Document Management					
	Performance Management					
	Claims Management					
Freight Management	Freight Payment				Insource	
	Freight Audit					
	Demurrage & Detention					
	Rating & Rate Management					
Analytics	Sizing			Insource		
	Network Optimization					
	Metrics		Insource			
	Routing & Load Planning					
	Data Maintenance					

were anticipating from access to lower wage rates in Asia, Latin America, and eastern Europe. The impact of geography on supply chain complexity and cost is grossly underestimated, and for novices in supply chain strategy, the impact can be catastrophic.

In this particular case we recommended two urgent interventions. One was an immersive education program for their supply chain managers, and the second was the quick exploration and implementation of a global supply chain service provider. Fortunately, both were successful and are still in place.

Figure 8.12   Supply chain complexity curves

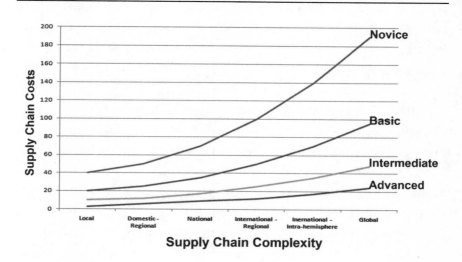

8.2 Justification and Selection

Outsourcing decisions are some of the most complex, emotional, and critical in developing supply chain strategy. The risk of service interruptions is very high, and as Dell found out the hard way, it is much easier to never outsource than it is to outsource and then re-insource. Toward that end, we have developed a variety of analysis and education tools to help our clients with the stress of the outsourcing decision. Our RightSource program has been used in nearly every major industry and is behind some of the world's largest supply chain logistics outsourcing projects including those at AT&T, Honda, Raytheon, Rio Tinto, Volkswagen, and United Technologies.

RightSource Diagnostic

The RightSource diagnostic puts each supply chain activity through a series of 30 questions related to the activity's suitability for outsourcing. The questions have been developed over nearly 30 years of guiding large and small organizations through this sometimes confounding decision-making process. The diagnostic is provided as Figure 8.13. Figure 8.14 is an example of how the RightSource diagnostic played out for a large food company. In that particular case the only clear-cut candidates for outsourcing were storage and returns. Those activities were put out for a successful bid, and they are now operated by two different third parties.

The RightSource diagnostic typically puts each activity into one of three buckets—definitely outsource, definitely insource, and maybe insource/outsource. The first two are easy. The murky middle is what causes the most consternation. For those, we may run a secondary diagnostic based upon two factors—cost and strategic advantage. If the activity is performed at a lower cost than external options and it does not create a strategic advantage, then we recommended maintaining the status quo with the activity. If the activity is performed at a lower cost than external options and it provides a strategic advantage, then we recommend investing in the activity. If the activity is performed at a cost higher than external options and it does not create a strategic advantage, then we recommend outsourcing the activity. If the activity is performed at a higher cost than external options and it does create a strategic advantage, then we recommend collaborating with an external alliance partner.

RightSource Methodology

If the decision has been made to have the new process or service performed externally, the right vendor must be selected. Unfortunately, there's no calculus for vendor selection, the motivations and financial incentives are often hidden, and the relationships between various parties are often suspect. As a result, this phase of supply chain strategy can get a little squirrelly.

With emotions running high, many jobs at stake, major financial impacts, and competing voices, it's a difficult choice. Unfortunately, many have made the wrong choice. In fact, based on the failure rate of outsourcing initiatives, it's more likely that an organization today will make the wrong choice. There are a wide variety of reasons.

Figure 8.13　RightSource diagnostic

	DEFINITELY INSOURCE	PROBABLY INSOURCE	SOURCING AGNOSTIC	PROBABLY OUTSOURCE	DEFINITELY OUTSOURCE
To what extent do the following activities provide a competitive advantage?	Greatly	Some	Little	None	Disadvantage
If an important customer learned that you were outsourcing the following activities, how would they respond?	Very Disappointed	Disappointed	No Reaction	Somewhat Excited	Excited
If the company was starting over, would you perform the following activities yourself?	Definitely	Probably	Can't Say	Probably Not	Definitely Not
To what extent do the following activities detract critical time, resources, and attention from the core mission of the company?	The activity is core.	None	Little	Some	Greatly
At what capacity are you currently operating in the following areas?	Always Operating at Optimal Utilization Levels	Nearly Always Operating at Optimal Utilization Levels	Sometimes Operating at Optimal Utilization Levels	Rarely Operating at Optimal Utilization Levels	Never Operating at Optimal Utilization Levels
If an influential stock analyst learned that you were outsourcing the following activities, how would they respond?	Dramatically Decrease the Stock Valuation	Decrease the Stock Valuation	No Response	Increase the Stock Valuation	Dramatically Increase the Stock Valuation
Are you currently aware of a competitor who successfully outsources the following activities?	No	Yes. One	Yes. A few	Yes. Some	Yes. Many
Are you currently aware of a 3PL who is successfully performing these activities in your industry?	No - It has been tried and failed.	No		Yes	Yes - It has been tried and was a success.
Are you anticipating performing the following activities in locations where you do not currently have distribution or manufacturing operations?	No - Never	No - Not in the immediate future.		Yes - Sometime soon.	Yes - Soon.
Are you anticipating a major upgrade in information systems in the following areas?	No, we just completed an upgrade.	No		Yes, in the near future.	Yes, very soon.
Would another company hire you to perform the following activities?	Yes, definitely.	Yes, probably.	Maybe	No	Definitely not.
Would a future CEO come from this area of the company?	Yes, definitely.	Yes, probably.	Maybe	No	Definitely not.
How does the productivity in the following areas compare with the general productivity expectations of the company?	Exceeds Expectations	Sometimes Exceeds Expectations	Meets expectations	Falls Below Expectations	Falls Far Below Expectations
How does the quality in the following areas compare with the general quality expectations of the company?	Exceeds Expectations	Sometimes Exceeds Expectations	Meets expectations	Falls Below Expectations	Falls Far Below Expectations
How does the financial performance in the following areas compare with the general financial performance expectations of the company?	Exceeds Expectations	Sometimes Exceeds Expectations	Meets Expectations	Falls Below Expectations	Falls Far Below Expectations
Are the transaction costs of these activities increasing or decreasing?	Decreasing Significantly	Decreasing	Remaining Constant	Increasing	Increasing Significantly
What would the impact of outsourcing the following activities be on corporate security?	A Major Threat	A Threat	No Impact	Would Help Security	Would Significantly Help Security
What would the risk of service interruption be if the following activities were outsourced?	High Risk of Disruption	Some Risk of Disruption	Minimal Risk of Disruption	No Risk of Disruption	Service Would Improve
How often do people working in the following areas interact with customers?	Very Frequently (Daily)	Frequently (Weekly)	Some (Monthly)	Rarely	Never
In the most recent customer satisfaction survey, how did customers rate corporate performance in the following areas?	Well Above Average	Above Average	Average	Poor	Very Poor
How much unique product knowledge is required in the following activities?	A Very Significant Amount	A Significant Amount	Some	A Little	None
What would the return on investment be if the following activities were upgraded to a world-class level?	Much Higher than Corporate Requirements	Higher than Corporate Requirements	At or Near Corporate Requirements	Below Corporate Requirements	Far Below Corporate Requirements
How far removed is the activity from the planned future core competencies of the company?	Very Close to Core Competencies	Close to the Core Competencies		Far from the Core Competencies	Very Far from the Core Competencies
What would the impact of outsourcing the following activities be on employee morale?	Devastating Across the Employee Base	Devastating to the Outsourced Employees	No Impact	Encouraging to the Employees	Very Encouraging to the Employees
If the activity was outsourced, how much capital would be made available for other uses?	None	Limited	Some	Somewhat Significant	Significant
To what degree do activity levels fluctuate in the following areas?	No Fluctuation	A Little Fluctuation	Some Fluctuation	Significant Fluctuation	Wild Fluctuation
Would outsourcing the activity provide access to world-class expertise?	No	Somewhat Likely	Likely	Most Likely	Definitely
Would outsourcing the activity provide access to best-of-breed IT capability?	No	Somewhat Likely	Likely	Most Likely	Definitely
To what degree would outsourcing the activity have on the risk of exposing a trade secret?	Definitely	Most Likely	Likely	Not Likely	None

Figure 8.14 RightSource Diagnostic for a large food company

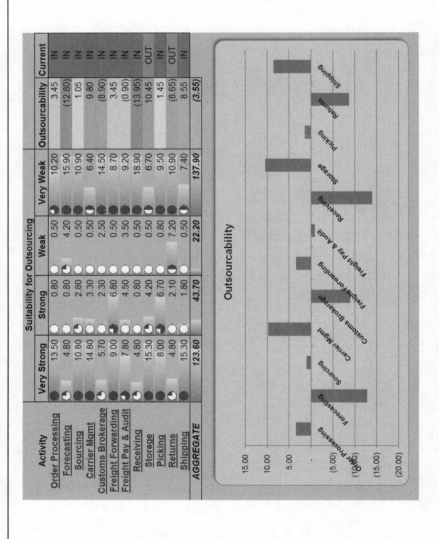

Activity	Suitability for Outsourcing				Outsourcability	Current
	Very Strong	Strong	Weak	Very Weak		
Order Processing	13.50	0.80	0.50	10.20	3.45	IN
Forecasting	4.80	0.80	4.20	15.90	(12.80)	IN
Sourcing	10.80	2.80	0.50	10.90	1.05	IN
Carrier Mgmt	14.80	3.30	0.50	6.40	9.80	IN
Customs Brokerage	5.70	2.30	2.50	14.50	(8.90)	IN
Freight Forwarding	9.00	6.80	0.50	8.70	3.45	IN
Freight Pay & Audit	7.80	4.50	3.50	9.20	(0.90)	IN
Receiving	4.80	0.80	0.50	18.90	(13.95)	IN
Storage	15.30	4.20	0.50	6.70	10.45	OUT
Picking	8.00	6.70	0.80	9.50	1.45	IN
Returns	4.80	2.10	7.20	10.90	(8.65)	OUT
Shipping	15.30	1.80	0.50	7.40	8.55	IN
AGGREGATE	123.60	43.70	22.20	137.90	(3.55)	

Outsourcability

First, there is an implicit assumption made in most organizations that any external entity with the word "logistics" in its name must be better at logistics than the internal logistics organization. Second, with all the advertising done by third-party logistics firms, all claiming to offer the world's best one-stop, do-it-all service package in every industry, a lot of pro-outsourcing momentum has been created. Third, no one wants to talk about the outsourcing adventures that have gone awry. Fourth, if you are on an internal team, who would really want to help an outside entity come in and take over their job? Finally, and I believe most importantly, for anyone other than an outsourcing provider or outsourcing consultant, the people working through the outsourcing decisions may have little or no experience in making outsourcing decisions. These are the individuals and teams we are most interested in helping.

RightSource Vendor Selection

We have had the opportunity to be a part of some of the world's largest supply chain vendor selections in computer hardware, software, material handling equipment, and 3PL services. Every time I think I've seen it all, some form of selection manipulation and/or naivite crawls out of a black barrel. One of the most naive approaches to vendor selection is retaining a hardware/software/3PL firm to help choose which hardware/software/3PL firm to use, and when the choice winds up being that company's hardware/software/3PL, the user is surprised at the lack of objectivity. Amazing! Sometimes a consulting firm with strong hardware/software/3PL "partnerships" is retained to help select which hardware/software/3PL vendor to use, and the user is surprised when the hardware/software/3PL selection happens to be one of those "partners." Amazing!

One vendor we worked with on their marketing strategy wanted to pay clients to use their system and give them a kickback on all additional systems they were able to help sell to other clients. I told them that if they were going to use that practice, then we needed to part ways immediately.

Fortunately the vendor repented and has become one of the most successful supply chain vendors in their market space.

During one of our large material handling vendor selections there was a change in the chief supply chain officer. The new officer was suspected of receiving kickbacks from one of the vendors that had been eliminated by the selection team. He insisted that that vendor be reconsidered. Needless to say, I was very suspicious of the individual and the vendor who was being reconsidered. We had to monitor the process very closely. Fortunately we had established credibility with the COO, the CEO, and the project team, and the new CSCO was not able to manipulate the selection.

In another supply chain disaster recovery case we worked on, the former VP of distribution had manipulated the business case for fully automating their DC. Though unproven and with all financial projections pointing to a business failure, the VP chose to be the guinea pig for a new vendor with a new type of automation. The project was a complete failure and nearly bankrupted the company. However, in the middle of the project, the project was heralded as a success by the vendor, the VP, and in the trade press. The VP was featured on the cover of one of the prominent supply chain trade journals and took a promotion into a higher-paying job with another company. I later ran into him and asked him what he had been trying to accomplish. He unapologetically said that he wanted to get his picture on the cover of a major industry trade journal and get a promotion with a higher-paying job in another company. Amazing!

With these potential shenanigans lurking as possibilities, our two main purposes in vendor selection are (1) objectivity in the selection and (2) long-term success in the relationship between the parties. The only way I have found to meet those two objectives is to faithfully complete the due diligence required to fully vet all candidates and formally evaluate each candidate at each decision gate. Completed RightSource selection matrices for two large outsourcing projects are provided as Figures 8.15 and 8.16.

Figure 8.15 Screenshot from the RightChain Vendor Selection System Vendor Selection Toolkit

Criteria	Weight	Vendor I	Vendor II	Vendor III	Vendor IV	Vendor V	Average
Company	8	1.79	15.55	16.08	29.65	16.21	15.86
Functionality	8	24.04	2.72	20.59	14.97	34.55	19.37
Technology	9	27.28	21.44	32.03	12.71	39.81	26.66
RFP	7.5	24.38	26.24	0.88	18.32	6.68	15.30
On-Site Presentation	8.5	3.02	41.81	17.42	12.95	22.58	19.56
References	8.5	11.27	11.65	9.69	11.60	11.86	11.21
Site Visit(s)	8	9.66	6.81	36.58	11.24	30.33	18.92
Financial Impact	9	15.77	22.30	4.28	29.03	20.16	18.31
Service Impact	10	34.35	11.61	14.67	44.90	34.82	28.07
AGGREGATE	8.55	187.13	179.13	173.36	214.71	245.34	199.93

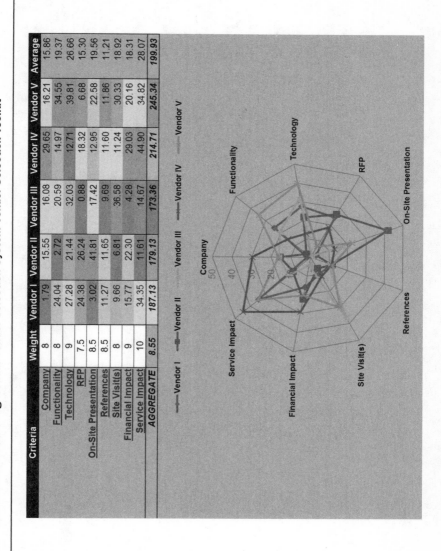

Figure 8.16 RightSource Selection Matrix

Categories	Evaluation Factors	Unweighted Evaluation				Weights	Weighted Evaluation			
		A	B	C	D		A	B	C	D
Price	Price	2.5	3	4.5	4	5	12.5	15	22.5	20
Quality/CI	Quality/Continuous Improvement	3	3	5	4	5	15	15	25	20
Culture	Culture	2	2	5	4	5	10	10	25	20
RFP	RFP Document	3	4	4	4	3.5	10.5	14	14	14
	RFP Presentation	3.5	3.5	4.5	4	4	14	14	18	16
	Bidders Conference	3	3.5	4	4	2.5	7.5	8.75	10	10
	RFP Compliance	1	4	4	4	5	5	20	20	20
Risk	Union Exposure/Risk	2	4	4	4	5	10	20	20	20
	US Compliance	4	4	3	3	5	20	20	15	15
Strategic	Competition	4	4	4	4	3	12	12	12	12
	Global Capability	4	3	4	4	4	16	12	16	16
	Spares?	4	3.5	3.5	3.5	4	16	14	14	14
Systems	Systems	3.5	3.5	3.5	3.5	4	14	14	14	14
References	References	2	3	4	4	5	10	15	20	20
	Site Visits	2	3.5	5	5	5	10	17.5	25	25
Experience	Industry Experience	4	4	4	4	4	16	16	16	16
	Production Support Experience	2.5	4.5	4.5	4.5	4	10	18	18	18
	Similar Production Support Experience	1.5	5	5	5	5	7.5	25	25	25
Industry Rankings	Gartner	3	3	4	4	4	12	12	20	20
Showcase	Facility	3	3	4	4	4	12	12	16	16
	Technology	3	3	3	3	4	12	12	12	12
	Visual Warehouse	3	3	4	5	3	9	9	12	15
Scores	Average	2.89	3.50	4.16	4.07		11.86	14.78	17.70	17.18
	Median	3.00	3.50	4.00	4.00		12.00	14.00	17.00	16.00
	High	4.00	5.00	5.00	5.00		20.00	25.00	25.00	25.00
	Low	1.00	2.00	3.00	3.00		5.00	8.75	10.00	10.00

CHAPTER 9

RightTech
Supply Chain Information Systems Strategy

"Buy truth, and do not sell it; buy wisdom,
instruction, and understanding."
—SOLOMON

There is a very direct correlation between the development of information technology and the development of supply chains. Specifically, as CPU speed, bandwidth, and economic efficiency has accelerated, the scope, scale, and integration of supply chains has followed suit (Figure 9.1). The scope and scale of supply chain logistics has moved from workplace logistics to facility logistics to corporate logistics to supply chain logistics to global logistics to galactic logistics. The integration of supply chains has moved from the factory floor to intracorporate supply chains to intracorporate business systems to intercorporate collaborative supply chain management (Figure 9.2). At this point, it would be difficult to imagine a supply chain functional or technical requirement that has not already been implemented or is not in the course of being implemented or just about to pop out of the R&D lab of a supply chain technology company. Development of supply chains and information systems technology is inextricably linked.

Figure 9.1   Supply chain and information technology development

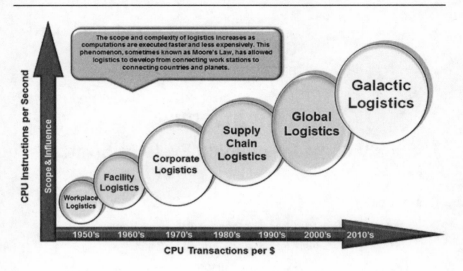

Figure 9.2   IT and interenterprise supply chain systems development

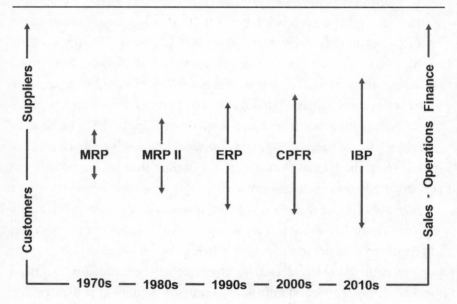

9.1 Supply Chain Information Systems Architecture

A supply chain information system includes the data, execution functionality, planning functionality, communications functionality, and interfaces
to plan, execute, and manage customer response, inventory, supply, transportation, and warehousing (Figure 9.3).

Whether packaged or as-a-service, within an ERP or connected best
of breed (BOB), the soft side of a supply chain information system is composed of data and functionality. Data includes transactional data, master
files, and patterns constructed from those two. Functionality includes
execution functionality, planning/optimization functionality, and measurement functionality. A high-level listing of the requirements in each
of those areas for customer oriented systems, inventory oriented systems,
supply oriented systems, transportation oriented systems, and warehouse
oriented systems is provided in Table 9.1.

Figure 9.3   Supply chain information systems architecture

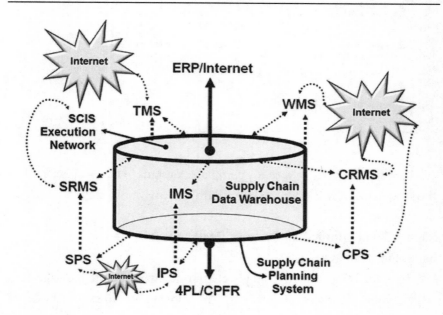

Table 9.1   Supply Chain Information System Requirements

		Customer Oriented Systems	Inventory Oriented Systems	Supply Oriented Systems	Transportation Oriented Systems	Warehouse Oriented Systems
Data	Transactions	Sales Order History	Deployment Order History	Purchase Order History, Production Order History	Transportation Order History	Warehouse Order History, Receipt History, Shipping History
	Master Files	Customer Master File	SKU Master File	Supplier Master File	Carrier Master File	Facilities Master File
	Patterns	Customer Activity Profile, Sales Order Profile	Inventory Activity Profile	Supply Activity Profile, Purchase Order Profile, Production Order Profile	Carrier Activity Profile, Transportation Order Profile, Lane Activity Profile	Warehouse Activity Profile
Function	Execution	Sales Order Management, Customer Transaction Management, Returns Authorization	Production Scheduling, Deployment, Supply Chain Visibility, MRP, DRP	E-Procurement, Purchase Order Management, Customs Compliance, Terms Management, Payment, Letters of Credit, Supplier Management	Freight Pay & Audit, Shipment Tracking, Rating, Routing, Yard Management, Transportation Compliance, Fleet Management, Carrier Management	Receiving, Putaway, Inventory Control, Storage, Order Picking, Packing, Shipping, Dock Management, Labor Management, Returns
	Planning and Optimization	Customer Service Policy, Service Optimization Design, Pricing Optimization, Revenue Management	Demand Planning, Sales & Operations, Planning, Lot Sizing, Collaborative Planning	Supply Planning, Sourcing Optimization, Lead Time Optimization, Terms Optimization	Network Optimization, Load Planning, Bid Optimization, Fleet Sizing, Mode Optimization	Slotting Optimization, Labor Optimization, Layout Optimization
	Measurement	Cost-to-Serve	Inventory Performance Measurement	Supplier Performance Measurement	Transportation Performance Measurement, Carrier Performance Measurement	Warehouse Performance Measurement

I am including three recently completed designs to help further explain the scope and workings of a supply chain information system.

Supply Chain Information Systems Design for a Large Beverage Company

We developed the following supply chain information system design for a large beverage company (Figure 9.4). The information flows are as follows.

Figure 9.4   Supply chain information systems design for a large beverage company

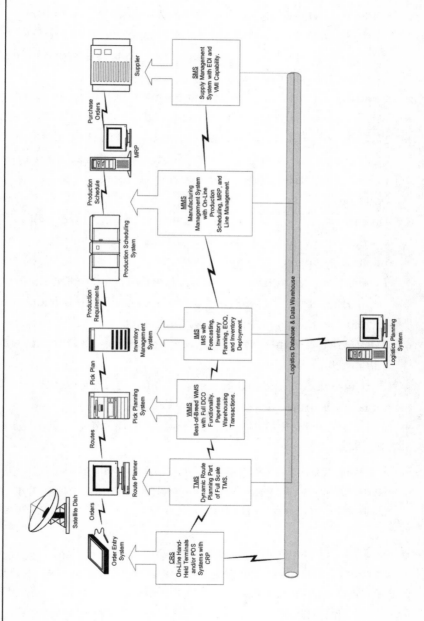

1. **Order execution.** A tablet-equipped route driver computes a replenishment order taking into account on-hand quantities, forecasted demand, and factory scheduling and collaborates it with HQ and the store manager. Once agreed upon, the order is approved and launched into the order pool for routing.
2. **Routing.** An on-demand routing optimization tool continually routes orders as they are placed in the order pool.
3. **Pick planning.** As soon as routes are finalized the in-process order picking plan is frozen and released to the WMS for labor management computations and replenishment planning, and pick tour building.
4. **Inventory.** As soon as the pick quantities are confirmed, projected warehouse inventory levels and warehouse replenishment requirements are updated.
5. **Production scheduling.** As soon as inventory and replenishment requirements are updated and confirmed, production schedules are revised to incorporate the new requirements.
6. **MRP.** MRP recognizes any shortages or overages and updates plans and purchase requirements accordingly.
7. **Purchase order.** Updated purchase requirements and orders are updated electronically.
8. **Data.** All related transactions are housed in the supply chain data warehouse.
9. **Decision support.** RightChain Analytics are continually running against any and all populated data to create scoreboards and optimizations for upcoming decision meetings.

Textiles Supply Chain Information System

In a recent ERP implementation, one of the world's largest textile companies took a giant step backward in functionality to take a small step forward in integration. The step backward nearly cost them their business. The functionality gaps created by the ERP implementation are illustrated in

Figure 9.5   RightTech Gap Analysis

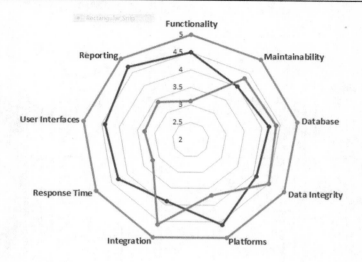

the RightTech Gap Analysis in Figure 9.5. The functionality gaps were costing the company nearly $70 million per year. We were retained to develop a business case for best of breed systems to supplement the ERP. The payback was 2.7 years (Figure 9.6). The system design is depicted in Figure 9.7.

9.2 Data Strategy

We recommend that a virtual or physical supply chain data warehouse (SCDW) serve as the foundation for specifying the entire supply chain information system. The reason is that if the underlying data structures are anticipated and developed ahead of the requirements for the other execution and planning systems, the design, selection, and implementation of those systems becomes much easier, less time consuming, and less likely to fail. In addition, it is the access to data that is typically the bottleneck, the cause of most system failures, and the underlying reason for most system

Figure 9.6 RightTech business case

Benefit Type	Metric	Cost-Benefit Scenario			
		a Best Case	b Most Likely Case	c Worst Case	d Expected Case
	Probability	10%	60%	30%	
Business Process Improvements	PV10	$6,902,449	$2,963,712	($908,416)	$ 2,195,948
	PV13	$8,093,909	$2,246,626	($1,297,137)	$ 1,768,225
	Exposure	($2,965,000)	($4,475,000)	($5,985,000)	$ (4,777,000)
	IRR	65%	28%	5%	25%
	ROI	570%	246%	119%	240%
	DROI	387%	167%	81%	163%
	Payback(yrs)	1.3	2.5	4.3	2.9
Business Process and IT Improvements	PV10	$9,040,914	$3,673,966	($434,913)	$ 2,977,997
	PV13	$7,739,547	$2,874,449	($878,588)	$ 2,235,048
	Exposure	($2,965,000)	($4,475,000)	($5,985,000)	$ (4,777,000)
	IRR	69%	32%	8%	28%
	ROI	620%	271%	131%	264%
	DROI	421%	184%	89%	179%
	Payback(yrs)	1.3	2.3	4	2.7
Business Process & IT Improvements and Millenium Cost Avoidance	PV10	$9,661,304	$4,707,949	$1,012,663	$ 4,094,698
	PV13	$8,339,755	$3,874,797	$521,898	$ 3,315,423
	Exposure	($2,266,720)	($3,311,200)	($4,355,680)	$ (3,520,096)
	IRR	81%	43%	17%	39%
	ROI	812%	367%	180%	355%
	DROI	551%	249%	123%	241%
	Payback(yrs)	1.1	1.8	3.1	2.1
Business Process, IT and Productivity Improvements and Millenium Cost Avoidance	PV10	$10,839,129	$5,476,814	$1,427,503	$ 4,798,252
	PV13	$9,380,884	$4,554,428	$888,593	$ 3,937,323
	Exposure	($2,266,720)	($3,311,200)	($4,355,680)	$ (3,520,096)
	IRR	87%	47%	19%	43%
	ROI	893%	403%	195%	389%
	DROI	606%	274%	133%	265%
	Payback(yrs)	1	1.7	2.9	2.0

Figure 9.7   RightTech systems design example

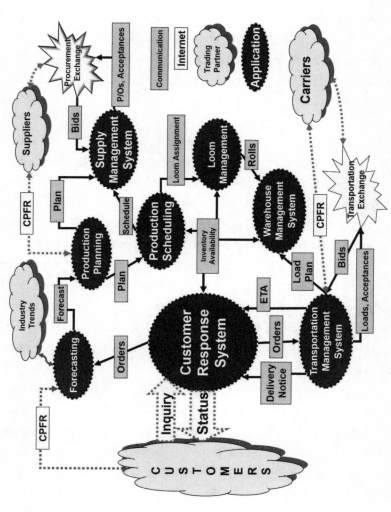
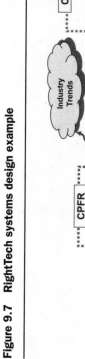

delays and response time problems. Finally, the execution and planning systems must be compatible with the selected provider's database. For all these reasons, we begin designing supply chain information systems by designing supply chain data structures.

Another reason we begin the SCIS design with the underlying data structures is that the process of supply chain activity profiling and data mining can't really begin until the supply chain data warehouse has been designed and populated. And it is in the process of supply chain data mining that we normally reveal the greatest opportunities for improvement in supply chain performance.

Suppose you were sick and went to the doctor for a diagnosis and prescription. When you arrived at the doctor's office, he already had a prescription waiting for you, without even talking to you, let alone looking at you, examining you, doing blood work, and so on. In effect, he diagnosed you with his eyes closed and a random prescription generator. Needless to say, you would not be going back to that doctor for treatment.

Unfortunately, the prescriptions for many sick supply chains are written and implemented without much examination or testing. For lack of knowledge, lack of tools, and/or lack of time, the majority of supply chain reengineering projects commence without any understanding of the root cause of the problems and without exploration of the real opportunities for improvement.

Supply chain activity profiling (or supply chain data mining) is the systematic analysis of supply and demand activities. Supply chain data mining and pattern recognition quickly identifies the root cause of material and information flow problems, pinpoints major opportunities for process improvements, and provides a foundation for objective decision making. Done properly, profiling and pattern recognition quickly reveal supply chain design and planning opportunities that might not naturally be readily evident. Supply chain data mining quickly eliminates options that really aren't worth considering to begin with. Many supply chain reengineering projects go awry because the project team explores concepts that never really had a chance in the first place. Profiling provides the right baseline to begin justifying new investments. Profiling gets key people involved. During the profiling process, it is natural to ask people from many affected groups to provide data, to verify and rationalize data, and to help interpret results.

For the most part, "People will only successfully implement what they design themselves." To the extent people have been involved, they feel that they have helped with the design process. Finally, profiling permits and motivates objective decision making as opposed to biased decisions made with little or no analysis or justification. I worked with one client whose team leader we affectionately called Captain Carousels. No matter what the data said, no matter what the order and profiles looked like, no matter what the company could afford, we were going to have carousels in the new design. You can imagine how successful that project was!

Supply chain data mining is key to the success of any supply chain improvement initiative, but it is normally the activity in a supply chain project that our clients have the least enthusiasm for and the internal IT group is least likely to support. To help overcome both barriers, we developed a streamlined methodology and web-based platform (Figure 9.8) to facilitate supply chain data mining. We begin with a standard representation of a supply chain data warehouse and data mining requirements. Those requirements are presented in Table 9.2. Organizations transfer the specified files, and our web-based tools produce an online supply chain activity profile. The profile is updated as often as our clients transmit the required files.

A supply chain activity profile is comprised of the profiles of the flow of material, information, and money in each of the supply chain logistics activities—customer service (customer activity profile), inventory management (inventory activity profile), supply (supply activity profile), transportation (transportation activity profile), and warehousing (warehouse activity profile). A short description of each follows.

Table 9.2   RightViews Supply Chain Activity Profiling, Data Mining, and Data Warehousing Requirements

Profile	Files/Sources	RightViews Queries	RightViews Profiles	RightChain Decisions
RightServe Customer Activity Profile	· Customer Order History · POS Data · Customer Master File · Item Master File	· **Sales by Customer and Customer Location** in $s, pallets, cases, pieces, weight, volume, frequency, orders, lines, deliveries · **Sales by SKU** in $s, pallets, cases, pieces, weight, volume, lines · **Sales by Customer and SKU** in $s, pallets, cases, pieces, weight, volume	· **Customer Activity:** ABC Customers by $Sales, Volume · **SKU Activity:** ABC SKUs by $Sales, Volume · **Customer-SKU Activity:** ABCxABC Customers & SKUs by $Sales, Volume · **Customer Order Profile:** $Sales, Volume, Cube, Weight, and Lines per Order	· Customer Response Measures · Customer Classifications · SKU Classifications · Customer-SKU Classifications · Customer Service Policy Design
RightServe Inventory Activity Profile	· Item Master File: Snapshots of On-Hand Inventory · POS Data · Customer Order File	· **On-Hand Inventory** in: Turns, Days-on-Hand, $Value, Cube, Space, Pieces by: Location and Commodity by Vendor, SKU Popularity, SKU Usage, and SKU Age · **Forecasting:** Lead Time Demand Variability and Forecast Accuracy by SKU by Location	· **Demand Variability** by SKU Popularity and SKU Age Inventory · **On-Hand Inventory** by Location and Commodity by: SKU Popularity Ranking, SKU Age Ranking, SKU Popularity and Age Rankings, and Vendor Rankings	· Inventory Performance Measures · SKU Categories for Inventory Management · Inventory Turnover and Fill Rate Targets by Logistics Segments · Forecasting Models by SKU Category · Inventory Reduction Opportunities by Logistics Segment
RightBuys Supply Activity Profile	· Purchase Order History File · Supplier Master File	· **Purchasing by Supplier** and Supplier Location in $s, cases, pieces, weight, volume, frequency, orders, lines, deliveries · **Purchasing by SKU** in $s, cases, pieces, weight, volume, lines · **Purchasing by Supplier and SKU** in $s, pallets, cases, pieces, weight, volume	· **Supplier Activity:** ABC by $Purchases, Volume, #SKUs · **SKU Activity:** ABC by $Purchasing, Volume, Frequency · **Supplier-SKU Activity:** ABCxABC by $Purchasing, Volume, SKUs · **Purchase Order Profile:** Purchasing, Volume, Cube, Weight, and Lines per Purchase Order	· Supplier Performance Measures · Supplier Categories · SKU Categories for Supply Planning · Supplier-SKU Rationalization · Sole vs. Primary/Secondary vs. Competitive Sourcing · Make-Buy Analysis · Supplier Service Policy Design

Profile	Files/Sources	RightViews Queries	RightViews Profiles	RightChain Decisions
RightTrips Transportation Activity Profile	· Shipping Manifest History File · Carrier Master File · Supplier Master File	· **From-To Matrix** between all pickup-deliver to points including: frequency, volume, weight, $value, carriers, carrier capacity, carrier availability, distance, time, freight paid, on-time delivery, damages, claims	· **Lane Activity Profile:** ABC Lanes by $Freight, Volume, Claims · **Carrier Activity:** ABC Carriers by $Freight, Volume, Shipments · **Inbound Transportation Activity:** ABC by $Freight, Volume, Value, Frequency · **Outbound Transportation Activity:** ABC by $Freight, Volume, Value, Frequency · **Carrier-Shipment Activity:** ABC x ABC by $Purchasing, Volume, SKUs · **Manifest Profile:** Shipping, Volume, Cube, Weight, and Lines per Manifest	· Transportation Performance Measures · Logistics Hierarchy Design · Logistics Network Design · Inbound Freight Management · Consolidation Design · Routing and Scheduling · Fleet Configuration · Mode and Carrier Selections · Potential Roles for Third Parties
RightHouse Warehouse Activity Profile	· Item Master File · Customer Order History File · Purchase Order History File	· SKU Activity by: popularity, usage, cases, pallets, cube, weight · Orders by $value, lines, cube, units	· **Order Profile:** Lines, Cube, Pieces, $Value, and Weight per Order Distribution · **Lines and Cube per Order Distribution** · **Item Activity Profile:** ABC SKUs by Picks, Usage, and Volume by SKU · **Item-Order Completion Profile** · **Inbound Activity Profile**	· Warehouse Performance Measures · SKU Categories for Warehouse Master Planning · Slotting · Storage Mode Selection · Order Picking Policies · Warehouse Layout

Figure 9.8   RightChain database design

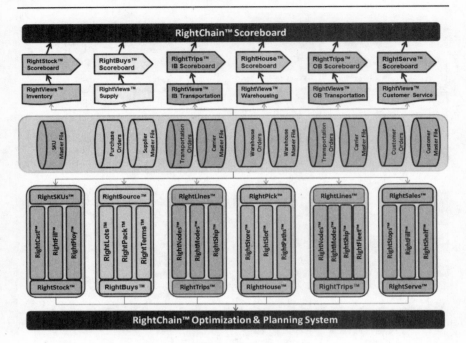

RightServe Patterns

The customer activity profile captures and illustrates sales activity by customer and by item in dollars, number of orders, number of order lines, units, weight, cube, truckloads, pallets, and cases. The customer activity profile is a key ingredient in developing one of the most important elements of a supply chain strategy—the supply chain service policy. Since not all customers and not all items create the same level or type of logistics demand, the supply chain strategy should reflect the unique logistics requirements of each customer and each item.

RightStock Patterns

My experience with inventory reduction initiatives is that there is rarely a single, major source of inventory buildups. Instead, inventory piles up in many places for many reasons, some valid and some not. The inventory activity profile pinpoints the major opportunities to reduce inventory and improve customer service at the same time. It identifies places in the supply chain and/or categories of merchandise where excess has accumulated. The inventory profile reports the turns, days-on-hand, and inventory investment for each item, item category, and vendor for each facility, region, in-transit, and in total.

RightBuys Patterns

The supply activity profile reveals opportunities for purchasing improvements by reporting purchasing activity in dollars, units, cases, pallets, truckloads, weight, volume, orders, and order lines by SKU, SKU category, supplier, and supplier location. The supply activity profile also serves as the basis for categorizing suppliers, supplier rationalization programs, inbound logistics planning, make-buy analysis, and purchase order profiling.

RightTrips Patterns

The transportation activity profile reveals opportunities for transportation strategy and process improvements by reporting for each transportation lane the units, cases, pallets, truckloads, weight, volume, and dollars moved in addition to lane statistics on carrier availability, carrier performance, on-time percentage, damage rates, and claims rates. The transportation activity profile is used in carrier rationalization programs, carrier performance measurement, transportation network design, routing and scheduling, and consolidation opportunities assessments.

RightHouse Patterns

The warehouse activity profile reveals patterns in item activity and customer orders that lead to improvements in storage system design, warehouse layout, and order picking. The warehouse activity profile includes an item activity profile and an order activity profile. The item activity profile reports for each item and item category the requests, units, cases, pallets, dollars, cube, and weight shipped per day, week, month, and year. The item activity profile is used in choosing and designing the storage system and housing for each item. The order activity profile is a distribution of the units, cube, cases, pallets, dollars, weight, and number of items per order and order type (regular, emergency, etc.). The order activity profile is used in designing order picking and shipping systems.

9.3 Functionality Strategy

A few years ago we were helping a large retailer develop their supply chain strategy. During one of the strategy meetings I was called into a one-on-one with their chief information officer. He wanted to meet with me to discuss their options for supply chain information systems and shared that they were considering a multibillion-dollar investment in an ERP solution to manage their supply chain. He asked me, "Dr. Frazelle, what do you think of that approach?"

To buy some time, I asked him a series of questions. First, "What are the main activities of your company?" He answered correctly, "buying, merchandising, inventory management, warehousing, and transportation." Second, "If you could use one word to describe all those activities, what would it be?" He answered correctly, "logistics." Third, "What is the weakest functionality in the ERP you are considering?" He answered correctly, "logistics." Lastly, "So what do you think about investing billions of dollars in a system whose weak point is where you need to be the strongest?"

To make a long, sad story short, they went ahead with the investment. The supply chain was so dysfunctional that at one point they had their own suppliers in their warehouses counting inventory for them. Their shelves wound up so empty that they required a substantial loan from the International Monetary Fund to recover from the implementation.

To help our clients think through their own functionality strategy, we frame the decision just like we would any other optimization decision—with objectives and constraints.

SCIS Functionality Objectives

1.   Minimize number of vendors
2.   Minimize number of applications
3.   Minimize number of interfaces

SCIS Functionality Constraints

1.   Meet or exceed functionality requirements
2.   Meet or exceed ROI
3.   Meet implementation timeline

Whatever mix of applications, vendors, and technologies meets those objectives and satisfies those constraints wins. If the supply chain requirements are simple, an ERP approach may be sufficient. If the supply chain requirements are highly complex and mission critical, then a best of breed-approach may be required (Table 9.3).

9.4 Communications Strategy

Each year we conduct a survey to determine industry priorities for supply chain systems functionality. Nearly every year the top three priorities are (1) paperless communications, (2) live inventory, and (3) productivity tracking.

Why is "paperless" the top priority? Many of the hurdles on the race to world-class supply chains are related to paper and paper handling. First, it is easy to lose paper. I do it every day. Second, you have to read paper. Reading supply chain documents usually requires searching through a

Table 9.3 BOB, Host, Breed Table

CURRENT

	Development		Breed		Hosting		Ownership		Payment		
	Build	Buy	ERP	BOB	Insource	Outsource	Own	3P	Own	Rent	Per X
Customer Service (CRMS)		X	X		X		X		X		
Inventory Planning & Management (IMS)		X		X	X						
Supply (SRMS)		X	X		X		X		X		
Transportation (TMS)		X		X		X		X		X	
Warehousing (WMS)	X			X	X		X		X		

RECOMMENDED

	Development		Breed		Hosting		Ownership		Payment		
	Build	Buy	ERP	BOB	Insource	Outsource	Own	3P	Own	Rent	Per X
Customer Service (CRMS)		X	X			X	X		X		
Inventory Planning & Management (IMS)		X		X		X		X			X
Supply (SRMS)		X		X		X		X			X
Transportation (TMS)		X		X		X		X		X	
Warehousing (WMS)		X		X	X			X		X	

maze of information for just a single line that matters for the transaction at hand. Transpositions creep in. Third, you have to write on paper. Fourth, things on paper cannot be communicated in real time. As a result, errors in inventory levels, product locations, task status, and/or order status are not known with real-time reliability, making it difficult or impossible to implement cross-docking and transaction interleaving. Fifth, paper is expensive to print and to handle and file. Sixth, it is easy to damage and smudge paper. Paperless supply chains and world-class supply chains go hand in hand!

Digital and real-time supply chains require an enabling set of devices and technologies. These devices are the data collection and communication devices forming the backbone of integrated supply chain information systems. Since the list of devices grows daily, it is impossible to present a perfectly current picture of the state of paperless warehouse technologies in book form. Logistics industry trade shows and related websites are the best and perhaps only continually updated presentation of the current state of paperless supply chain technology.

That said, though the menagerie of devices is changing and being upgraded rapidly, the general categories of technologies have remained fairly stable. First, to support paperless supply chains we need a way to automatically identify supply chain objects (containers, documents, vehicles, and locations). We call those means automatic identification technologies including optical characters and readers, bar codes and bar code readers, radio frequency tags and readers, smart cards and smart card readers, and vision systems. Second, we need a means to communicate information to supply chain operators. Those means we call automatic communication technologies including radio frequency data communications, digitized voice, virtual displays, and task by light systems.

Paperless supply chain communication devices are the interface between supply chain operators and supply chain management systems. The decisions made in those brief and myriad interactions govern the productivity, accuracy, and speed of the entire supply chain. Hence, the design

Figure 9.9 Taxonomy of supply chain communication systems

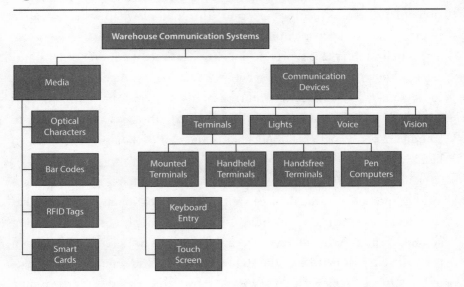

and selection of those devices and systems is critical to the success of the overall operation (Figure 9.9).

Automatic Identification Systems: Characters, Codes, Tags, and Cards

There are four primary automatic identification systems in use in supply chains: optical characters and readers, bar codes and bar code readers, radio frequency identification (RFID) tags and readers, and smart cards and smart card readers.

Optical Characters

Though rare, optical characters are still employed in some supply chain operations. Optical characters are human- and machine-readable. The digits at the bottom of a bank check are the most common use of optical characters. Optical character recognition (OCR) systems read alphanumeric data encoded in optical characters so that people as well as computers can interpret the information (Figures 9.10 through 9.12). Much like a

Figure 9.10   Optical characters

```
A B C D E F G H I J K L M N O P Q R S T U V W X Y Z
1 2 3 4 5 6 7 8 9 0  $  +  <  >  /  \  "  .  -  ,
```

Figure 9.11   Sorter induction operator scanning optical characters in a large Japanese book distributor

Figure 9.12   OCR reader scanning optical characters in a large Japanese book distributor.

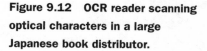

bar code, an OCR label is read with a handheld or automated scanner. OCR systems operate at slower read rates than bar code systems and are priced about the same. OCR systems are attractive when both human- and machine-readable capabilities are required.

Bar Codes and Scanners

A bar code system includes a bar code *symbology* to encode and decode a series of alphanumeric characters to and from dark and light spaces, bar code *readers* to interpret the bar code symbology, and bar code *printers* to reliably and accurately print bar codes on labels, cartons, and/or picking and shipping documents.

Bar Code Symbologies

A bar code is a series of printed rectangles and intervening spaces (Figure 9.13). The structure of unique rectangle/space patterns represents various alphanumeric characters. The same pattern may represent different alphanumeric characters in different symbologies or codes.

The codes themselves fall into one of five major groupings: one-dimensional (1D) linear bar codes, stacked linear bar codes, two-dimensional (2D) matrix codes, postal codes, and QR codes.

Linear, 1D bar codes are the most common type of bar code. All the information contained within the code is organized horizontally and read and decoded as the code is read from left to right by a scanner. An example from Boots Pharmacy is provided as Figure 9.14. An example from L.L. Bean is provided as Figure 9.15.

Figure 9.13 Linear, one-dimensional (1D) bar code

Figure 9.14   Linear bar codes in use at Boots Pharmacy, London

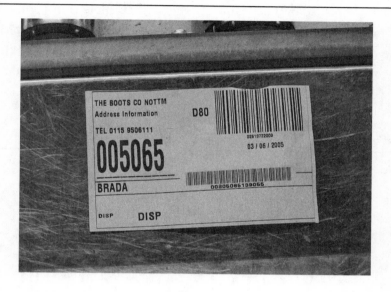

Figure 9.15   Linear bar codes in use for product identification and sorter induction (L.L. Bean, Freeport, Maine)

As the name implies, stacked linear bar codes are simply 1D linear bar codes stacked on top of one another. An example is in Figure 9.16. The main advantage over the simple 1D codes is the ability to encapsulate a large amount of alphanumeric data in a small footprint. Stacked linear bar code readers must be able to simultaneously read the code horizontally and vertically.

Figure 9.16   Stacked linear bar code

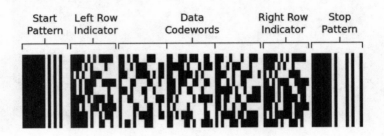

Two-dimensional bar codes, sometimes referred to as high density codes, are overlapping linear bar codes, one horizontal and the other vertical in the same field. These codes permit the automatic encoding of nearly a printed page's worth of text in a square inch of page space. Examples include Code 49, Code 16k, PDF 417, Code One, Datamatrix, UPS's Maxicode, and the currently popular QR code. QR codes are the current latest rage in the bar code world. Quick Response (QR) codes (Figure 9.17) are a type of 2D or matrix code developed in Japan and now in popular use due to their information density and ability to encode URLs.

Figure 9.17 QR code

Bar codes can be effectively used to automatically identify products, containers, locations, operators, equipment, and documents. However, one barcode "gotcha" is the tendency to get caught up in bar coding for the sake of bar coding. The key to success is to minimize the amount of bar coding required to achieve the objectives of digital communications. If there is too much bar coding and too much bar code scanning (Figure 9.18), the costs and time to print and scan all the codes can quickly negate potential productivity and accuracy benefits.

Figure 9.18   Over-labeled and over-coded carton

Bar Code Readers

Bar codes are read by both contact and non-contact scanners. As the name implies, contact scanners must contact the bar code. They may be portable or stationary and typically come in the form of a wand or a light pen (Figure 9.19). The wand/pen is manually passed across the bar code. The scanner emits either white or infrared light from the wand/pen tip and reads the light pattern that is reflected from the bar code. This data is stored in solid-state memory for subsequent transmission. *Contact readers* are excellent substitutes for keyboard or manual data entry. Alphanumeric information is processed at a rate of up to 4 to 24 inches per second, and the error rate for a basic scanner connected to its decode is 1 in 1,000,000 reads.

Figure 9.19   Pen (or wand) bar code scanner

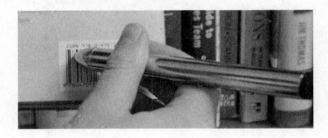

Non-contact readers may be handheld (Figures 9.20 and 9.21), hands-free (Figure 9.22) or stationary (Figure 9.23) and include fixed-beam scanners, moving-beam scanners, and charged couple device (CCD) scanners. Non-contact scanners employ fixed-beam, moving-beam, video camera, or raster scanning technology to take from one to several hundred looks at the code as it passes. Most bar code scanners read codes bidirectionally by virtue of sophisticated decoding electronics that distinguish the unique start/stop codes peculiar to each symbology and decipher them accordingly. Further, the majority of scanner suppliers now provide equipment with an auto-discrimination feature that permits recognition, reading, and verification of multiple symbol formats with no internal or

Figure 9.20   Handheld bar code scanner (Green Foods, Tokyo, Japan)

Figure 9.21   Long-distance handheld bar code scanner (Sears, Atlanta, Georgia)

Figure 9.22   Hands-free ring scanner (Caterpillar, Atlanta, Georgia)

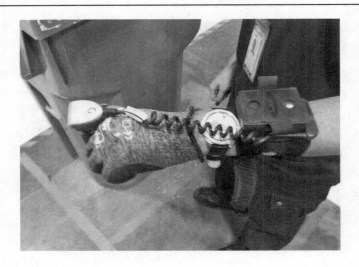

Figure 9.23   In-line bar code scanner

external adjustments. Finally, suppliers have introduced omni-directional scanners (Figures 9.24 and 9.25) for industrial applications that are capable of reading bar codes passing through a large view-field at high speeds, regardless of the orientation of the bar code. Those scanners are commonly used in high-speed sortation systems.

Figure 9.24   Omni-directional bar code scanning

Figure 9.25   Omni-directional bar code scanner for tilt-tray sorting (L.L. Bean, Portland, Maine)

Fixed-beam readers use a stationary light source to scan a bar code. They depend on the motion of the object to be scanned to move past the beam. Fixed-beam readers rely on consistent, accurate code placement on the moving object.

Radio Frequency Tags

Radio frequency identification (RFID) tags encode data on a chip that is encased in a tag (Figures 9.26 through 9.30). When a tag is within range of a special antenna, the chip is read and decoded by a tag reader. RFID tags can be programmable or permanently coded. Some tags are permanently coded and can be read only within a small range.

Figure 9.26   RFID tag

Figure 9.27   Tagged pieces in tagged cartons on a tagged pallet (Lindsay and Reade)

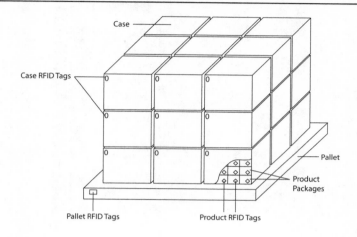

Figure 9.28   Inbound pallet RFID tag reader at a Marks & Spencer DC outside London

Figure 9.29   RFID tags for tote tracking (Marks & Spencer, London)

Figure 9.30   RFID tag reader reading the contents of outbound totes (Metro, Munich, Germany)

As a result of their durability, RFID tags are often used for permanent identification of containers, essentially acting as container license plates. RF tags are also attractive in harsh environments where printed codes may deteriorate and become illegible.

Smart Cards and Smart Card Readers

Magnetic stripes commonly appear on the back of credit or bank cards. They are used to store a large quantity of information in a small plastic footprint. The magnetic stripe is readable through dirt or grease. Data contained in the stripe can be changed. The stripe must be read by contact, thus eliminating high-speed sortation applications. Magnetic stripe systems are generally more expensive than bar code systems. In warehousing, magnetic stripes are used on smart cards in a variety of paperless applications. Smart cards are now used in logistics to capture information ranging from employee identification to the contents of a trailer load of material (Figure 9.31) to the composition of an order picking tour. For example, at a large cosmetics distribution center, order picking tours are downloaded onto smart cards (Figure 9.32). The smart cards are in turn inserted into a smart card reader built into each order picking cart. In so doing, the picking tour is illuminated on an electronic map of the warehouse appearing on the front of the cart.

9.2 Automatic Communication Systems

The basic information required by operators to complete a warehousing task are the identification and quantity of the material to move, the origin, and the destination. Today there are a nearly overwhelming variety of means of communicating that information, including lights, radio frequency (RF) data communications, digitized voice, and virtual displays.

Figure 9.31   Optical memory card used for automated truck manifesting an RF tag used in container identification

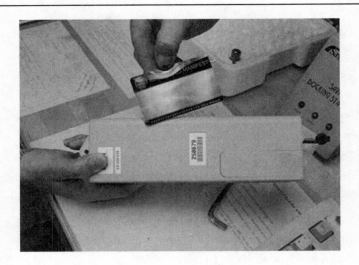

Figure 9.32   Smart cards used in an order picking application at Shiseido's Tokyo distribution center. Each card's magnetic strip holds a picking tour. The smart cards are read by a smart card reader attached to each intelligent picking cart.

Radio Frequency Data Communications

Lift-truck mounted (Figures 9.33 and 9.34), handheld (Figure 9.35), and hands-free radio data terminals (RDTs) are reliable tools for both inventory and vehicle/driver management. RDTs incorporate a multicharacter display, full keyboard, and special function keys. They communicate and receive messages on a prescribed frequency via strategically located antennae and a host computer interface unit. Beyond the basic thrust toward tighter control of inventory (Figure 9.36), improved resource utilization is most often cited in justification of these devices. Further, the increasing availability of software packages that permit RDT linkage to existing plant or warehouse control systems greatly simplifies their implementation. The majority of RDTs installed in plants and warehouses use handheld wands or scanners for data entry, product identification, and location verification. This marriage of technologies provides higher levels of speed, accuracy, and productivity than could be achieved by either technology alone.

Lights and Displays

As mentioned, there are many ways to communicate the basic information required to complete a warehousing transaction.

Light directed operations use indicator lights and lighted alphanumeric displays to direct warehouse operators in order picking, putaway, and/or sortation (Figures 9.37 through 9.40). The most popular use is in broken case picking from flow racks, shelving, and/or carousels. In the case of flow rack or bin shelving, a light display is placed at the front of each pick location (in the place of a location label). The light is illuminated if a pick is required from that location. The number of units to pick appears on the same display or on a display at the top of the flow rack or shelving bay.

In carousel picking, a light tree is placed in front of each carousel. A light display appears on the tree to correspond to every picking level on the carousel. As a carrier is positioned in front of the order picker, the light display corresponding to the level to be picked from is illuminated.

Figure 9.33   Vehicle-mounted radio frequency terminal with touch-screen capability at Happinet's Tokyo distribution center

Figure 9.34   Vehicle-mounted RF terminal (Verizon, Atlanta, Georgia)

Figure 9.35   Handheld RF data terminal (Caterpillar, Atlanta, Georgia)

Figure 9.36   Cycle counting via RF terminal with pen computing (LifeWay, Nashville, Tennessee)

Figure 9.37 This pick-to-light system at Bertelsmann's Gutersloh distribution center directs the operator to picking locations from the three pallet locations behind with weigh checking to prohibit mis-picks.

Figure 9.38 Pick-by-light with next task director display (Bertelsmann, Gutersloh, Germany)

Figure 9.39   Pick-by-light (LifeWay, Nashville, Tennessee)

Figure 9.40   Pick-by-light and put-by-light to retail store totes aided by next-pick and next-put director and motion detector to prevent mis-picks and mis-puts (AT&C, Tokyo, Japan)

Lights can also be used to direct case picking and pallet storage and retrieval operations.

Voice Headsets

The use of synthesized voice is increasingly popular in warehouse operations. In stationary systems, a synthesized voice is used to direct a stationary warehouse operator. For example, at a wholesale grocery distribution center, carousel operators are directed by lights, and a broadcast synthesized voice speaks the correct picking location and quantity.

In mobile voice-based systems, warehouse operators wear a headset with an attached microphone (Figures 9.41 and 9.42). Via synthesized voice, the WMS talks the operator through a series of transactions. For example, for a pallet putaway, the lift truck operator hears a command to putaway a particular pallet into a particular warehouse location. When the transaction is complete, the operator speaks, "putaway complete" into the microphone. Then the system speaks the next transaction to the operator. If the operator forgets the transaction, he simply speaks, "repeat transaction" and the system repeats the instruction.

The advantages of voice-based systems include hands-free operations, the operator's eyes are free from terminals or displays, and the system functions whether or not the operator is literate. Another advantage is the ease with which the system is programmed. A simple Windows-based software package is used to construct all necessary transaction conversations. To operate every area of the warehouse with a voice-based system would require conversations for receiving, putaway, restocking, order picking, and shipping. Once those conversations have been developed, the system is a WMS unto itself. This approach can be an inexpensive way to achieve a majority of the functionality of a typical WMS.

Vision Systems

Vision system cameras take pictures of objects and codes and transmit the images for interpretation. Vision systems "read" at moderate speeds,

Figure 9.41   Lift truck operator with voice headset

Figure 9.42   Voice picking from flow rack inside a cold room

ith accuracy highly dependent upon the quality of light in the "reading" environment. Obviously, vision systems do not require contact with the object or code.

A large European direct to consumer retailer recently installed a vision system at receiving (Figure 9.43). The system is located above a telescoping conveyor used to convey inbound cartons from a trailer into the warehouse (Figure 9.44). The system recognizes those inbound cartons with missing bar codes, reads the product and vendor number on the carton, and directs a bar code printer to print and apply the appropriate bar code label.

Virtual "Heads Up" Displays

Virtual (or "heads up") displays (Figure 9.45) present an operator with virtual overlays on the warehouse floor, products, or layouts to direct an

Figure 9.43   Vision system used to automate receiving inspection at Quelle's logistics center in Leipzig, Germany

Figure 9.44   Automated picking and shipping inspection (Nu Skin, Nagoya, Japan)

operator through travel paths and/or to perform specific transactions on specific products. The displays can also be used to present the operator with a virtual computer display and/or to take an operator on a virtual tour of a 3D warehouse layout. That application can be used in training warehouse operators in working the full range of warehouse transactions in each area within the warehouse.

Figure 9.45   Data goggles (Knapp Logistics)

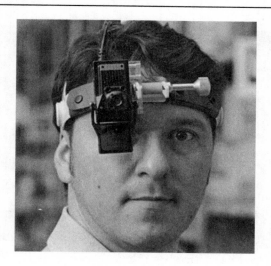

The choice of a supply chain communication technology should be made for each supply chain activity since the human-machine interaction requirements for each activity are unique. For example, picking is handling intensive and hence is best automated with hands-free communication technology, such as voice headsets or pick-to-light. Piece picking is handling and search intensive at high frequency and lends itself to light direction. Cycle counting or any kind of inspection is forms based and as such lends itself to pen computing. The type, conditions, and frequency of the communications in each supply chain activity should guide the technology selection. An example supply chain communications plan developed for a recent client is depicted in Figure 9.46.

Figure 9.46   Logistics chain communications plan

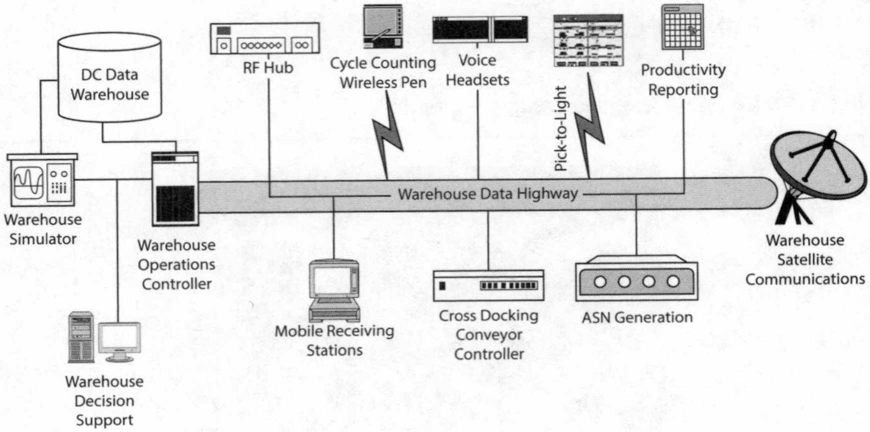

9.5 Justification and Selection

Our approach to supply chain information system justification is very simple. We consider the practices that the new system will permit that could not otherwise be implemented and their resulting impact on resource requirements and service. We assign a savings to the reduction in resources and to the quality improvements to learn if there is an attractive return on investment.

I have provided a couple of justification examples. In the first (Figure 9.47) is a rather simple payback analysis for pick-to-light systems in a warehouse. The second (Figure 9.48) is a return-on-investment analysis for a new warehouse management system.

Figure 9.47   Pick-to-light justification analysis

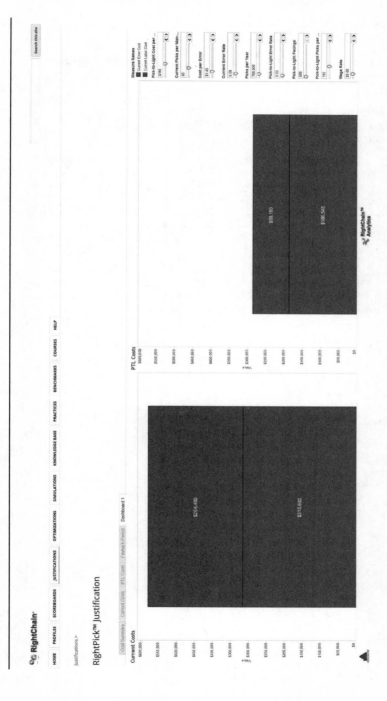

Figure 9.48   WMS business case

	Justification Scenarios			
	I	II	III	IV
	Labor	I + Space	II + Inventory	III + Accuracy
Gross Annual Savings	$ 2,741,457	$ 3,065,787	$ 3,264,518	$ 3,279,121
Maintenance (@18% of License)	$ 202,701	$ 202,701	$ 202,701	$ 202,701
Net Annual Savings	$ 2,538,755	$ 2,863,085	$ 3,061,817	$ 3,076,420
Initial Licensing	$ 1,126,119	$ 1,126,119	$ 1,126,119	$ 1,126,119
Terminals/Headsets	$ 1,040,748	$ 1,040,748	$ 1,040,748	$ 1,040,748
Outside Implementation Services	$ 775,000	$ 775,000	$ 775,000	$ 775,000
Internal Implementation Services	$ 928,000	$ 928,000	$ 928,000	$ 928,000
Server Hardware	$ 175,000	$ 175,000	$ 175,000	$ 175,000
TOTAL INVESTMENT	$ 4,044,867	$ 4,044,867	$ 4,044,867	$ 4,044,867
Payback vs Net Annual Savings	1.59	1.41	1.32	1.31

CHAPTER 10

RightTeam
Supply Chain Organization Strategy

"Do you see a man skilled in his work? He will serve before kings;
he will not serve before obscure men."

—SOLOMON

Less than one-third of all supply chain projects ever attain their intended goals within budget or schedule. Those projects include reengineering supply chains, reconfiguring facilities, outsourcing to third-party logistics providers, and restructuring logistics networks. If the project involves software, the success rate is less than 15 percent!

In considering the 100-plus projects I have been involved in personally, and the many more I have secondhand knowledge of through our professional education program, I can say without hesitation that the fundamental reason a project, program, or enterprise fails is organizational dysfunction. I was first made starkly aware of this when the managing partner of one of the nation's largest supply chain consulting firms abruptly resigned and went back to school to study industrial psychology and Christian counseling. I was introducing him to an industry audience sometime after he completed his course of study, and I asked him why he quit so suddenly and why he chose his program of study. He shared that most of the supply chain assignments his firm had completed had resulted in thick presentations and very limited results. His observation was that the barrier to implementation was nearly always organizational dysfunction.

A few years ago I conducted a workshop for the operating committee of one of the world's largest industrial conglomerates. The heads of operations for each business unit plus the company's COO participated. We had a question and answer session at the end of the workshop. The COO asked the first question. "Dr. Frazelle, we have quite a bit of conflict in these meetings. Especially lately. Why is that?" I asked him what the charter of the group was. He said, "We have two main objectives. The first is to reduce inventory. The second is to lower our unit costs." I said politely, "You just answered your own question. Your main methods of reducing unit cost, far-flung global sourcing from cheap labor sources and buying in large quantities to receive discounts, increase your inventory levels. The objectives are at odds with one another, so you are at odds with one another." They asked me what they should do about it. I encouraged them, like I encourage all our clients, to take a step back and reconsider their objectives and their approach. I suggested that their objectives would preferably be to maximize return on invested capital (ROIC), improve perfect order percentage, spend whatever was required in total supply chain cost to support those objectives, and invest in whatever inventory level was required to accomplish those objectives. Sometimes that inventory level will be higher than we currently have, and sometimes it will be lower. Inventory is not an end in itself; it is a means to an end.

We witness this conflict in nearly every client situation we encounter. In all but the wisest and most mature organizations, highly qualified professionals are required to do the impossible. They are required to respond to a barrage of typically uncoordinated initiatives from across the organization. Those initiatives normally include many of the following. Increase SKUs. Increase customization. Increase inventory availability. Reduce headcount. Reduce customer response times. Reduce transportation costs. Reduce purchase costs through global sourcing. Reduce manufacturing costs. Mitigate increasing supply chain risk with multiple sources. All of these naturally work to increase inventory levels. Yet, facing prevailing Lean thinking, they are still required to reduce inventory.

It is the stress inherent in those uncoordinated and often conflicting objects in the backdrop of organizational misalignment, a lack of education and professional development, and a lack of planning that ultimately dooms projects and discourages professionals. For that reason, our supply chain organization focus is on alignment, education, and planning.

10.1 Alignment Strategy

A few years ago I received a phone call from the VP of distribution from one of the nation's largest retailers. I was surprised that he was calling to ask for our assistance with a new supply chain strategy because I knew from our benchmarking work that their company was one of the country's most efficient retailers. When I got on-site I started to understand their dilemma.

I asked the VP of distribution how he was compensated. He said that his bonus was based on continuing to lower the delivered cost per unit to their retail stores. I asked him how he accomplished that. He said that it was by choosing inexpensive transportation modes and inexpensive carriers within those modes, maximizing container utilization by holding containers at their warehouses until they were completely full, and maximizing warehouse labor utilization by holding and releasing store replenishment orders in large batches. I told him that I remembered from my benchmarking work that they were evidently doing a good job along those lines. He agreed but said his problem was that their distribution was too efficient. I asked him to explain. He said that their vice president of retail's bonus was based on increasing sales per square foot in the stores and maximizing in-store availability. He said that their distribution program had resulted in $250 million in lost sales the prior year, and they needed a way to align the objectives of distribution and retail. That's code for "My business partner and I are ruining each other's lives." I told him that aligning corporate objectives was what we do for a living and that we could help. To make a six-month-long supply chain strategy story short, by incorporating lost sales cost, inventory carrying cost, transportation cost, and warehousing cost in their RightChain objective function, we were able to develop a supply chain strategy that put more than $50 million on their bottom line by cutting their lost sales by $240 million and optimizing (not minimizing) their total logistics cost.

For political, technical, and cultural reasons, bringing the supply organization into alignment is easier said than done. Based on the organization's culture, existing organization structure, and business environment, the team begins to naturally gravitate toward a preferred model. The model alternatives include:

- Functional organization
- Process organization
- Matrix organization
- Integrated supply chain organization
- Global supply chain organization
- Business unit supply chain organization
- Distributed supply chain organization
- Hybrid model

Functional Organization Model

The functional or "silo" organization model is a carryover from post–World War II manufacturing organizations and is an extension of the academic disciplines that are still maintained in many U.S. universities. A typical functional organization concept from a recent retail client is illustrated in Figure 10.1.

Figure 10.1   Functional organization model for retail operations

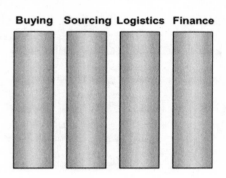

The premise of the silo/functional organizational model is that if each silo is optimized, then the entire enterprise performance will be optimized. In most cases the premise turns out to be false. Customers and shareholders are not interested in silo performance. Customer/shareholder value is only really enhanced when the functional, political, and technical silos are shattered and restructured to focus attention on customer, shareholder, and employee satisfaction. A few years ago we named one of our major supply chain initiatives "Project Jericho" because the initiative was a catalyst for bringing down the old walls in the organization.

Process Organization Model

The process organizational model structures people, metrics, and systems around critical business processes. Figure 10.2 illustrates a supply chain process organizational model with silo overlays. The model features five key business processes—brand development, consumer development, customer development, supplier development, and supply chain management—that focus the corporate resources—marketing, manufacturing, and logistics—on customer service.

Figure 10.2   Process organizational model with silos

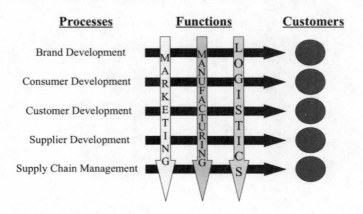

Matrix Organization Model

The matrix organizational model (Figure 10.3) is an attempt to combine functional and process models. It is oftentimes a compromise organization structure. My personal experience and the experience of most of our clients is that the matrix model serves neither the interests of the customers, shareholders, or internal management. As the Proverb says, "You cannot serve two masters."

Integrated Supply Chain Organizational Model

The integrated supply chain organizational model (Figure 10.4) is focused on the processes of customer satisfaction, supply development, and supply chain cost/capital management. The model requires a chief supply chain officer (CSCO) or supply chain vice president to be responsible for the four key total supply chain performance indicators—total supply chain cost, perfect order percentage, total supply chain cycle time, and supply chain productivity. The CSCO has three direct reports, one each in charge of customer response (customer service and order processing), supply (inventory planning and procurement), and logistics (transportation and

Figure 10.3   Matrix organization structure

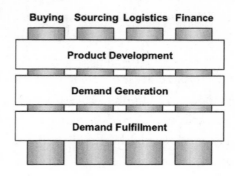

Figure 10.4   Integrated supply chain model

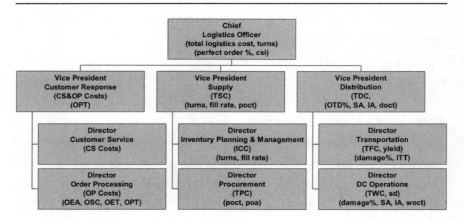

warehousing). The results with this model have been impressive, and this is a common recommendation for us to make to our clients.

There are two reasons I believe this model works particularly well. First, the organization structure is cleanly aligned with well defined, reliable, and benchmarkable supply chain performance indicators. Any time performance metrics are vaguely presented and/or the organizational structure is misaligned with their own metrics, the total organizational performance will suffer. Second, individual temperaments and giftings in supply chain organizations tend to fall into the three categories—service, supply, and logistics. The customer service team is typically and necessarily comprised of the happiest, most joyful, and most optimistic professionals in a supply chain. These are the individuals who are most adept at customer recovery and can patiently leave a complaining customer smiling at the end of a difficult conversation or series of e-mails. The supply team is typically and necessarily made up of the nerdy analysts with impressive academic credentials, expert spreadsheet skills, and thick glasses. These are the individuals that are the checks and balances between the high-minded objectives of the sales and marketing organization and the conservative concerns of the finance organization. The distribution team is typically and necessarily made up of the rolled-up shirtsleeves crowd that is not afraid to get their hands dirty driving a lift truck or fixing a tractor. These are the individuals who will get the job done, period. The integrated supply chain organizational model tends to work in concert with God-given gifts and inclinations.

Global Supply Chain Organization Model

The global supply chain organizational model is an extension of the integrated supply chain model. In essence, the global supply chain model includes an integrated supply chain organization for global supply chain planning and policy making, regional (e.g. North America/NAFTA, Europe/EU, Asia-Pacific, and Latin America) supply chain planning and policy making, and in-country/local (e.g. Canada, Spain, Korea, Peru) supply chain planning and policy making. Each level has an individual responsible for total supply chain, customer response, supply, and distribution performance. In a typical global supply chain organization model, the global supply chain management team makes global policy/plans (communication standards, metrics definition, system selections, best-practice templates, vision setting, etc.), and the regional/local management teams adopt those global standards to the unique regional/local conditions. The global supply chain organization model has been adopted successfully by Coca-Cola, Nestlé, 3M, Colgate, and a variety of pharmaceutical firms.

A recommended global supply chain organization structure from a recent client in the health and beauty aids industry is provided in Figure 10.5.

Figure 10.5   Global supply chain organization model

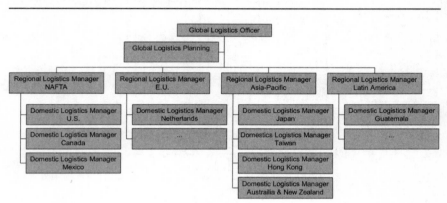

Business Unit Supply Chain Organization Model

One of the most difficult questions to answer in supply chain organization design and development is if and when a business unit should have its own supply chain organization. The classic trade-off is between the leveraging of assets that is available when multiple business units share supply chain assets (distribution centers, transportation fleets, inventory, supply chain information systems, and supply chain personnel) and the control that may be lost to a particular business unit when a designated supply chain infrastructure is not dedicated to their particular needs. The evaluation usually comes down to an analysis of the supply chain synergies that are available across the business units. Those synergies are created when different business units are logistically similar in key areas including order profiles, response time requirements, customer base, supplier base, carrier

Figure 10.6   Business unit supply chain organization model

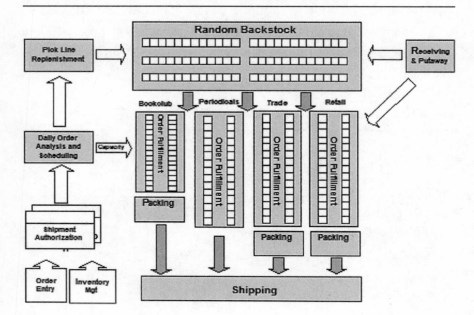

base, and inventory profiles. If those similarities are not present, it most often is advisable to dedicate a supply chain organization to a business unit. Otherwise, the supply chain similarities can be leveraged to create high efficiencies in the leveraging of supply chain assets across business units. Most business unit managers will go along if the benefits of the leveraging are passed along to the business unit, if the supply chain manager is competent and politically astute, and if there is no major barrier to customer satisfaction in the cross business unit model.

A recent client in the book distribution business was able to achieve both objectives simultaneously (Figure 10.6). The supply chain organization at LifeWay supplies retail stores, mail-order customers, and thousands of churches with a variety of Christian media including books, tapes, CDs, videos, magazines, and Bible lessons. All three business units are supplied from a common inventory and distribution center. However, each business unit is supported with a stand-alone order picking area designed to accommodate the unique order profiles and customer service requirements of the unique business units. The processed orders then flow through a common sorting systems for outbound deliveries.

Distributed Supply Chain Organizational Model

The distributed supply chain organizational model (Figure 10.7) eliminates any formal supply chain organization other than a chief supply chain officer (CSCO). Instead, logisticians are recruited and developed by the CSCO and placed in the other areas of the corporation with the responsibility to incorporate sound supply chain practices into the traditional corporate activities of marketing, research and development, sales, manufacturing, information systems, finance, and so on. The model works similar to the concept of total quality management, where TQM experts (black belts) are placed in each area of the corporation to introduce quality management disciplines.

Figure 10.7   Distributed supply chain organization model

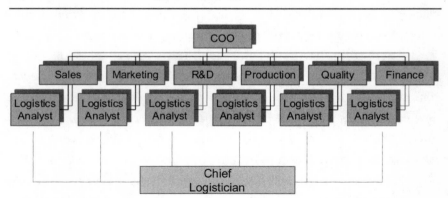

10.2 Supply Chain Professional Development

Imagine that you were a tourist on your first visit to San Francisco. You had always heard of the Golden Gate Bridge, and you chose a hotel as close to the bridge as possible. You awoke early on your first morning in San Francisco and decided to get out on your bike to see the bridge. You were up so early that no one else was awake. No one was walking or riding their bikes. It was so early, there were not even any cars moving about or on the bridge.

You ride your bike up the bridge, and you are deciding whether or not to ride across to the other side. All your life you have wanted to cross the Golden Gate Bridge, and this is your chance. You look across and it's a long, long way to the other side. You look down, and it's a long, long way down. You are trying to gather information about the safety of your crossing, and suddenly your scan comes across the plaque honoring the person responsible for designing the bridge and planning the project. You read that it's their very first bridge design and that they had stumbled into bridge design after other stints in marketing and sales. What just happened to your comfort level in crossing the bridge? What would you have liked to have read on that plaque? "A veteran leader of large-scale bridge designs and implementations with advanced degrees in civil engineering and urban planning."

What does this have to do with supply chain education? A lot!

Supply chains are like bridges—planning bridges, software bridges, communication bridges, product flow bridges, cash flow bridges, document flow bridges—that connect internal and external consumers, suppliers, sales, operations, and finance. The large majority of those bridges are planned, constructed, and maintained by hardworking, well-meaning professionals who have no formal training in bridge building. With less than 10 percent of supply chain professionals having any formal training in supply chain logistics, is it any wonder that less than 30 percent of all supply chain logistics projects are successful?

One of my favorite Solomonisms is the promise that if we *train up a child in the way he should go, when he is mature, he will not depart from it*. The concepts of supply chain logistics are relatively new. Any organization getting started is a relative child in supply chain logistics. However, Solomon's promise is that if we train the child, when the child matures, the child will not depart from the training. That's why it takes time for organizations to break through to sustained supply chain success. That's why it is important to incorporate training early and often. That's why we integrate training into every consulting engagement. That's why it typically takes several months for all the RightChain principles and concepts to permeate corporate culture.

One of my driving motivations for establishing The Logistics Institute and the Supply Chain Management Series was my observation that the level of understanding of supply chain concepts was underdeveloped in most organizations. Yet, it is that understanding or lack thereof that ultimately determines the success or failure of supply chain projects. Since less than one-third of supply chain projects ever meet their intended goals, industry is paying a high price for this lack of understanding. We created The RightChain Institute to raise the level of understanding of supply chain concepts and to increase the likelihood of supply chain projects yielding their intended results through supply chain professional development.

The turnover of supply chain professionals (especially in supply chain services companies) is extraordinarily high. The key to maintaining high levels of supply chain performance is retaining high-performing supply chain professionals. One key to retaining those high performers is to challenge them professionally. A key to challenging them is to continue to develop their supply chain education and skills.

Toward that end, the very best supply chain organizations maintain formal career paths and development programs for their supply chain professionals. We have worked with a variety of supply chain organizations that maintain a dedicated staff focused solely on developing the supply chain workforce. We worked closely with one large organization to develop an internal supply chain institute to help the supply chain professionals maintain their cutting-edge understanding and implementation of advanced supply chain concepts.

10.3 Planning Strategy

A large company in Silicon Valley retained us a few years ago to help them craft a supply chain strategy. We were about 90 minutes into the kickoff meeting with the COO when there was a loud, urgent knock on the meeting room door. Right after the knock someone barged in, looked at the COO, and announced, "Steve, we have a problem with a customer's fab line. We've shorted them on several parts, and the compliance penalty is about to kick in. We need to figure out how to get them back up and running as soon as possible." The COO looked at me and asked if we could help them address the issue. I agreed, and we spent the next few days helping them resolve the issue. They were well satisfied at the end of the week. Our team flew back to Atlanta.

The next month we flew back out to San Jose to restart the project. We were about 60 minutes into the kickoff meeting with the COO when there was a loud, urgent knock on the door. Someone barged into the room, looked at the COO, and announced, "Steve. We have a problem with a customer's fab line. We're late delivering some key parts, and their compliance penalty is about to kick in. We need to figure out how to expedite some parts as soon as possible." The COO looked at me and asked if we could help them resolve the issue. I reluctantly agreed. We spent the next few days resolving the issue. They were very well satisfied with the week's work.

The next month we flew out to San Jose to restart the project. We were about 30 minutes into the kickoff meeting with the COO when someone barged into the meeting room, looked at the COO, and announced, "Steve. We've got an upset customer on the phone. We shipped them the wrong parts, and they are about to kick in our noncompliance penalty." The COO looked at me and asked if we could help with the issue. I said, "No. You hired us to help you craft a supply chain strategy that would make sure no one ever knocks on that door. We are happy to help you with that, but we will not be accomplices to this kind of chaos."

As soon as I said it, I assumed we would be fired. The COO was enraged. He said, "We hired you to help us." I said, "Yes. You hired us to help you. But, it's not helping you for us to jump through hoops every time your supply chain creates a shortage, delay, or error. We can help you eliminate the causes of the shortages, delays, and errors, but we need to pack our bags and go back to Atlanta if every time we meet someone knocks on that door." I am not sure anyone had ever told Steve no. It was a shock to him. He calmed down after a few minutes and asked if I was serious. I said, "You hired us to help develop a strategy that minimizes the supply chain chaos and disorder that has become your norm. It has become your norm to the point that you are numb to it, maybe even addicted to it, and can no longer even imagine a supply chain world without it." I also reminded him that their director of logistics had just suffered a psychological breakdown.

There was a very long silence. The next thing he said floored me. He said, "OK. You're right. I never thought about it that way. What do you need?" I explained that we needed his undivided attention for three hours every other week, two of his best analysts full-time for a few months, and unfettered access to their supply chain data. After four months we had optimized their supply chain strategy and implemented a disciplined process to maintain the strategy. The chaos and disorder died down. The cost overruns stopped. The seesaw of excess inventory and dire shortages stopped.

Supply chain management is by nature a firefighting business. Many days on-site with our clients are like adventures into a high-stakes whack-a-mole game. Unfortunately, many organizations reward that kind of firefighting at the exclusion of long-range planning. The goal of the planning process and organization is to stop playing and rewarding those who play supply chain whack-a-mole. Doing so requires the creation of and commitment to a supply chain planning organization and process.

CHAPTER 11

RightPlan
Supply Chain Planning Strategy

"The plans of the diligent lead surely to plenty,
But those of everyone who is hasty, surely to poverty."
—SOLOMON

I have been blessed to meet many prominent people in the course of my speaking engagements. One of those is General Gus Pagonis. He was the general in command of the U.S. Armed Forces during the liberation of Kuwait. He tells the story of their initial setup in the Kuwaiti summer when temperatures range between 110 and 120 degrees. During the setup he assigned five analysts to an air-conditioned trailer where they were ordered to run war simulations and to inform the general of any planning contingencies they had not already considered. One August afternoon one of the analysts ran out of the simulation trailer and approached General Pagonis. After getting permission to speak, he informed the general that they needed to order tens of trailers of long underwear. On first thought, that seems absurd. When the general challenged the analyst to explain, the story went like this. The simulations predicted the war would be fought in the Kuwaiti winter. Winter temperatures in Kuwait dip into the teens. With the war in full fight, inbound logistics capacity would not allow anything but ammunition, fuel, and food to be received. If our troops were going to be properly clothed for the fight, the order had to be placed immediately. The order seemed so absurd in the summer heat that it had be approved by General Colin Powell. To make a long story short, the order was approved. The long underwear was received. The initial conflict to expel Iraqi troops from Kuwait began with an aerial and naval bombardment on January 17, 1991, and continued for five weeks. This was followed by a ground assault on February 24. I don't know how much impact the long underwear had on the victory, but it didn't hurt.

How did the U.S. Army know to place the order? They dedicated people, time, and resources for planning!

Integrated Supply Chain Planning

Sales and operations planning (S&OP) and its planning relative known as integrated business planning (IBP) receive a lot of attention as potential panaceas for inventory optimization and rationalization. Done properly, it can help along those lines. The key, usually missing, is "done properly."

Over the last few years I have attended, reviewed, and even facilitated several S&OP/IBP meetings. Sometimes sales is not there. Sometimes operations is not there. Sometimes planning is not there. Sometimes inventory is not discussed. Sometimes logistics is not involved. Sometimes the meeting morphs into a seminar, or worse. Sometimes the meeting doesn't happen. Reliable data is the exception rather than the rule. The decision support tools necessary to answer difficult questions are rarely available. Though seemingly a "standard" in the industry, I have found S&OP/IBP to have as many different meanings as there are companies.

Despite those disappointments, I was encouraged recently at two client sites. Pratt & Whitney Canada coined the term SIOP for sales, inventory, and operations planning. Coca-Cola Consolidated coined the term T&OP, transportation and operations planning. They both recognized something was missing from S&OP and launched out on their own. Those two clients in particular pressed us to craft a planning program that filled in the gaps of traditional S&OP and IBP programs.

As I mentioned early on, there are a variety of valid perspectives on inventory—(1) financial, service, and operations; (2) strategic, tactical, and execution; (3) customer service, manufacturing, sourcing, transportation, and warehousing. Each of those perspectives needs to be addressed, optimized, and rationalized in the planning process and meetings. In addition, though traditional S&OP has focused primarily on inventory, I recommend that it be expanded to consider the total supply chain and its ability to support the financial and service requirements of the business.

We developed the RightChain planning process for integrated supply chain planning (ISCP) to help companies move beyond S&OP/IBP to integrated supply chain planning and optimization. The components of our planning program are illustrated in Figures 11.1 through 11.5. The planning process is illustrated in Figure 11.6 and described in steps 1 through 7. The program connects the short, middle, and long-term; sales, operations, and finance; employees, customers, and shareholders; up, down, and horizontal; and systems, process, and people.

Via organization, data, systems, analytics, metrics, and policies, integrated supply chain planning collaborates, optimizes, and synchronizes demand, supply, logistics, and financial planning. More specifically, under ISCP, demand planning encompasses product portfolio management, customer portfolio management, demand orchestration, and demand forecasting. Supply planning encompasses global sourcing optimization, supplier portfolio management, supply orchestration, and supplier capacity management. Logistics planning encompasses logistics network optimization, inventory optimization, collaborative transportation planning, and logistics capacity planning. Financial planning encompasses cost, price, and rate forecasting; currency and trade optimization; value based accounting; and terms optimization. Integrated supply chain planning connects those dots and includes integrated supply chain scenario

Figure 11.1   Integrated demand, supply, logistics, and financial planning

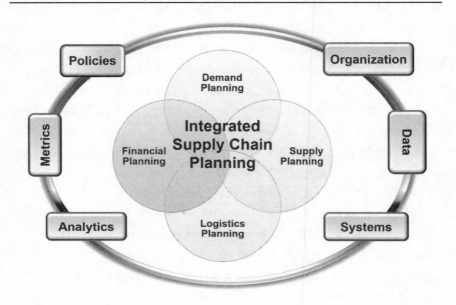

Figure 11.2   High-level components of RightChain planning

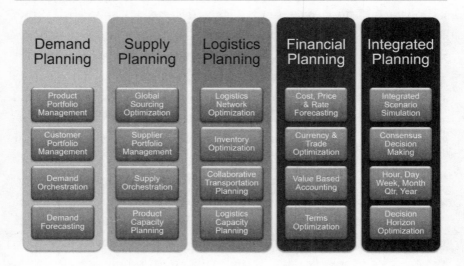

Figure 11.3   Detailed components of RightChain planning

PLANNING AREAS			Demand Planning	Supply Planning	Logistics Planning	Financial Planning	Integrated Supply Chain Planning
PORTFOLIO MANAGEMENT		Activity	Product Portfolio Management	Commodity Portfolio Management	Port Portfolio Management	Investment Portfolio Management	Risk Portfolio Management
			Customer Portfolio Management	Supplier Portfolio Management	Mode Portfolio Management		BU Optimization
			Product-Customer Portfolio Management	Commodity-Supplier Portfolio Management	Carrier Portfolio Management		
FORECASTING		Activity	Demand Forecasting	Supply Forecasting	Logistics Forecasting	Financial Forecasting	Integrated Forecasting
		Cost & Rates	Price Elasticity Forecasting	Commodity Cost Forecasting	Freight Rate Forecasting	Cost, Price & Rate Forecasting	Market Intelligence
		Capacity	Maximum Demand	Product Capacity	Network Capacity	Cash/Capital Capacity	Plan Capacity
COLLABORATION		Internal	Consensus Forecasting	Consensus Capacity Planning	Consensus Logistics Planning	Consensus FP	Consensus Planning
		External	Forecast Sharing	Capacity Sharing	Collaborative Logistics	Collaborative Finance	CPFR
		Shaping	Demand Shaping	Supply Shaping	Freight Shaping	Price Shaping	Plan Shaping
		Development	Customer Development	Supplier Development	Carrier/Port Development	Partner Development	Planning Development
RISK		Risk Assessment	Demand Risk	Supply Risk	Logistics Risk	Financial Risk	Plan Risk
		Flexibility	Pull In / Push Out	Supply Flexibility	Logistics Flexibility	Financial Flexibility	Plan Flexibility
		Contingency Planning	Demand Contingency Plan	Supply Contingency Plan	Logistics Contingency Plan	Financial Contingency Plan	Integrated Contingency Plan
POLICY		Policy	Customer Service Policy	Supplier Service Policy	Carrier/3PL Service Policy	Financial Policies	Planning Policies
		Terms	Purchasing Terms	Buying Terms	Transit Terms	Financial Terms	Planning Terms
			Demand Policy	Supply Policy	Logistics Policy	Trading Policy	

Figure 11.4 Detailed components of RightChain planning, continued

PLANNING AREAS		Demand Planning	Supply Planning	Logistics Planning	Financial Planning	Integrated Planning
ANALYTICS	Optimization	Backcasting	Sourcing Optimization	Network Optimizaiton	Backtesting	Horizon Optimization
		Lag Optimization	Allocation Optimization	Product Flow Optimization	Currency & Trade Optimization	Plan Optimization
			Packaging Optimization	Mode/Carrier Optimization	Cash Flow Optimization	
					Entry/Exit Optimization	
			INCOTERMS Optimization			
			Inventory Optimization			
	Simulation	Simulated Buying Behavior	Simulated Processing Behavior	Simulated Network Behavior	Simulated Market Behavior	Plan Simulation
		Demand Stream Simulation	Supply Stream Simulation	Logistics Stream Simulation	CPR Simulation	Business Simulation
	Attributes	Large Scale Optimization, High Speed Simulation, Animation & Visualization, Shadow Pricing, Early Warning Systems				
	Activity Skills	DP Skills	SP Skills	LP Skills	FP Skills	IP Skills
	Enabler Skills	IP Data, IP Metrics, IP Analytics, IP Systems, IP Organization - Awareness, Intermediate & Advanced				
	Attributes	Aligned Structure, Conducive Culture, Clear Roles, Excellent Casting				
ORGANIZATION	Meetings	DP Meeting	SP Meeting	LP Meeting	FP Meeting, Pre-S&OP, ES&OP	
		Customer Conference	Supplier Conference	Carrier Conference	Partner Conference	Planning Conference
	Attributes	Coordinated Calendars, Committed Participation, Decision Focused, Meticulous Preparation, Diligent Follow-up, Adhered Agendas				
METRICS	Financial	Revenue	Expense, Capital	Expense, Capital	EBIT/ROIC/EVA	
	Accuracy	Forecast Accuracy	Supply Accuracy	On-Time Accuracy	Rate/Price Accuracy	Plan Accuracy
	Variance	Demand Variance	Schedule Variance	On-Time Variance	Budget Variance	Plan Variance
	Availability	Contract Compliance	Supplier Fill Rate	Carrier Fill Rate	Cash Availability	Plan Availability
	General	Balanced Scales, Span the Bridge, Value Focused, Aligned Accountability, Command & Control				
SYSTEMS	Execution Systems	Order Processing	Production Scheduling	Logistics Execution	Financial Execution System	Planning Execution System
	Planning Systems	Advanced Forecasting System	Advanced Production Systems	Advanced Logistics System	Advanced Financial System	APO/APS
	Data	Data Integrity, Data Cleansing, Automated Reconciliation, Big Data Mining				
	Visibility	Demand Visibility	Supply Visibility	Logistics Visibility	Financial Visibility	Plan Visibility
		Customer Orders	Purchase Orders	Shipment Tracking	Bid Tracking	Early Warning
		Inventory Visibility			Real Time Markets	
	Attributes	IP DSS Filters, Planning Execution Integration, Enterprise Integration, Real-Time, On-Demand, Mobile, Early Warning Systems				

Figure 11.5   RightChain planning principles

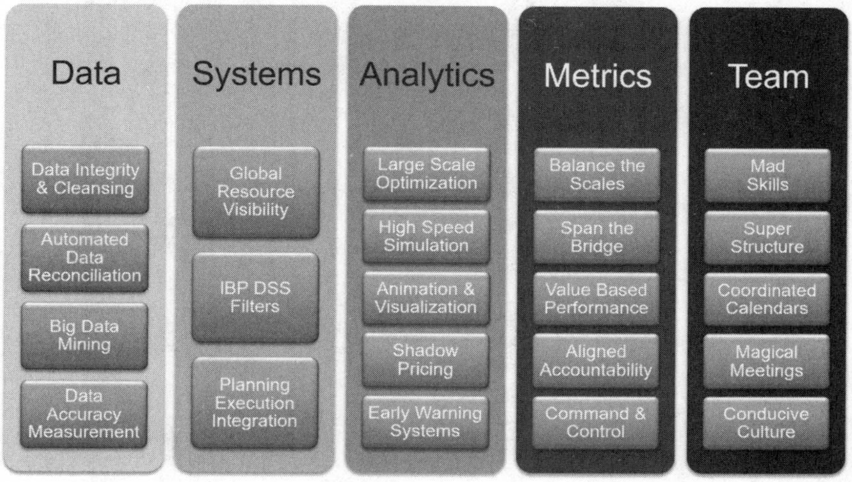

Data	Systems	Analytics	Metrics	Team
Data Integrity & Cleansing	Global Resource Visibility	Large Scale Optimization	Balance the Scales	Mad Skills
Automated Data Reconciliation	IBP DSS Filters	High Speed Simulation	Span the Bridge	Super Structure
Big Data Mining	Planning Execution Integration	Animation & Visualization	Value Based Performance	Coordinated Calendars
Data Accuracy Measurement		Shadow Pricing	Aligned Accountability	Magical Meetings
		Early Warning Systems	Command & Control	Conducive Culture

simulation; consensus decision making, supply chain scheduling, and time frame optimization.

An overview of our RightChain integrated supply chain planning program is presented in Figure 11.6 and explained below.

1.   **Cadence and Gates.** Supply chain requirements and capacity must be rationalized and optimized in the short, middle, and long term. Therefore, the RightChain program works in daily (Gate I), weekly (Gate II), monthly (Gate III), quarterly (Gate IV), and annual (Gate V) buckets accordingly. A very disciplined RightChain calendar (Figure 11.7) synchronizes and schedules the daily, weekly, monthly, quarterly, and annual meetings, taking into account the traditional annual meetings, quarterly earnings reports, monthly budgets, weekly production schedules, and daily operating agendas.

2.   **Organization Levels.** All levels of the organization are impacted by, should participate in, and should be held accountable to RightChain

Figure 11.6   RightChain planning process

	Daily	Weekly	Monthly	Quarterly	Annually
Cadence >	EXECUTION	EXECUTION/TACTICAL	TACTICAL	TACTICAL/STRATEGIC	STRATEGIC
Time Frame >	Manager	Manager/Director	Director	Director/VP	Director/VP/C-Level
Participation >					
GATE >	I	II	III	IV	V
Demand & Requirements — Customer Response	Sales Orders Update → Shipping Update, MRP/DRP Update	Pre-Concensus Forecasting →	Concensus Forecasting, Demand Planning	Customer Valuation, Customer Satisfaction, CSP Update, SKU Valuation	Long Range Demand Planning, Portfolio & Channel Strategy, Customer Service Policy, Customer Conference
Optimization & Rationalization — Inventory	Inventory, ABC Cycle Count, Perpetual Inventory	Management RightChain™, Inventory Scheduling, Supply Signal Update	Director RightChain™, Smoothing, Concensus Planning, Inventory Planning	Executive RightChain™, Deployment Review, Material Flow Plan, Supply Chain Scoreboard Review	Strategic RightChain™, Network Strategy, Flow Strategy, Supply Chain Strategy
Supply & Capacity — Manufacturing, Supply, Transportation, Warehousing	Production, Purchase Orders, Bills & Manifests, Receipts & Pick Sheets	Manufacturing Scheduling, Supply Scheduling, Transportation Scheduling, Warehouse Scheduling	Manufacturing Planning, Supply Planning, Transportation Planning, Warehouse Planning	Manufacturing Review, Sourcing Review, Transportation Review, Warehousing Review	Long Range Capacity Strategy, Sourcing Strategy & Supplier Conference, Transportation Strategy & Carrier Conference, Warehousing Strategy & 3PL Conference
METRICS — Finance, Service, Inventory, Stability	Sales, OTD, POP, Inventory Accuracy, No. of Changes	Sales, OTD, POP, $s, Days, Turns, No. of Changes	EBIT, ROS, Cash, ROIC, OTD, POP, IVA, GMROI, IPC, $s, Days, Turns, % Changes	EBIT, ROS, Cash, ROIC, OTD, POP, IVA, GMROI, IPC, $s, Days, Turns, % Changes	EBIT, ROS, Cash, ROIC, OTD, POP, IVA, GMROI, IPC, $s, Days, Turns, % Changes

Figure 11.7   RightChain planning calendar

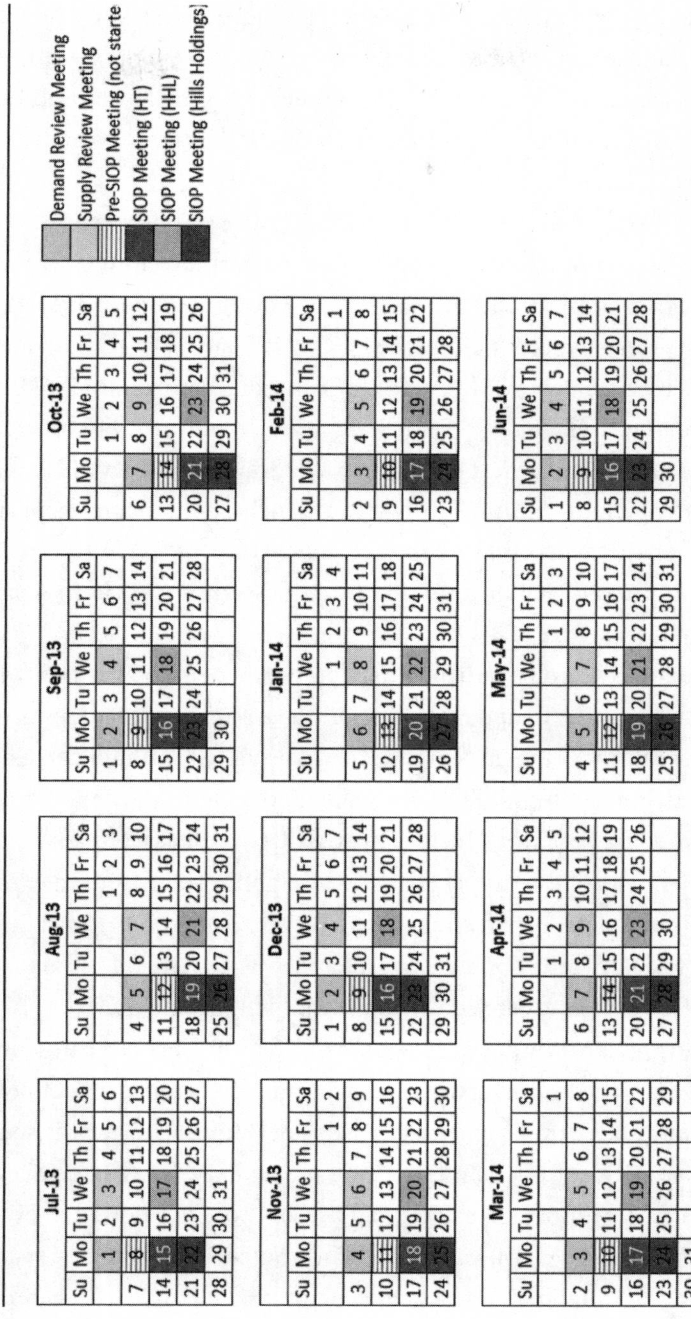

Legend:
- Demand Review Meeting
- Supply Review Meeting
- Pre-SIOP Meeting (not starte[d])
- SIOP Meeting (HT)
- SIOP Meeting (HHL)
- SIOP Meeting (Hills Holdings)

Jul-13

Su	Mo	Tu	We	Th	Fr	Sa
	1	2	3	4	5	6
7	8	9	10	11	12	13
14	15	16	17	18	19	20
21	22	23	24	25	26	27
28	29	30	31			

Aug-13

Su	Mo	Tu	We	Th	Fr	Sa
				1	2	3
4	5	6	7	8	9	10
11	12	13	14	15	16	17
18	19	20	21	22	23	24
25	26	27	28	29	30	31

Sep-13

Su	Mo	Tu	We	Th	Fr	Sa
1	2	3	4	5	6	7
8	9	10	11	12	13	14
15	16	17	18	19	20	21
22	23	24	25	26	27	28
29	30					

Oct-13

Su	Mo	Tu	We	Th	Fr	Sa
		1	2	3	4	5
6	7	8	9	10	11	12
13	14	15	16	17	18	19
20	21	22	23	24	25	26
27	28	29	30	31		

Nov-13

Su	Mo	Tu	We	Th	Fr	Sa
					1	2
3	4	5	6	7	8	9
10	11	12	13	14	15	16
17	18	19	20	21	22	23
24	25	26	27	28	29	30

Dec-13

Su	Mo	Tu	We	Th	Fr	Sa
1	2	3	4	5	6	7
8	9	10	11	12	13	14
15	16	17	18	19	20	21
22	23	24	25	26	27	28
29	30	31				

Jan-14

Su	Mo	Tu	We	Th	Fr	Sa
			1	2	3	4
5	6	7	8	9	10	11
12	13	14	15	16	17	18
19	20	21	22	23	24	25
26	27	28	29	30	31	

Feb-14

Su	Mo	Tu	We	Th	Fr	Sa
						1
2	3	4	5	6	7	8
9	10	11	12	13	14	15
16	17	18	19	20	21	22
23	24	25	26	27	28	

Mar-14

Su	Mo	Tu	We	Th	Fr	Sa
						1
2	3	4	5	6	7	8
9	10	11	12	13	14	15
16	17	18	19	20	21	22
23	24	25	26	27	28	29
30	31					

Apr-14

Su	Mo	Tu	We	Th	Fr	Sa
		1	2	3	4	5
6	7	8	9	10	11	12
13	14	15	16	17	18	19
20	21	22	23	24	25	26
27	28	29	30			

May-14

Su	Mo	Tu	We	Th	Fr	Sa
				1	2	3
4	5	6	7	8	9	10
11	12	13	14	15	16	17
18	19	20	21	22	23	24
25	26	27	28	29	30	31

Jun-14

Su	Mo	Tu	We	Th	Fr	Sa
1	2	3	4	5	6	7
8	9	10	11	12	13	14
15	16	17	18	19	20	21
22	23	24	25	26	27	28
29	30					

decisions. Participation by levels including manager, director, and executive are highlighted in Figure 11.6. Meeting types are labeled as Management RightChains, Director RightChains, and Executive RightChains to reflect the nature of the decisions considered in the work sessions.

3. **Players.** At each gate in the RightChain planning process, appropriate representatives from the major multidisciplinary areas of the corporation should be meeting. For example, Executive RightChain meetings would include the CFO/VP finance, COO/VP operations, CEO/president, CSMO/VP sales and marketing, CMO/VP manufacturing, and CSCO/VP supply chain. Director RightChain meetings would include their counterparts at the director level. Management RightChain meetings would include their counterparts at the management level. We often convene meetings in a RightChain Command Center featuring full access to supply chain scenario analytics. (Figure 11.8)

4. **Demand and Requirements.** Forecasted demand has typically focused on customer demand in units or dollars and is often developed solely by sales. Customer demand should be vetted through consensus forecasting, and should be extrapolated to include all supply chain units of measure including pieces, cases, pallets, cube, weight, and loads. The elements of the supply chain service policy such as fill rate, response time, delivery frequency, and so on also act as constraints on the supply chain and should be considered as well. All of these are reflected in the swim lane labeled "Demand and Requirements."

5. **Supply and Capacity.** Capacity in "S&OP" has typically focused on unit manufacturing capacity. Capacity should reflect not only manufacturing capacity, but also sourcing capacity, transportation capacity, warehousing capacity, IT capacity, and financial capacity to fund inventory investments. Each of those is a potential bottleneck in total supply chain capability. Each potential bottleneck is considered in the "Supply and Capacity" swim lane.

Figure 11.8   RightChain command center at a large client site
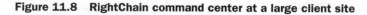

6. **Performance Measures.** Traditional S&OP performance metrics
    are focused on operational inventory indicators like inventory days-
    on-hand or turns. However, a supply chain schedule, plan, and
    strategy impacts many more metrics including inventory financial
    performance, EBIT, ROIC, workforce productivity, supply chain
    asset utilization, revenue, total supply chain cost, customer service,

complexity, and so on. Our full-blown RightChain Scoreboard considers the full range of interrelated metrics. It is organized by metrics related to providing customers with excellent customer service, employees with a great place to work, and shareholders with excellent financial returns.

7. **Tools and Data.** One of the typical hindrances to successful S&OP/ IBP meetings is the lack of real-time decision support tools to answer the tough and sometimes meeting-squelching questions that arise. We developed the RightChain Analytics Portal to support real-time data mining and decision making at each planning stage. In the example in Figure 11.9 we are optimizing and simulating the impact of various supply chain scenarios on the inventory levels in a global aerospace supply chain. In the example in Figure 11.10 we are optimizing and simulating the impact of various trading and supply chain scenarios on global coal mining production.

Figure 11.9   RightPlan optimization in aerospace

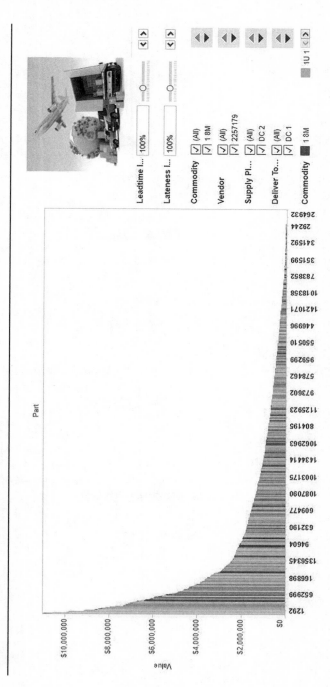

Figure 11.10 RightPlan optimization in natural resources

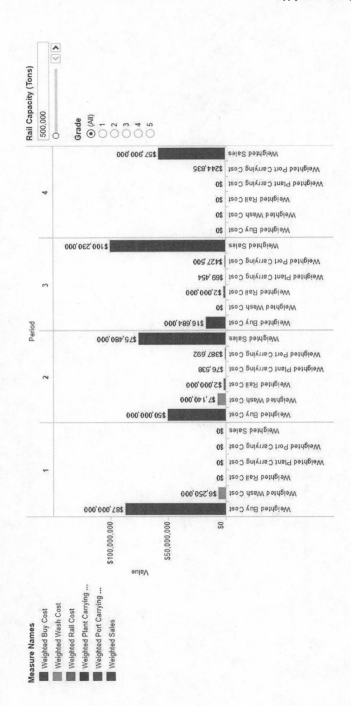

INDEX

Page numbers followed by *f* and *t* refer to figures and tables, respectively.

ABOUT THE AUTHOR

Dr. Frazelle is one of the world's foremost authorities on supply chain strategy. He is President and CEO of RightChain™ Incorporated and Executive Director of RightChain™ Institute. RightChain™ is a global supply chain professional services firm with teams in Atlanta, Georgia; Tokyo, Japan; San Jose, Costa Rica; Lima, Peru; and Sydney, Australia. RightChain™ is responsible for more than $5 billion in financial gains for its clients and was recently named one of the Top 20 Supply Chain Technology Providers.

Dr. Frazelle was founding director of The Logistics Institute at Georgia Tech, at the time the world's largest center for supply chain education and research and was recently named executive director of The LOGOS Institute for Advanced Supply Chain Studies at Meiji University in Tokyo. As an educator, Dr. Frazelle has trained more than 50,000 supply chain professionals in the principles of world-class supply chain logistics; as a consultant he has assisted more than 100 companies and government agencies in the implementation of RightChain™ principles; as an author he has authored, co-authored, and/or contributed to more than seven books on supply chain logistics; and as a professor he has lectured at Cornell, Northwestern, the University of Wisconsin, Waseda University, Meiji University, the National University of Singapore, Swinburne University, and the Kyushu Institute of Technology. His books, *Supply Chain Strategy, World-Class Warehousing,* and *Inventory Strategy* are published in seven languages including Chinese, English, Japanese, Korean, Spanish, Portuguese, and Russian.